D1453464

VIETNAM
RIGHT? or WRONG?

J. Randolph Maney, Jr.

(Cover) Reflections from the Wall at dawn on the Mall,
courtesy of Alison Malzahn.

BookLocker
Trenton, Georgia

Print ISBN: 978-1-958877-65-4
Ebook ISBN: 979-8-88531-335-3

Published by BookLocker.com, Inc., Trenton, Georgia.

Printed on acid-free paper.

Library of Congress Cataloguing in Publication Data
Maney, Jr., J. Randolph
VIETNAM: RIGHT? or WRONG? by J. Randolph Maney, Jr.
Library of Congress Control Number: 2022923855

BookLocker.com, Inc.
2023

First Edition

dedicated to

my daughters

Alison & Kristin

ACKNOWLEDGEMENTS

This book has gone through various iterations and probably would never have made it to print if it was not for the veteran editor and author John Bowman who took the time to advise and encourage me along the way. I would also like to thank Ron Cleaver, Stan Durkee, Bill Saffa, Bill Wark and Bill Thomas for their input and suggestions. I cannot thank Andrew Murphy enough for each of the very helpful maps in this book and thanks also goes to the United States Marine Corps for permission to use their map of Operation Starlite published by Colonel Rod Andrew, Jr., *The First Fight, U.S. Marines in Operation Starlite, August 1965* (Quantico VA, Marine Corps History Division). I am also most grateful to the Vietnam Center and Sam Johnson Vietnam Archive at Texas Tech University for allowing me to use photographs from their extensive archives.

The thoughtful edits and suggestions by Susan Towne and my wife Tucker were also greatly appreciated and add much value to this presentation. I am also very thankful to Tomas Benton and Marianne Kelsey Orestis for allowing me the use of their works to help tell the story of what happened on the ground in Vietnam.

CONTENTS

PROLOGUE

Those who cannot remember the past are condemned to repeat it.

George Santayana
American Philosopher

It would be hard for anyone watching the evening news on April 29, 1975, to forget the sight of desperate refugees trying to board a Huey Slick as it lifted off in Saigon during the fall of South Vietnam. Likewise, it would be hard for anyone watching the evening news on August 16, 2021, to forget the sight of desperate refugees clinging to the side of an Air Force C-17 as it lifted off the runway in Kabul during the fall off Afghanistan.

The U.S. departures from Vietnam and Afghanistan were similar in that they were both chaotic.[i] They were also similar in that, in both instances, the United States was able to evacuate over a hundred thousand allies but had to leave hundreds of thousands behind.[ii]

Besides these similarities there was also a difference: America wanted to help those left behind in Afghanistan but when it came to Vietnam there was not much of an appetite to do so. As the end approached in Vietnam, for example, then Senator Joseph R. Biden (D) made it clear he would "…vote for any amount [to get] the Americans out.." but, he added, "I don't want it mixed up with getting the Vietnamese out."[iii]

The lack of a domestic desire to help our South Vietnamese allies became even more apparent when Saigon fell. That same day, President Gerald R. Ford urged Congress to appropriate $507 million to transport and care for the 120,000 South Vietnamese who had escaped the war-torn country. Congress completely rejected that request the following day;[iv] "unbelievable,"[v] Ford said.

But, things began to change in July 1986 when Ho Chi Minh's hardline deputy, Le Duan, died. After his death all of Vietnam's wartime leaders resigned from the politburo by year's end, clearing the way for a younger more reconciliatory generation of leaders to ascend to power.[vi] By 1987, Vietnam's new leadership "deeply coveted normalization with the United States…,"[vii] and by 1987 the United States had come to appreciate its obligation to the Vietnamese it had left behind.

As a result of negotiations with this new more mellow Vietnamese leadership Vietnam went from being an enemy of the United States under the Trading with the Enemy Act in 1993, to having this classification lifted in 1994, to normalized relations in 1995, to exchanging Ambassadors in 1997, to entering into Most Favored Nation (MFN) status in 2001.[viii]

In 1975, it would have been hard to believe the president of the United States would be in Hanoi in 2000 telling a cheering crowd that, "…America is now the home to one million Americans of Vietnamese ancestry."[ix] But, as a result of cooperation between the two countries, that is what happened.

**President William J. Clinton in Hanoi on November 18, 2000.
(National Archives)**

In 1983, when Vietnam's average per capita income was $150 a year,[x] it would also have been hard to believe that *USA Today* would be calling Ho Chi Minh City (Saigon) a "cosmopolitan city [buzzing] with entrepreneurial energy in 2015."[xi] And, finally, it would have been hard to believe that a Vietnamese automaker would be announcing the opening a $6.5 billion electric vehicle plant in North Carolina in 2024.[xii] But, as a result of cooperation between the two countries, that is what happened.

Today there are further similarities between the end in Vietnam and the end in Afghanistan. In 2022, after a year under Taliban rule "[t]he Afghan people [like the Vietnamese in 1976] are living a human rights nightmare;"[xiii] furthermore, Afghanistan's economy (like Vietnam's in 1976) is on the brink of devastation[xiv] and in need of international funding.[xv] Likewise, no one today believes that the president of the United States will ever be in Kabul telling a cheering crowd that

America is now the home for a million new Americans of Afghan ancestry. But the possibility does exist.

The possibility exists because, in spite of the "nightmare" in Afghanistan, the United States and the Taliban are still engaged in negotiations.[xvi] Since the United States already feels an obligation to those it left behind all that may be needed now is a younger "more reconciliatory" leadership in Afghanistan. In 1975, no one thought the hard line communist leadership in Vietnam would ever mellow, but with time it happened. Hopefully the same thing will happen in Afghanistan, sooner rather than later.

An added incentive for the Taliban to mellow sooner rather than later is Russia's desire to rebuild its empire. Kabul should well remember Russia's invasion in the 1980s and America's assistance that helped save it from becoming a Russian satellite near the end of the Cold War. In the face of what may be the coming of a second Cold War, it would be mutually advantageous for Afghanistan and the United States to become partners once again, sooner rather than later.

But this book is not about the beginning of a second Cold War: it is about Vietnam and the role it played in ending the Cold War that began in 1947.

PREFACE

Every day in Vietnam, Dave Gagermier religiously kept a diary; whether in trial or out on firebases hunting down witnesses, he still made time for his diary entries. This seemed like a lot of work to me and I once asked him why he kept this diary so meticulously. Because, he said, "Someday I am going to write a book and," he added, "If you ever read it you might even find yourself in there somewhere."

After Vietnam I moved to Virginia and Dave to Indiana and we exchanged Christmas cards for a while but, as often happens, this came to an end somewhere along the way. After Vietnam, I did not hear anything further about Dave's book but I did recently learn about his untimely passing from Bob McNamara, a mutual friend.

I met Bob over forty years ago when he moved to Virginia from Indiana and, to make small talk after being introduced, I mentioned that I knew one person in Indiana and that person, I said, was Dave Gagermier. After a very long pause, and a sideways look, Bob said, "Are you kidding me, Dave is my best friend." Then it was my turn to pause, and ask if he was kidding me? He was not. What are the chances of that?

Unlike Dave, I did not keep a diary or plan on writing a book until a few years ago when I started reading the Pentagon Papers and became interested in the decision-making process that led us into Vietnam. At that time I began writing down my own thoughts and, to put things in perspective, I did so in the form of a timeline.

The timeline by itself, however, seemed pretty sterile so I asked a few Vietnam Veterans to take a look at the manuscript and give me some feedback, which they did. One, for example, said it "looked like a bunch of 3x5 cards stacked on top of each other" and, to make it more interesting, another suggested that I put in some personal experiences.

With these comments in mind, I went back through the manuscript and reduced the timeline (took out some of the 3x5 cards) and added some personal experiences. Regardless of the form, however, the focus of the book is on whether the United States did the right thing by going into Vietnam.

In the 1960s, opinions varied around the country and in the halls of Congress where, for example, Congressman Donald Riegle (R/D) was so opposed to the war he could not bring himself to tell constituents of his, who had lost their son in Vietnam, that their loss "was in their interest or in the national interest or in anyone's interest."[xvii]

Many then, and today, share the former Congressman's point of view. In fact, in June 2022, as the 50th anniversary of the "Watergate break-in" approached, the *Washington Post* said in a front-page article that:

> Watergate, along with the Vietnam War, marked a dividing line between old and new, ushering in a changed landscape for politics and public life -- from a period in which Americans trusted their government to a period in which the trust was broken and never truly restored. ...[xviii]

The Watergate incident, with good reason, caused Americans to lose trust in their government, but I hope to show here that the Vietnam War, with all its warts, is a different matter.

I do not write as a "combat veteran" in the following pages because, as it should be understood from the outset, I am not a combat veteran. I write, instead, as a lawyer by: setting the stage; laying out the relevant facts as I see them (along with some trivia); arguing the case, and then making a summation.

Christmas 1969 at Camp Enari, Vietnam: from left to right, Cliff Wentworth, Richard Holt, John Erch, and Dave Gagermier.

INTRODUCTION

In 1965, after four years in ROTC at the University of Richmond, I was commissioned a 2nd Lieutenant in the United States Army and in September 1968, shortly after graduating from the University of Richmond School of law, I entered the Judge Advocate General's Corps (JAG Corps). Thereafter, my class of 200 newly minted Captains was given additional legal training at the Army's "JAG School," then annexed to the University of Virginia law school, and now a stand-alone campus facility.

At JAG School we were taught how to prosecute and defend cases under the Uniform Code of Military Justice, and how to handle many other legal matters unique to the Army that are not ordinarily found on state bar exams. After four months of training, we were sent on our way.

Fort Sam Houston, in San Antonio, Texas was my first stop, and life was good there. My wife, Tucker, and I were in post housing with others our age; I had a regular paycheck and my brother, his wife, and my parents lived in town. Our quarters were small, but the back yard was a chip shot from the 10th tee box on the Ft. Sam golf course. Particularly nice was the half day we had each week for PT (Physical Training), which included golf if you walked and carried your bag.

My office at Ft. Sam Houston consisted of a metal desk in a big hallway shared with three other new JAGs. My first assignment there was to determine whether injured soldiers had incurred their injuries in the line of duty (LOD) or not (NLOD), one of those unique legal matters not found on the bar exam.

While this did not seem like important work to my friends and family it was important to those who were injured because a NLOD determination meant you had to pay for your own medical expenses. Take, for example, the situation that came up later in Vietnam when a soldier tried to sneak into downtown An Khe for an evening with the ladies but instead was seriously injured when the perimeter guards heard noise in the wire and opened fire.

This was a NLOD type injury and the commanding general wanted the consequences enforced to deter similar activity by others. Fortunately, (or unfortunately) for this soldier his injuries were so serious he had to be medevacked to Japan and the matter was not pursued.

But I am getting ahead of myself. Back at Fort Sam Houston I soon moved on to more traditional legal work like writing wills, preparing powers of attorney and dealing with domestic relation problems. Then, after about three months, I was assigned to represent Richard Reynolds[*] who was in serious trouble.

Reynolds, a high school football star, was a big guy who had just been drafted … by the army that is. In a nutshell, it was alleged that Reynolds and two others had lain in wait at an isolated stop sign on Post. It was further alleged that when an unaccompanied female stopped at this sign Reynolds opened the car door; grabbed the woman's purse, and fled with his accomplices. It did not help matters that Reynolds was in possession of the stolen purse when he was later apprehended; nor did it help that the victim was the Post Commander's wife.

While I was inexperienced, I did know that the robbery charge facing Reynolds was serious and that he probably would be prosecuted in a

---

[*] Some names have been changed; this is one them.

general court-martial where the maximum sentence, if convicted, was ten years in prison and a dishonorable discharge. I also knew that if Reynolds was tried by a special court-martial the maximum sentence (at the time) was six months in the local stockade with no discharge.

Therefore, I knew enough to immediately try to convince the prosecutor that justice would best be served if this case was prosecuted in a special court-martial, or essentially as a misdemeanor. That is eventually what happened and, at trial, Reynolds was convicted and "got the max." I would see him again later.

The next criminal matter to come my way was a young soldier who was about to be included as a defendant in a rather sensational murder case. The suspect, however, insisted he was not guilty (I will call him NG) and I believed him. But, convincing the Criminal Investigation Division (CID) was another matter.

CID, however, finally agreed it would not include NG in their prosecution referral if he could pass a polygraph test. I accepted their terms and, after the test was administered, the polygrapher concluded NG was being truthful. Accordingly, per the agreement, NG was not referred for prosecution.

Submitting NG to a government administered polygraph examination, without testing him first, was a big risk but the case was moving fast, and once charged with murder things can go sideways in a hurry. So now, right out of law school, I was doing the kind of work I wanted to do plus I was able to play golf and softball in the evenings, and spend time with my family on the weekends. Life, as I say, was good.

Then, in July 1969, just as I was getting ready to play golf on a PT afternoon, I got a phone call from my "office-mate" whose grey metal desk was next to mine in the hallway. He had called to ask if I wanted him to open a letter from JAG's Office of Personnel that had just been placed on my desk, and I did.

I suspected the letter included orders to Vietnam, but I still wanted to know when I would be leaving. My suspicions were soon confirmed and I shortly learned that my departure date was 23 August; I decided not to play golf that afternoon.

Shortly after I got this letter, Ed Collins, who had been in the office for three years, received similar orders with the same departure date. This meant we could compare notes as we prepared to go. For starters, we both had to clear our desks as best we could and we both had to complete a week of "in-country" training in the 100-degree Texas heat which was a good preview of coming attractions. In my case, I also had to get four impacted and infected wisdom teeth pulled; I knew my PT days were over.

One good thing about the departure date was that my wife and I were able to join our new friends, Tim and Karen Harper, on a road trip to the west coast. The plan was to drive from San Antonio to San Francisco stopping when we felt like it, with two days in Las Vegas definitely on the agenda.

When we got to Las Vegas, I spent the first day standing in line to get tickets to see Elvis Presley who was in the middle of his 1969 "comeback tour." As expected, he put on a great show, and also, as expected, we had a great road trip to San Francisco, with the exception of my wife's car sickness (which turned out to be morning sickness).

In San Francisco, Tim and Karen dropped us at the airport and my wife caught a flight back to San Antonio. From there my brother was kind enough to drive our car (a VW bug), a stray dog I had picked up, and my wife back to her home in Fairfax, Virginia. Ed Collins, who had flown in from Massachusetts that morning, met me at the airport and we spent the rest of the day with one of his Notre Dame classmates.

After a day of beer and Notre Dame stories Ed's friend dropped us at the Greyhound bus station in San Francisco for the last leg of our trip to Oakland's Army Air Terminal. And, while waiting in line for our bus to Oakland, I could faintly hear the Doors front man, Jim Morrison, singing *Light My Fire* on someone's distant boom box. This turned my thoughts to an earlier time.

Eight years had passed since 1961, when Jim and I graduated from high school in Alexandria, Virginia, and since then our lives had taken distinctly different paths. I was in San Francisco … on my way to Vietnam, and Morrison was in L.A. … on his way to the Rock & Roll Hall of Fame.

But when the P.A. system announced that the night's last bus to the Army Air Terminal in Oakland had been canceled my reminiscing stopped and reality returned since this development meant we were going to miss our flight to Vietnam. As Ed and I discussed this turn of events a nearby Army Sergeant added that, in addition to being AWOL, anyone who missed a scheduled flight to Vietnam had to pay for the next one.

It did not take us long to figure out that, while expensive, a cab to Oakland would not cost as much as a flight to Vietnam so we, along with an infantry lieutenant in line with us, grabbed our duffle bags; ran out front, and hailed a taxi. Just before the cab pulled away from the curb a war protestor in front of the station ran over; stuck his head in the front window, and yelled to no one in particular, "Die First."

A send off like this on August 23, 1969, was not surprising as that same week more than 400,000 people would gather on a dairy farm outside of Woodstock, New York where they would protest "the war" and make love (not necessarily in that order) during a 32 act, 3-day, rock concert.

Also adding to the turbulence of the time was the trial of the so-called "Chicago Seven"[*] which was set to begin in a month. The defendants in that case had been charged with, among other things, conspiring to incite a riot, a year earlier, at the 1968 Democratic National Convention in protest of the Vietnam War. And, when the trial finally began the situation was so volatile the National Guard had to be called in to keep the peace.

There were no bands playing for those leaving for Vietnam in the fall of 1969 and when they came back, if they did, there was no one "thanking them for their service." The late 1960s was definitely a turbulent time, as more and more Americans were starting to believe the United States should never have gone to Vietnam in the first place.

This belief crested in 1985 when over 70% of the country felt that way. However, polls now show that many Americans have begun to realize that this war was more confusing than first meets the eye, and in the coming pages I hope to show why.

---

[*] The trial actually started with eight defendants but one, Bobby Seale, was later severed.

CHAPTER ONE
The Setting

At the end of World War II France thought French Indochina, as constituted in 1940, would be returned to them as a colony. This, however, created a problem because President Franklin D. Roosevelt had previously said he did not believe French Indochina should be returned to France as a colony, an opinion he repeated at the Cairo Conference in December 1943.[xix]

But, at the Yalta Conference in February 1945, Roosevelt partially changed his position and proposed, instead, that France be made trustee of Indochina "with the proviso that independence was the ultimate goal."[xx] This modification, however, did not satisfy Charles de Gaulle, Chairman of the Provisional French Republic, who, upon learning of Roosevelt's position, sent him the following communiqué on March 13, 1945:

> If the public here [in France] comes to realize that you are against us in Indochina there will be terrific disappointment, and nobody knows to what that would lead. We do not want to fall into the Russian orbit, [in Europe] but I hope you do not push us into it.[xxi]

A few weeks after Roosevelt received de Gaulle's communiqué, he also received a Secret report from the OSS (Office of Strategic Services - - precursor to the CIA) warning him about the threat posed by a rapidly rising Russian Empire. In this April 2, 1945, report Roosevelt was informed that:

> Russia [would] emerge from the present conflict [World War II] as by far the strongest nation in Europe and Asia---strong enough, if the United States should stand aside, to dominate Europe and at the same time to establish her hegemony [dominance] over Asia. Russia's natural resources and manpower are so great that within relatively few years she can be much more powerful than either Germany or Japan has ever been. In the easily foreseeable future Russia may well outrank even the United States in military potential.[xxii]

Ten days later Roosevelt died.

Upon Roosevelt's death, Vice President Harry S. Truman became president of the United States. Among the many matters sitting on Truman's desk when he assumed office was the "de Gaulle/Indochina problem," which was aggravated by the fact the French Communist Party was France's largest and most militant political party,[xxiii] making it quite possible France could fall into the "Russian orbit" if pushed.

There was also a problem in Asia where Nationalist China (America's "forgotten ally" in the Pacific) "wanted an independent Korea and Vietnam to be [governed] under a joint Sino-American tutelage."[xxiv] This was further complicated because Roosevelt, after first promising Manchuria (now northern China) to Nationalist China, instead handed it over to Russia at the Yalta conference in return for Stalin's promise to join in the war against Japan if Germany should surrender.[xxv] In spite of, or maybe because of, these competing demands Truman decided that U.S. policies in Indochina would be dictated by military needs.[xxvi] Therefore, he left decisions regarding territorial control of Southeast Asia to the Combined Chiefs of Staff of the allies in the Pacific (the United States, Great Britain and Nationalist China).[xxvii]

On May 8, 1945, Germany surrendered to end World War II in Europe and two months later, with the threat of a ruthless Stalin* on his mind, Truman, traveled to Potsdam, Germany to participate in the "Potsdam Conference" that opened on July 7, 1945.[xxviii]

Traveling to Potsdam, where territorial control of post-war Europe would be under consideration, Truman knew the Soviet army occupied most of Eastern Europe and he knew he would not be able to change

---

* Stalin was, indeed, ruthless. He presided over the starvation of over 3.5 million Ukrainians between 1931 and 1934 during the *Holodomor* (a word derived from the Ukrainian words for hunger - - *holod* and extermination - - *mor*). In addition, he liquidated a million people who opposed his policies and sent ten million others to forced labor camps.

the borders where "the Red Army stood." He also knew he would not be able to revisit agreements made at Yalta.[xxix] He, therefore, had two goals in mind.

First, Truman wanted to ensure that Russia kept its "Yalta promise" to join in the war against Japan. General Dwight D. Eisenhower on the other hand, did not think America should give the Russians anything for their assistance in the Pacific[*] as he, unlike General Douglas MacArthur, thought their help was no longer needed. Therefore, on July 20, 1945, Eisenhower advised Truman not to invite Russia into the war in the Pacific.[xxx] This advice, however, came two days too late.

Secondly, Truman wanted to dismantle Germany on his, instead of Stalin's terms,[xxxi] because he believed Stalin had his eyes set on taking control of Germany.

As Stalin was travelling to Potsdam, he was thinking about the twenty-seven million Russians killed during World War II,[xxxii] leaving him of the opinion he was entitled to the territory on which his Army stood and more. Consequently, when Stalin got to Potsdam he refused to budge on most issues, causing post-war Europe to tilt toward Russia.

At Potsdam, British Prime Minister Winston Churchill, Soviet Generalissimo Stalin and President Truman presided over a gathering that would change post-World War II borders. It was said that Truman and Churchill "made the big concessions because they had little choice—Russian occupation of Eastern Europe was indeed a fait accompli... and because they hoped to achieve harmony with Stalin."[xxxiii]

---

[*] Eisenhower thought that no power on earth could keep the "Red Army" out of (the war against Japan) unless victory came before they could get in.

While Stalin did not concede much at Potsdam, Truman did convince him to partition Germany into four zones of military occupation (the American, British and French zones in the West and the Soviet zone in the East) [xxxiv] This configuration, Truman believed, would make it difficult for Russia to take control of Germany (and it did).

Furthermore, Stalin agreed at Potsdam to partition the city of Berlin (located deep in East Germany) into the Soviet (Eastern) and allied (Western) zones.[xxxv] In addition to reshaping European borders at Potsdam, decisions were also made about post-war Asia, where the war continued. Decisions were being made before the war's end in Asia because, in spite of Japan's resolve, the major allies in the Pacific (Nationalist China, Great Britain and the United States) were becoming more optimistic about the final outcome.

Optimism was beginning to run high on Truman's part because on the eleventh day of the Potsdam Conference, July 18, 1945, Russia agreed to join the war against Japan no later than August 15, 1945, supposedly with no strings attached.[xxxvi] Truman's optimism further increased three days later on July 21 when he received a coded message advising him of the first successful nuclear test at Los Alamos, New Mexico.[xxxvii] This was also good news to the Chairman of the U.S. Joint Chiefs of Staff, General George C. Marshall, who thought an invasion of Japan would result in 250,000 American deaths,[xxxviii] other estimates ran as high as a million.[xxxix] After considering Marshall's concerns and other matters Truman, on July 25, 1945, ordered the use of "the bomb" if necessary.[xl]

However, prior to dropping this bomb the Pacific allies called upon Japan to unconditionally surrender or face "utter devastation of the Japanese homeland."[xli] This "Declaration" or demand was delivered on July 26, 1945, over the airwaves and in leaflets dropped on ten cities, including Tokyo.[xlii] Early on July 27, 1945, the Declaration was heard by the Japanese on the radio and, after an all-day cabinet meeting, Japan's prime minister rejected its terms; calling them beneath contempt.[xliii]

Upon Japan's defeat, if it came to pass, the Combined Chiefs of Staff of the allied commands in the Pacific decided at Potsdam that, what was formerly French Indochina would for "operational purposes" be divided at the 16th parallel with Japan surrendering the northern half to China and the southern half to Great Britain.[xliv] This provision was set forth in General Order No. 1.

Japan's options began to narrow when an atomic bomb was dropped on Hiroshima on August 6, 1945.[xlv] With no surrender forthcoming, a second bomb was dropped on Nagasaki on August 8, at which point the Soviets, anticipating Japan's surrender, jumped into the War in the Pacific on the same day.[xlvi] On August 10, 1945, Japan advised it would accept the terms of the Potsdam Declaration if their Emperor could remain the Sovereign.[xlvii]

In a cable to Washington on the evening of August 10, Great Britain agreed to accept Japan's terms; on August 11, Nationalist China and, reluctantly, Australia agreed. However, "(t)he Soviets appeared to be stalling in the hope of having some control over Japan and to drive further into Manchuria."[xlviii]

Indeed, while waiting for Japan's official surrender, Stalin, a day after joining the war in the Pacific, began marching through Manchuria toward Korea with two Army Divisions.[xlix] The United States, with its closest troops on Okinawa 600 miles away, could only watch as Russia gobbled up this territory.[l]

To address this immediate "Russia problem" the War Department held emergency meetings on August 10 and 11. After these meetings Washington recommended (to Russia) that Japan surrender that part of Korea south of the 38th parallel to the U.S. and that part north of the 38th parallel to Russia; Russia (surprisingly) accepted.[li]

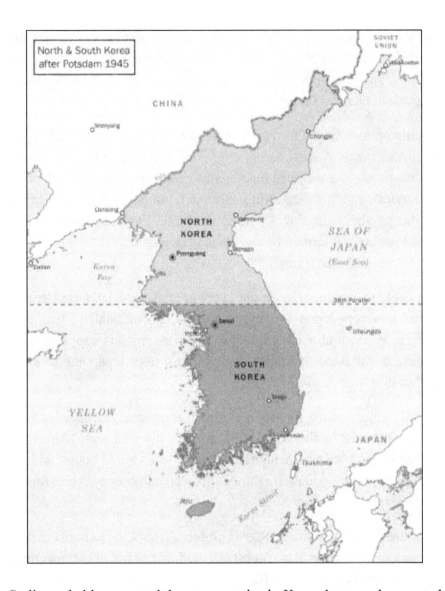

Stalin probably accepted the compromise in Korea because he wanted to save his army for a planned invasion of Japan. However, "pressure from Truman—and the implicit threat of the atomic bomb—caused Stalin to reverse course just…before his scheduled invasion, and northern Japan was spared the fate of North Korea in the postwar years."[lii]

After being informed that its Emperor could remain as Sovereign, Japan surrendered[liii] on August 14, 1945. The surrender documents, however, were not finalized until signed on September 2, 1945, during a ceremony aboard the USS Missouri where the previously agreed upon terms of Japan's surrender of Korea were formalized in General Order No. 1.[liv]

With the assistance of General MacArthur, exiled patriot Syngman Rhee (69) was brought back to South Korea in October 1945, to help rule the country.[lv] Also in 1945 the guerilla chieftain, Kim Il Sung,[*] was handpicked by the Soviets to become North Korea's head of state.[lvi]

On October 24, 1945, fifty different countries officially established the United Nations,[lvii] but this did not necessarily mean all these countries would cooperate with each other, and they did not. In February 1946, for example, the U.S. State Department asked the Charge d' Affaires of its embassy in Moscow, George Kennan,[**] why the Soviet Union was opposing the recently formed World Bank and International Monetary Fund.[lviii]

On February 22, 1946, Kennan responded to this inquiry with a 5,000-word telegram, the so-called "Long-Telegram." In this telegram he advised, among other things, that the:

> …Basic Features of Post War Soviet Outlook, as Put Forward by Official Propaganda Machine, Are as Follows:

---

[*] Kim Il Sung was the grandfather of Kim Jung-Un, North Korea's current head of state.
[**] Keenan had lived in Moscow before and after World War II.

(A) USSR still lives in antagonistic "capitalist encirclement" with which in the long run there can be no permanent peaceful coexistence. As stated by Stalin in 1927 to a delegation of American workers:

"In course of further development of international revolution there will emerge two centers of world significance: a socialist center, drawing to itself the countries which tend toward socialism, and a capitalist center, drawing to itself the countries that incline toward capitalism. Battle between these two centers for command of world economy will decide fate of capitalism and of communism in entire world."

*****

[And, said Kennan in summary]:

...we have here a political force committed fanatically to the belief that with US there can be no permanent *modus vivendi*, [agreement] that it is desirable and necessary that the internal harmony of our society be disrupted, our traditional way of life be destroyed, the international authority of our state be broken, if Soviet power is to be secure. This political force has complete power of disposition over energies of one of world's greatest peoples and resources of world's richest national territory, and is borne along by deep and powerful currents of Russian nationalism... this is admittedly not a pleasant picture... but I would like to record my conviction that problem is within our power to solve – without recourse to any general military conflict...[lix]

*****

Thus, began the Cold War concept of containing communism,[lx] and stopping the: "(a)bolition of private property."[lxi]

In a March 1946 speech, Churchill, also concerned about Russian dominance, dejectedly, noted that:

From Stettin to the Baltic to Trieste to the Adriatic, *an iron curtain had descended across the Continen*t. Behind the line lie all the capitols of the ancient states of Central and Eastern Europe. Warsaw, Berlin, Prague, Vienna, Budapest, Belgrade, Bucharest, and Sofia, all these famous cities and the populations around them lie in what I must call the Soviet sphere, and all are subject in one form or another, not only to Soviet influence, but to a very high and, in many cases, increasing measure of control from Moscow.[lxii] (Emphasis mine)

*****

[And, he added] no one knew 'the limits, if any to [the] expansive and proselytizing tendencies' of the Soviet Union and its Communist International [Comintern].[lxiii]

Churchill was a private citizen when he gave this speech having been defeated eight months earlier in Great Britain's general election (while he was representing Great Britain at the Potsdam Conference). Even so, he called it "the most important speech of his career."[lxiv]

In 1947, Great Britain informed Truman it could no longer afford to financially help Turkey and Greece defend themselves against attempted communist takeovers.[lxv] Upon receiving this information Truman went before a joint session of Congress and asked for financial aid to help both countries resist the spread of communism. In making this request, he said:

> the United States [is] compelled to assist 'free peoples' in their struggles against 'totalitarian regimes,' because the spread of authoritarianism would 'undermine the foundations of international peace and hence the security of the United States.[lxvi]

Congress responded with a $400 million bill which Truman signed into law on May 22, 1947, stating that, "The conditions of peace include, among other things, the ability of nations to maintain order and independence and to support themselves economically."[lxvii] Thus began the Truman Doctrine of containment and an official declaration of the "Cold War."

On February 24, 1948, with the Soviet army poised on its border, the Czech Republic (a symbol of democracy in Central Europe since World War I) fell to a communist coup d'etat and became a Soviet satellite overnight.[lxviii]

Accordingly, the United States expanded the Cold War a little over a month later with a $12 billion European Recovery Program (the Marshall plan) designed to help rebuild Western Europe.[lxix] In announcing the coming program, Secretary of State Marshall said, "Our policy is directed not against any country or doctrine, but against hunger, poverty, desperation, and chaos."[lxx]

Then, on June 11, 1948, the Senate passed the "Vandenberg Resolution," which advised the president to seek security through regional mutual defense agreements.[lxxi] This approach would eventually be employed by the United States and would turn out to be an important part of America's foreign policy in the coming years.

On July 20, 1948, Syngman Rhee was elected president of the Republic of (South) Korea[lxxii] and, in September 1948, North Korea declared that henceforth it would be known as the Democratic People's Republic of Korea, and that the guerilla chieftain Kim Il Sung would be its premier. When Rhee and Kim took office, each avowedly intended to join the two "Republics" into a single Korea under their own control.[lxxiii]

In October 1948, the Soviets recognized the Democratic People's Republic of Korea (North Korea) as the only lawful government in Korea.[lxxiv] In December 1948, the UN General Assembly responded by declaring that the Republic of Korea (South Korea) was the only lawful government in Korea.[lxxv]

Meanwhile, back in Germany in 1948 the United States, Great Britain and France unified their separate German zones into one zone which they renamed West Germany. This, Stalin declared, was a violation of the Potsdam Agreement[lxxvi] causing him to withdraw from the four-power administration of Berlin and order the United States, Great Britain, and France (the allies) to leave the city.[lxxvii] To back up his order Stalin placed a blockade around West Berlin, on June 26, 1948, thereby, stopping the flow of all essential goods into the city. In addition, he stationed 40 army divisions in East Germany in preparation for battle.[lxxviii]

The United States responded in July 1948 by stationing three groups of strategic bombers in Great Britain.[lxxix] And, with tensions running high, the allies, before taking military action, put an embargo of their own on East German exports and air-lifted food and other vital supplies into West Berlin.[lxxx] The same month (July) the United States began discussing the formation of a mutual defense treaty with Great Britain, France, Belgium, the Netherlands, Luxemburg and Canada.[lxxxi]

On November 29, 1948, British diplomat Harold Nicolson, "reflecting the anxiety of the times," wrote in his diary that:

> Russia is preparing for the final battle for world mastery and that once she has enough bombs she will destroy Western Europe, occupy Asia, and have a final death struggle with the Americans. [The odds of peace continuing he guessed were] not one in twenty.[lxxxii]

In April 1949, the North Atlantic Treaty Organization (NATO) was formed. Its original members* were: Belgium, Canada, Denmark, France, Iceland, Italy, Luxemburg, the Netherlands, Norway, Portugal, the United Kingdom, and the United States.[lxxxiii]

On September 30, 1949, Stalin peacefully ended his blockade of Berlin and, even though West Berlin was not strategically important, the allied resistance to the siege "became a symbol of willingness to oppose further Soviet expansion in Europe."[lxxxiv]

"The Soviet Union made no further conquests in Western Europe or the Near East after its post-war military occupation of Eastern and Central Europe. But containment was not employed early enough in the Far East..." [lxxxv] because, it was correctly noted, the Truman administration did not know as much about Asia as it did about Europe.[lxxxvi]

---

* By 2022 the following countries had joined the original NATO members: Greece, Turkey, Germany, Spain, the Czech Republic, Hungary, Poland, Bulgaria, Estonia, Latvia, Lithuania, Romania, Slovakia, Slovenia, Albania, Croatia, and Montenegro.

And, in February 1949, Truman made his first big mistake in Asia when he decided to stop sending military supplies and economic aid to Nationalist China. He made this decision because Secretary Marshall for some reason had come to believe Nationalist leader, Chiang Kai-shek, a World War II ally, (who had just lost 14 million people fighting Japan)[lxxxvii] was not much better than the Chinese Communist leader Mao Zedong.[lxxxviii]

Senator Arthur Vandenberg (R)[*] disagreed with this assessment, and noted in his diary at the time: "If, at the very moment when Chiang's Nationalists are desperately trying to negotiate some kind of peace with the communists, we suspend all military shipments to the Nationalists, we certainly shall make any hope of negotiated peace impossible. We shall thus virtually notify the communists that they can consider the [Chinese civil] war ended and themselves as victors."[lxxxix] Senator Vandenberg, as it turned out, would be correct.

Additional communist gains were made in Asia in 1945 when Kusnasosro Sukarno, a communist backed nationalist, declared that he intended to take control of Indonesia, a heavily populated chain of islands spanning one-eighth of the world's globe in Maritime Southeast Asia.[xc]

On September 23, 1949, the Soviets successfully tested an atomic bomb giving them the same firepower as the United States.[xci] Furthermore, as predicted by Senator Vandenberg, Mao, who acknowledged Stalin as the leader of the worldwide communist

---

[*] Senator Vandenberg was the President pro tempore of the Senate from 1947 to 1949, and architect of the Vandenberg Resolution, that had advised the president to seek security through regional mutual defense arrangements.

revolution, seized control of Nationalist China[xcii] and brought China into the communist fold on October 1, 1949.

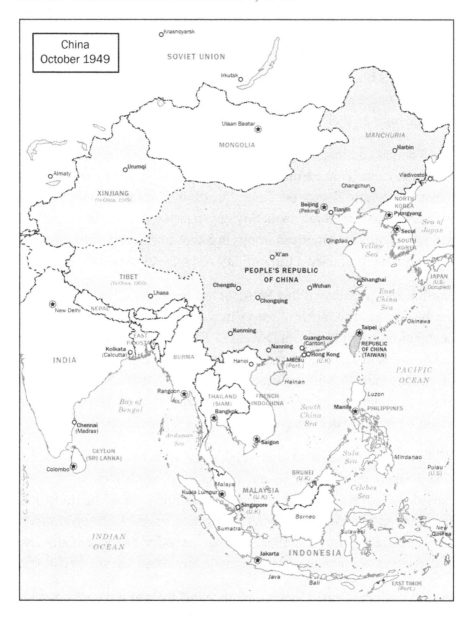

"The 'loss' of [mainland] China to communism at a pivotal moment in the early Cold War … had especially unsettling consequences. It extended to East Asia a conflict that had been confined largely to Europe. In one stroke it appeared to shift the global balance of power against the United States."[xciii] According to the Pentagon Papers, the Republicans blamed this loss squarely on the Truman Administration (correctly) saying that cuts in assistance to the Chinese Nationalists had undermined their ability to defend themselves.[xciv]

The Truman administration was soon to be tested again when Kim Il Sung, after receiving permission from Stalin, launched an invasion to "liberate" South Korea on June 25, 1950.[xcv] Truman, now under pressure to do something about Soviet expansion in Asia, immediately authorized the few American troops in Korea to respond militarily and he, thereafter, promised a full military response to the invasion.[xcvi]

North Korea's breach of this Potsdam territorial demarcation line was the beginning of a bitter three-year war that was at an impasse in negotiations when President Dwight D. Eisenhower, promising an end to hostilities in Korea, entered office in January 1953. The likelihood of ending these hostilities was enhanced on March 5, 1953, when Stalin died and his successor, George Malenkov, used the occasion of Stalin's funeral to declare a need for "peaceful coexistence."[xcvii]

Within weeks, consistent with Malenkov's declaration, the Soviet Union voted to withdraw its assistance from North Korea.[xcviii] This caused the North Koreans to fear further fighting would be futile and such proved to be the case. After a few more months of negotiations the war ended on July 27, 1953, with an armistice that essentially left both nations where they were geographically when the war began.[xcix]

Even though the United States did not "win" the war it did stop Soviet expansion; moreover, as historian Richard H. Rovere said:

the United States proved [in Korea] that its word was as good as its bond—and even better, since no bond had been given. History will cite Korea as the proving ground of collective security, up to this time no more than a plausible theory. [History] will cite it as the turning point of the world struggle against Communism.[c]

As the Korean War was winding down in Asia another struggle against communism was heating up. It is a separate, but intertwined, story; it is the Vietnam story.

CHAPTER TWO
200 BCE to 1955

The evolution of modern-day Vietnam began around 200 BCE when Trieu Da, a former Chinese general, took control of an area in southernmost China that ran from the Red River delta (near modern day Hanoi) down the coast as far south as (modern day) Da Nang. This area was mainly populated by a group of people known as the Viets who had been driven there by the Chinese.[ci]

After taking control of this territory Trieu Da renamed his new kingdom Nam Viet,[*] and killed all those loyal to the Chinese emperor. Nam Viet remained independent for about 300 years until it was reconquered by China in 111 CE, and would remain under Chinese control for about one thousand years.[cii]

However, after a series of uprisings, the territory would regain its independence in 939 at which time it became known as Dai Viet. Between 1100 and 1200 Dai Viet fought the Islamic kingdom of Champa on the central coast and the Khmer (Cambodian) empire to its west, but its biggest rival was the Mongul dynasty in the north which had taken power in China in 1200.[ciii]

Dai Viet, was able to maintain its independence until 1407 when it was reconquered by China. But, after only eleven years the Chinese were driven out and the territory once again became known as Dai Viet.[civ]

The rulers of Dai Viet, in need of more land, then began to expand southward and continued to do so, for 300 years with in-fighting along the way.[cv] The in-fighting began when the Mac Family, led by the

---

[*] "Nam" meaning "south or southern."

27

governor of modern-day Hanoi, deposed the Le family and took control of Dai Viet in 1527; this conflict was resolved after 50 years of civil war when the Le family regained control.[cvi]

A power struggle, however, picked up again in the late 1500s this time it was between the Nguyen family in the south and the Trinh family in the north. During this struggle, the Nguyen family erected two walls along the 17th parallel (basically the line drawn by the Geneva Accords in 1954) dividing it from the Trinh family. For 200 hundred years each family vied for total control until a revolution broke out and the entire territory passed to the Tay Son family in the 1700s.[cvii]

In the late 1700s three brothers from the Tay Son family took control of Dai Vet and divided it into three separate states.[cviii] This resulted in political chaos and continuous fighting[cix] until 1802 when Gia Long united the three states;[cx] renamed the territory Vietnam,[cxi] and declared himself Emperor.

This unified period lasted for about sixty years and was said to have been "filled with great tyranny, intrigue and bloodletting..."[cxii]

In 1858, France and Spain sent military forces to Vietnam in response to the alleged persecution of their Catholic missionaries.[cxiii] After four years, Spain left but France remained and took control of the three eastern provinces in Cochinchina in 1862.[cxiv] In 1863, Cambodia, at its request, became a French protectorate,[cxv] and in 1867 France took control of the three western provinces in Cochinchina (southern Vietnam).[cxvi]

In 1883, the northern and central territories in Vietnam (Tonkin and Annam) signed a treaty with France that made them French protectorates, and in 1887 France combined Tonkin, Annam and Cochinchina with Cambodia and formed the Indochinese Union or

French Indochina.^{cxvii} In 1893, Laos was added to this Union.^{cxviii} (See Map p.7)

In February 1930, Vietnamese troops opposed to French rule mutinied but were quickly suppressed.^{cxix} In 1932, Bao Dai became the figurehead ruler of Tonkin, Annam and Cochinchina when France made him Emperor of this territory (once again called Vietnam).^{cxx}

In September 1940, Japan's military took control of Vietnam, but reached an agreement with Vietnam's Vichy French* government that permitted Bao Dai to remain the administrative "ruler."^{cxxi} In 1941, however, Tokyo went from just using the bases in Vietnam to demanding a presence that was tantamount to the occupation of Indochina.^{cxxii} When this happened the United States became very concerned because at that time Southeast Asia supplied the U.S. with about ninety percent of its crude rubber and seventy-five percent of its tin. In addition, U.S. oil companies produced twenty-seven percent of the sizeable amount of oil produced in the East Indies.^{cxxiii}

Consequently, President Roosevelt informed the Japanese Ambassador to the United States that he was becoming very alarmed about Japan's presence in Indochina and told him that:

> ...if the Japanese Government would refrain from occupying Indochina with its military and naval forces ... [he] would assure [them] that he would do everything within his power to obtain from the Governments of China, Great Britain the Netherlands and ...the United States ... a binding and solemn declaration [of neutralization] provided Japan would undertake

---

* When Germany overran France in World War II it established a Nazi government in Vichy, France; therefore, the French who sympathized with Germany, were often referred to as "Vichy French."

the same commitment, to regard Indochina as a neutralized country…[cxxiv]

At the same time Secretary of State Cordell Hull directed his Under Secretary of State, Sumner Wells, to make it clear to the Japanese Ambassador that:

…the occupation of Indochina by Japan possibly means one further important step to seizing control of the South [China] Sea area, including trade routes of supreme importance to the United States controlling such products as rubber, tin and other commodities. This was of vital concern to the United States.[cxxv]

According to Wells, the "Secretary said that if we did not bring out this point [the American public would] not understand the significance of [Japan's] movement into Indochina."[cxxvi]

However, Japan did not respond favorably to the request for a non-aggression pact, and the "United States reacted vigorously, not only [by] freezing Japanese assets under [its] control but also [by] imposing an embargo on supplies of oil to Japan."[cxxvii]

On August 2, 1941, Acting Secretary of State Wells "deplored Japan's 'expansionist aims' and impugned Vichy" in a press release that read:

Under these circumstances this Government is impelled to question whether the French Government at Vichy in fact proposes to maintain its declared policy to preserve for the French people the territories both at home and abroad which have long been under French sovereignty.

This Government, mindful of its traditional friendship for France, has deeply sympathized with the desire for the French people to maintain their territories and to preserve them intact.

In its relations with the French Government at Vichy and with the local French authorities in French territories, the United States will be governed by the manifest effectiveness with which these authorities endeavor to protect these territories from domination and control by these powers which are seeking to extend their rule by force and conquest, or by threat thereof.[cxxviii]

Behind the scenes the United States continued to propose the neutralization of Indochina if Japan would withdraw its forces.[cxxix] This was how things stood in Indochina on December 7, 1941, when the Japanese bombed Pearl Harbor.

At about that time, a man known as Ho Chi Minh, (after many other aliases) came back into the picture. Ho, was born Nguyen Tat Thanh, in Annam in 1890,[cxxx] but left Vietnam in 1911 and traveled the world before deciding to call France his home in 1917.[cxxxi]

In 1920, he became a founding member of the French Communist Party;[cxxxii] in 1924 he moved to Russia, and in 1930, while in Russia, he formed the Vietnamese Communist (VC) Party.[cxxxiii] In all, he "spent three decades [abroad] as a paid agent of the Communist International [Comintern]."[cxxxiv]

In 1938, after working at the Lenin and Stalin Schools in Moscow,[cxxxv] Ho was sent to Nationalist China by the Comintern to spread the communist message;[cxxxvi] however, he was jailed immediately upon arrival because of his communist past. But in 1941, Ho was released when he promised Chiang Kai Shek he would join China in its war against Japan,[cxxxvii] a war that had been going on since 1937.[cxxxviii]

After a thirty-year absence, at the age of fifty-one, Ho migrated back to northern Vietnam (Tonkin) in 1941.[cxxxix] There he assembled approximately 5,000 guerillas ostensibly to fight the Japanese,[cxl] and armed them with weapons given to him by the United States and China.[cxli] It was not long before these guerrillas became known as Vietminh "an abbreviation for Viet Nam Doc Lap Dong Minh Hoi (the Revolutionary League for the Independence of Vietnam.)"[cxlii] This turned out to be the perfect situation for Ho because the Japanese were basically "inert"[cxliii] in Tonkin, so instead of fighting the Japanese, he proceeded to eliminate any non-communist opposition in the area.[cxliv]

By mid-August 1945, Ho Chi Minh and his Vietminh had seized control of Hanoi and demanded and received the resignation of Bao Dai.[cxlvcxlvi] "(A)nd for many years thereafter the Viet Minh... systematically murder(ed) all of those political opponents who would not accept their authority, and even some...who were in political alliance with them."[cxlvii]

On September 2, 1945, the same day Japan officially surrendered on the USS Missouri, Ho Chi Minh unveiled a Declaration of Independence in Hanoi which proclaimed that a new Democratic Republic of Vietnam (DRV) would henceforth constitute the only government in Vietnam.[cxlviii]

Ignoring Ho's unilateral declaration, Japan, as agreed to at Potsdam and as provided for in General Order No. 1, surrendered that part of Indochina north of the 16th parallel to China on September 2, 1945. On the same day, again pursuant to General Order No. 1, Japan surrendered that part of Indochina below the 16th parallel to Great Britain.[cxlix]

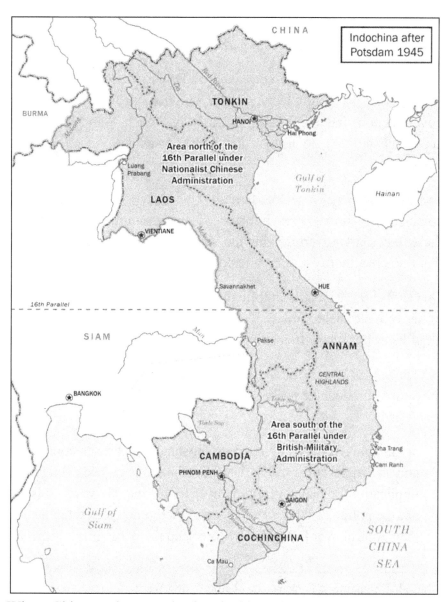

When China took control of Indochina above the 16th parallel it inserted a 50,000-man occupation army into the territory.[cl] Ten days later, on September 12, 1945, Britain landed occupation forces in the form of a loyal battalion of Gurkhas Indian soldiers and a company of French soldiers below the 16th parallel.[cli]

This force was under the command of British General Douglas D. Gracey who, just before leaving India, said that, "[t]he question of the government of Indochina [was] exclusively French,"[*] and added that, "civil and military control by the French [was] only a question of weeks."[clii]

By September 23, 1945, Britain (which was sympathetic to colonization) allowed French forces to return to southern Vietnam and these forces, after overthrowing the Vietminh around Saigon, declared that French authority had been restored in southern Vietnam.[cliii]

On October 9, 1945, Britain formally ceded control of Indochina south of the 16th parallel to France,[cliv] and by March 4, 1946, it would have all of its troops out of Indochina.[clv]

In October 1945, the United States took a wait and see attitude about the return of Indochina to France saying in an official policy statement that it had:

> no thoughts of opposing the reestablishment of French control and no official statement by US GOVT has questioned even by implication French sovereignty over Indochina. However, it is not the policy of this GOVT to assist the French to reestablish their control over Indochina by force and the willingness of the

---

[*] Since Indochina was a French colony before World War II, the return of this colony to France was, from the perspective of Britain and France, consistent with the Atlantic Charter signed by Roosevelt and Churchill and issued on August 14, 1941. This Charter provided, among other things, that no territorial changes during World War II would be made after the war without the wishes of the people concerned. By January 1, 1942, twenty-six governments (including the Soviet Union) had pledged support for the Charter's principles.

US to see French control reestablished assumes that French claim to have the support of the population of Indochina is borne out by future events.[clvi]

With France taking control of the DRV in the south, Ho sought help from the United States, China, Russia and Great Britain in two different February 1946 letters.[clvii] In these letters he was quick to point out that it was he, and his Vietminh, who had opposed Japan during World War II, and it was the French who had in fact aided the Japanese.[clviii]

In addition, Ho sent separate letters to President Truman, through Secretary of State, Marshall. In these letters he offered various trade incentives and the possibility of a naval base at Cam Rahn Bay in return for U.S. help. He further said he would never forget the U.S. role in defeating Japan and added that he was not a "puppet of Moscow."[clix]

Ho's effort to gain control of Vietnam was backed by local OSS officers who had saved his life with anti-malaria medication during the war.[clx] These officers, who had become friends with Ho after saving his life, vouched for his claim of independence from Moscow[clxi] and added that, regardless of Ho's ideology, he should be listened to because he had become the "'symbol of nationalism and the struggle for freedom to the overwhelming majority of the population.'"[clxii]

Other intelligence reports, however, indicated that Ho remained a loyal follower of Moscow and that his apparent independence from the Kremlin was only because Stalin trusted him to carry out the Soviet mission.[clxiii] Accordingly, the OSS district chief in China recommended against giving "help to individuals such as Ho who were known communists and therefore sources of trouble."[clxiv]

In the end, Secretary Marshall decided that even if Ho was personally pro-West, as he claimed to be, his philosophy would eventually be "supplanted by philosophies and political organizations emanating from the Kremlin," and this, he felt, was unacceptable.[clxv] The State Department, therefore, decided to maintain a position of neutrality, leaning toward France.[clxvi]

By March 1946, France was back in control of southern Indochina (which included South Vietnam), but it still did not have a French soldier in northern Indochina due to the considerable presence of the Chinese.[clxvii] Therefore, France, in order to gain control of northern Indochina, negotiated a treaty with China (the Franco-Chinese treaty) that provided for China's departure.[clxviii] In this treaty, China agreed to sell northern Indochina to France and leave by March 15, 1946, in return for which France agreed to convey Shanghai, Tientsin, Hankow, Canton and the territory of Kwanchouwan to China. In addition, France agreed to give China a free port in Haiphong and custom free transport of its goods to the port. Finally, France agreed to sell the Yunnan railroad to China and substantially improve the status of all Chinese nationals living in Vietnam.[clxix]

This purchase included the DRV (North Vietnam) and Ho, not getting any responses to his requests for help, took another approach on March 6, 1946. This approach was to sign a treaty with France known as the Ho-Sainteny agreement or the Franco-Vietnamese Accords, which provided that the DRV would join the French Union as an independent state and welcome French troops as replacements for the departing Chinese soldiers.[clxx]

In other parts of the world, the Philippines, previously a U.S. Commonwealth, became a Republic on July 4, 1946.[clxxi] And in August 1946, the United States, responding to Turkey's request to counter a Soviet demand for joint control of the Turkish Straits, sent a naval task force to the area to show its support.[clxxii]

Back in Vietnam, relations between France and the DRV became strained in December 1946 when the Vietminh attacked Hanoi's electric power plants, and attempts to seal the Ho-Sainteny agreement ended when the French retaliated.[clxxiii] Thus, began the French/Indochina War.

In February 1947, the U.S. Ambassador in Paris was instructed to respond to a French emissary who had complained about the U.S. decision not to supply arms to France for use in the French/Indochina war. As instructed, the Ambassador sent a telegram to the French saying that the U.S. understood their position, but added that:

> … At same time we cannot shut our eyes to fact that there are two sides [to] this problem and that our reports indicate both a lack [of] French understanding of other side (more in Saigon than in Paris) and continued existence [of] dangerously outmoded colonial outlook and methods in area. Furthermore, there is no escape from fact that trend of times is to effect that colonial empires in XIX Century sense are rapidly becoming thing of past… On the other hand, we do not lose sight of fact that Ho Chi Minh has direct Communist connections and it should be obvious that we are not interested in seeing colonial empire administration supplanted by philosophy and political organizations emanating and controlled by Kremlin….

> Frankly we have no solution to problem to suggest. It is basically matter for two parties to work out themselves and from your reports and those from Indochina we are led to feel that both parties have endeavored to keep door open to settlement. We appreciate fact that Vietnam started present fighting in Indochina on

December 19 and that this action has made it more difficult for French to adopt a position of generosity and conciliation. Nevertheless, we hope that French will find it possible to be more than generous in trying to find a solution.[clxxiv]

In short, the U.S. told France that it thought colonialism was a thing of the past, but that it did not want to see colonialism supplanted by communism. Therefore, France was asked to work out a solution in Indochina other than colonialism or communism.

In March 1949, France and Bao Dai, who had been reinstated as emperor, signed a treaty (the Elysée Agreement) that recognized South Vietnam or the State of Vietnam (consisting of Co Chin China and most of Annam) as an independent state within the French Union.[clxxv] However, in reaching this agreement, France did not relinquish control of Vietnam's army or provide it with any autonomy.[clxxvi]

In June 1949, the United States announced its support for the Bao Dai government.[clxxvii]

In December 1949, Ho went to Moscow to participate in the celebration of Joseph Stalin's seventieth birthday and, at that time, "pleaded [with Stalin] for military and diplomatic help from the Soviet-bloc." Stalin agreed and "given the realities of geography…assigned the responsibility for the logistical aspects of this task to China."[clxxviii] In January 1950, Mao and Stalin agreed to provide economic and military assistance to Ho Chi Minh.[clxxix]

On February 1, 1950, Truman's Secretary of State, Dean Acheson, expressed his displeasure with the Soviets, saying that the Kremlin's recognition:

of Ho Chi Minh's communist movement in Indochina comes as a surprise. The Soviet acknowledgement of this movement should remove any illusions as to the 'nationalist' nature of Ho Chi Minh's aims and reveals Ho in his true colors as the mortal enemy of native independence in Indochina.[clxxx]

Within the week, the State of Vietnam, the Kingdom of Laos and Cambodia were recognized by the United States and Great Britain as independent states.[clxxxi]

China and the Soviet Union signed a mutual defense and assistance treaty on February 15 which prompted China's Premier, Zhou Enlai, to say that "the linking of the two communist nations created a force that was 'impossible to defeat.'"[clxxxii]

Within two weeks of the China/USSR treaty Truman's "National Security Council" issued an internal report stating:

It is important to United States security interests that all practicable measures be taken to prevent further [communist] expansion in Southeast Asia. Indo-China is a key area of Southeast Asia and is under immediate threat …

The neighboring countries of Thailand and Burma [Myanmar] could be expected to fall under Communist domination if Indo-China were controlled by a Communist-dominated government. The balance of Southeast Asia would then be in grave hazard.[clxxxiii]

This NSC Report, then, drew the line against "further communist expansion in Southeast Asia."[clxxxiv]

In April 1950, the National Security Council incorporated Kennan's Long Telegram and the Truman doctrine into NSC-68, a 58-page memorandum, classified Top Secret and not declassified until 1975.[clxxxv] NSC-68 emphasized "the global nature of the Cold War, making the frequently quoted observation that, 'The assault on free institutions is world-wide now…and a defeat anywhere is a defeat everywhere.'"[clxxxvi]

On April 10, 1950, General Omar Bradley, Chairman of the Joint Chiefs of Staff, informed the Secretary of Defense that Southeast Asia, from a military point of view, was:

> ….*a vital segment in the line of containment of Communism* stretching from Japan southward and around to the Indian Peninsula... The security of the three major non-Communist base areas in this quarter of the world-Japan, India, and Australia-depends in a large measure on the denial of Southeast Asia to the Communists. If Southeast Asia is lost, these three base areas will tend to be isolated from one another, … (Emphasis mine)

The memorandum continued saying:

> d. The fall of Indochina would undoubtedly lead to the fall of the other mainland states of Southeast Asia.
> e. The fall of Southeast Asia would result in the virtually complete denial to the United States of the Pacific Littoral of Asia.
> f. Soviet control of all the major components of Asia's war potential might become a decisive factor affecting the balance of power between the United States and the USSR, and
> g. A Soviet position of dominance over the Far East would also threaten the United States position in Japan... The feasibility of retention by the United States of its offshore island bases (e.g. the Marshall Islands and the Mariana's including Guam, Tinian and Saipan) could thus be jeopardized.[clxxxvii]

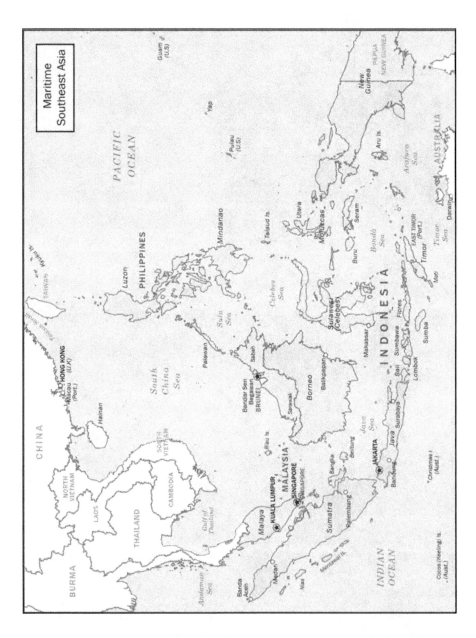

In addition to worrying about a "line of containment" in Asia, the United States was also worried about its "line of containment" in Europe with a war-weary France, and its large communist bloc, threatening to vote the Communist Party into office in the next election.[clxxxviii]

These concerns were continuing to grow on February 16, 1950, when France requested military and economic assistance from the U.S.[clxxxix] In response, on May 1, 1950, the U.S. approved a $10 million financial package to help France with its efforts in Vietnam, Cambodia and Laos.[cxc]

In the spring of 1950, John Foster Dulles, before becoming Eisenhower's Secretary of State, called on the United States to protect the anti-communist Peoples Republic of China on Taiwan saying, "If we do not act, it will be everywhere interpreted that we are making another retreat because we dare not risk war."[cxci]

In June 1950, Truman, contemporaneous with his defense of South Korea, also sent the Seventh Fleet to the Taiwan Strait to protect the Peoples Republic of China from invasion by the Chinese Communists.[cxcii]

On July 26, 1950, the U.S. committed another $15 million to France's war effort in Indochina.[cxciii] A week later an American Military Assistance Advisory Group (MAAG-1), consisting of 35 men, arrived in Saigon to screen French requests for military aid and to assist in the training of the South Vietnamese army.[cxciv] The following year the United States would agree to provide aid directly to South Vietnam, and U.S. civilian personnel would join the U.S. military personnel already there.[cxcv]

In the Philippines, a communist dominated rebel group known as Huks (Hooks) began attacking the hometown of the defense minister, Ramon Magsaysay, in November 1950.[cxcvi] These attacks, however, were repelled by September 1951, largely due to the anti-guerilla tactics jointly employed by Lieutenant Colonel Edward G. Landsdale[*] and Magsaysay.[cxcvii]

In July 1952, the United States officially recognized the State of Vietnam (South Vietnam) as a sovereign country by changing the American Legation in Saigon to an embassy.[cxcviii]

On November 4, 1952, Dwight D. Eisenhower became president elect of the United States.[cxcix] With his election, the fighting in Vietnam ceased "to be regarded as a colonial war and…[became] a war between Communism[**] and the 'free world'" where "(t)he possibility of direct Chinese intervention [became] a matter of urgent preoccupation for many of Eisenhower's closest advisors, in particular Secretary of State John Foster Dulles and Vice President Richard M. Nixon."[cc]

On January 20, 1953, Eisenhower was sworn in as president of the United States.

Colonel Landsdale's success fighting communists in the Philippines caught the attention of Lieutenant General John W. O'Daniel (Commander of the Army in the Pacific) causing him to send Landsdale to South Vietnam in June 1953 to assess the situation. After making his assessment, Landsdale recommended that France quit calling its effort in Vietnam a "colonial struggle" and call it, instead, a "war of free and independent Vietnamese, advised and aided by the

---

[*] Lansdale joined the army in October 1945, and he, then a Major, was sent to the newly independent Philippines as an OSS "advisor." In 1947 he transferred to the Air Force in the same capacity and earned a "reputation as an innovative and effective agent of American Cold War foreign policy [where he was] credited with almost single-handily preventing a communist takeover of [the Philippines]" which earned him a promotion to full colonel ahead of his peers in January 1952.

[**] It has been opined that anti-communism hysteria was being fueled at the time by the witch-hunts of Senator Joseph McCarthy, which peaked in 1954.

French Union, fighting to free the country of Chinese-Communist controlled forces which are made up of brother Vietnamese."[cci]

Landsdale, who was to become an early fixture in Vietnam, said that a person without an understanding of Vietnam's formative years (1950-1963) was like "a spectator arriving in the middle of a complex drama, without true knowledge of the plot or of the identity and motivation of those in the drama."[ccii]

While Russia called for a "peaceful coexistence" when the Korean Armistice was signed,[cciii] China merely shifted its aid from Korea to the Vietminh and went from supplying them with 10 tons of arms and ammunition a month to supplying them with 1,500 tons a month.[cciv]

In September 1953, First Secretary Nikita Khrushchev became head of the communist party and in 1955 he ousted Premier Malenkov and replaced him with Nikolai Bulganin.[ccv]

On September 2, 1953, Secretary Dulles, in response to China's increased assistance to North Vietnam, noted that "a single communist aggressive front extended from Korea on the North to Indochina on the South" saying:

> Communist China has been and now is training, equipping, and supplying the Communist forces in Indochina. There is a risk that, as in Korea, Red China might send its own army into Indochina. The Chinese Communist regime should realize that such a second aggression could not occur without grave consequences which might not be confined to Indochina. I say this soberly...in the hope of preventing another aggressor miscalculation.[ccvi]

This statement implied "that the United States would administer a punishing nuclear blow to China without necessarily involving its land forces in an Asian war."[ccvii]

Senator Mike Mansfield (D) a member of the Senate Foreign Relations Committee conducted an on-the-spot inspection of Asia in 1953, and after the inspection reported back to the Committee, saying:

> World Peace hangs in the balance [along the avenues of Communist expansion in the Far East.] Hence the security of the United States is no less involved in Indochina than in Korea. [Our aid in the conflict was being given in recognition of Indochina's] great importance to the non-communist world and to our own national security.[ccviii]

On September 30, 1953, the Eisenhower administration added $385,000,000 to the $400,000,000 already budgeted for Vietnam and, by April 1954, U.S. aid to Indochina constituted one-third of the administration's foreign aid budget ($1,133,000,000 out of $3,497,000,000).[ccix]

On November 10, 1953, Ramon Magsaysay, with the covert help of Colonel Lansdale, was elected president of the Philippines prompting Eisenhower to say, "This is the way we like to see an election carried out."[ccx] For his work in "directing a brilliant campaign to arrest and reverse the spread of communist influence" in the Philippines, Landsdale became the fourth recipient of the National Security Medal.[ccxi]

In an unfortunate November move, French General Henri Navarre sent 12,000 troops into Dien Bien Phu, a fortified area on a valley floor in northern Vietnam. General Navarre intended by this move to draw the

North Vietnamese into frontal combat.[ccxii] Unfortunately for France, the communists would "take the bait."

Much else was also happening at that point in time. Cambodia and Laos were granted independence from the French Union in 1953 and 1954 respectively,[ccxiii] and in 1954 they were recognized as independent nations in the Final Declaration of the Geneva Accords.[ccxiv]

In Guatemala, President Eisenhower used covert means to help overthrow the pro-Marxist regime of Jacobo Arbenz Guzman in 1954.[ccxv]

In February 1954, the Soviet Union, the United States, France, and Great Britain agreed to meet the following month in Geneva, Switzerland to discuss the situation in both Korea and Vietnam. The meeting was called to reach "a peaceful settlement of the Korean question" and to discuss "the problem of restoring peace in Indochina."[ccxvi]

The following month, on the Ides of March, French soldiers found themselves surrounded and under attack by 40,000 communist troops at Dien Bien Phu, prompting the Chairman of the U.S. Joint Chiefs, Admiral Arthur W. Radford, to propose intervening with a nuclear strike. However, he later modified this proposal and recommended, instead, a massive air strike, followed by precision bombing and the insertion of paratroopers along with the mining of the Haiphong Harbor.[ccxvii]

On April 7, 1954, Eisenhower said that if Indochina fell to communism it would be the beginning of "falling dominoes." Here for the first time, a public name was given to the domino theory.[ccxviii]

However, even though concerned about the situation in South Vietnam, Eisenhower (unlike Truman in Korea) refused to unilaterally intervene without Congressional approval, and Congress would not give its approval unless Great Britain committed.[ccxix] Great Britain, however, refused to commit because it "believed that France could salvage a reasonable settlement in the ongoing talks in Geneva."[ccxx]

Without assistance from either Great Britain or the United States France suffered a humiliating defeat at Dien Bien Phu on May 7, 1954.[ccxxi] This defeat was not only a defeat on the battlefield; it was also a "devastating blow to an already shaky morale at home."[ccxxii]

Even though North Vietnam won a great victory at Dien Bien Phu, it was in no position to immediately continue with other campaigns because it, too, suffered enormous losses (25,000 casualties with 10,000 KIAs) during the eight-week battle.[ccxxiii]

At this time another fervent Vietnamese nationalist, by the name of Ngo Dinh Diem, came back on the scene.[ccxxiv] Diem, born in Hue in 1901, could trace his roots back to the first king of Vietnam,[ccxxv] and his father was the grand chamberlain of the royal court of Annam.[ccxxvi] However, when the French removed Emperor Thanh Thai from the throne in 1907, Diem's father resigned his position in protest;[ccxxvii] moved to the country, and began life as a farmer.[ccxxviii] There Diem grew up, both as a Catholic and a Confucian,[ccxxix] trudging with his father "through the rice paddies behind a water buffalo and a plough."[ccxxx]

At his father's insistence, Diem also attended Catholic schools where, among other things, he learned French, Latin and classic Chinese.[ccxxxi] He then went on to Lycee Ouoc Hoc, a Vietnamese secondary school that Ho Chi Minh had attended before him.[ccxxxii] By virtue of his academic excellence, Diem was offered a scholarship to study in

France in 1918 but, unlike Ho Chi Minh, he remained in Vietnam, and continued his studies at the School of Law and Administration in Hanoi.[ccxxxiii]

Diem graduated first in his class in 1921,[ccxxxiv] and began his career in the public sector as a "district chief" riding circuit on horseback mediating disputes[ccxxxv] where he, influenced by his rural upbringing, did a good job taking care of the peasants.[ccxxxvi]

By 1926, at the age of 28, Diem had become one of South Vietnam's 41 province chiefs[ccxxxvii] where he supervised three hundred villages as the police chief, judge, tax collector and public works administrator all rolled into one.[ccxxxviii] As province chief he indirectly encountered the older Ho Chi Minh who, at the time, was in Hong Kong orchestrating communist insurrections in provinces throughout Vietnam, including Diem's.[ccxxxix] Diem had nothing but contempt for France,[ccxl] but he was also an ardent anti-communist;[ccxli] therefore, "without needless excess" he put down the insurrection in his province by rounding up and arresting every communist he could find.[ccxlii]

Diem's austerity and dedicated service made him such a successful province chief Emperor Bao Dai offered him the position of interior minister in 1933.[ccxliii] Diem, however, was reluctant to accept this offer because the French held very tight control over cabinet level positions; however, when France said it would let him carry out his own reforms, he agreed to take the position.

But, in spite of its promise, France, after only a few months, refused to act on Diem's proposal to elect a representative assembly.[ccxliv] Therefore, Diem, like his father before him, resigned his post in protest[ccxlv] saying that Emperor Bao Dai was "nothing but an instrument in the hands of the French."[ccxlvi]

"Diem's career as a colonial administrator was over, but his reputation as a Catholic and a nationalist had been greatly enhanced."[ccxlvii] The French responded to Diem's resignation by taking away his academic degrees and decorations for government service and considered arresting him.[ccxlviii] But they, instead, let him return to his hometown of Hue where, as a mandarin, he remained active in local court politics, and continued to oppose French colonialism.[ccxlix]

Exiled in Hue, Diem took the opportunity to expand his view of Confucianism by collaborating with Phan Boi Chu, an anti-colonial Confucian revolutionary, under house arrest. It was during this time that Diem came to understand Confucianism was "a kind of social philosophy that was flexible and adaptable to Vietnam's contemporary problems."[ccl]

In 1942, Diem formed a political organization known as the "Association for the Restoration of Vietnam"[ccliccli] which was made up of exiled Vietnamese nationalists and Japanese ex-patriots who opposed both the communists and the French. The organization operated for about two years during which time it tried to convince Japan to give Vietnam its independence.[ccliii] Japan, however, declined to act on this entreaty and the Vichy French began arresting the organization's members[ccliv] at which time Diem went underground.[cclv]

In March 1945, Bao Dai once again turned to Diem and asked him to serve as the prime minister of his "nominally sovereign Vietnam," but Diem declined the offer [cclvi] and instead formed a "Third Force" as an alternative to Bao Dai and Ho Chi Minh. This Third Force also proved to be unsuccessful and Diem became a fugitive; wanted by both the French and the communists.

In late 1945, Diem was captured and imprisoned by the Vietminh, and in early 1946 he found himself in front of Ho Chi Minh in Hanoi[cclvii] where the following conversation ensued:

Diem: What do you want of me?

Ho: I ask of you what you have always wanted of me—your cooperation in gaining independence. We seek the same thing we should work together.

Diem: You are a criminal who has burned and destroyed the country, and you have held me prisoner.

Ho: I apologize for the unfortunate incident. When people who have been oppressed revolt, mistakes are inevitable and tragedies occur…You have grievances against us but let's forget them.

Diem: You want me to *forget* that your followers killed my *brother*? (Emphasis in original)

Ho: I knew nothing of it. I had nothing to do with your brother's death. I deplore such excesses as much as you do… I have brought you here to take a position of high importance in our government.

Diem: My brother and his son are only two of the hundreds who have died—and hundreds more who have been betrayed. How can you dare to invite me to work with you?

Ho: Your mind is focused on the past. Think of the future—education, improved standards of living for the people.

Diem: You speak a language without conscience.[cclviii]

Diem refused Ho's offer in 1946 because he believed communism would "destroy the Vietnamese political, social and religious traditions that he revered."[cclix] This refusal was taken at great personal risk because, as Diem well knew, the Vietminh had just murdered one of his brothers and a nephew by burying them alive as part of their political purge.[cclx]

However, Ho, apparently in an attempt to make it look like the Vietminh were dissolving,[cclxi] released Diem instead of incarcerating or killing him. This decision, it is said, was "the biggest mistake Ho ever made."[cclxii]

After World War II ended and the French again gained control in Indochina Diem, unsuccessfully, attempted to convince France to give Vietnam the same status in the French Union that India and Pakistan had in the British Commonwealth.[cclxiii] While France would not make this concession it did offer to put Diem in charge of the country in 1945[cclxiv] (the "Diem solution"); however, the terms of the offer were unsatisfactory, and he turned it down.

In need of someone from Vietnam to head the country, France, once again, turned to Bao Dai and put him in charge (the "Bao Dai solution"). In March 1948, Diem traveled to Hong Cong where he tried to convince Bao Dai to gain a measure of independence from France, While Bao Dai could not be persuaded to seek this independence he did offer Diem the post of prime minister in his new government in 1949.[cclxv]

However, Diem again declined because the other posts were being filled with French sympathizers. In declining, he said:

> The national aspirations of the Vietnamese people will be satisfied only on the day when our nation obtains the same

political regime which India and Pakistan enjoy [in the British Commonwealth]... I believe it is only just to reserve the best posts in the new Vietnam for those who have deserved best of the country; I speak of those who resist.[cclxvi]

Diem then quit communicating with the Vietminh, and with Bao Dai, saying:

it should be known that the present struggle is not only a battle for the political independence of the Fatherland but also a social revolution...to restore independence to the peasants and workers of Vietnam. In order that each and every person in Vietnam can have sufficient means to live in a [manner] befitting the dignity of a man who is truly free. I advocate social reforms that are sweeping and bold, with the condition that the dignity of man will always be respected and will be free to flourish.[cclxvii]

Diem had hoped to offer his country an alternative to communism and colonialism, through a Third Force,[cclxviii] but by 1950 the Soviet Union and China were backing Ho Chi Minh and the U.S. and France were backing Bao Dai. This left Diem odd man out. Since the Vietminh had issued orders for his assassination[cclxix] and, since the French obviously were not in his corner,[cclxx] Diem left Vietnam with the hope of gathering support for his "Third Force" elsewhere. He went first to Japan in August 1950 and then to the United States to try to gain support for his nationalist cause.[cclxxi]

Unable to obtain backing for his cause in either place he tried his luck in Europe but was unsuccessful there too. Therefore, he returned to the United States in December 1950 and, after three years of lobbying, his efforts began to pay dividends.[cclxxii]

Gaining interest but no promises in the United States, Diem decided to return to Europe and try to regain contact with Bao Dai. On the eve of his departure in May 1953, Justice William O. Douglass held a lunch in his honor, a lunch that was attended by a number of Washington luminaries including Senator John Kennedy (D) and, in particular, Senator Mike Mansfield (D) who left the luncheon "with the feeling that if anyone could hold South Vietnam, it was somebody like Ngo Dinh Diem."[cclxxiii]

Once in Europe Diem began setting the stage for his return to Vietnam with the help of his brothers, Ngo Dinh Can, Ngo Dinh Nhu and Ngo Dinh Luyen, and events there played into his hands.[cclxxiv] By October 1953, many South Vietnamese leaders were demanding total independence from France, prompting Bao Dai to meet with the nationalist Diem in Europe to determine whether they could work together.[cclxxv]

When, the French fell on the battlefield at Dien Bien Phu, it became clear to Bao Dai that France might capitulate at the conference table during the upcoming Geneva Conventions. Therefore, with his options running out, Bao Dai once again turned to Diem.[cclxxvi] At this time he offered Diem the position of premier with full control over civilian and military matters[cclxxvii] and, in so doing, told him that he did "not have the right to avoid (his) responsibilities."[cclxxviii]

On May 8, 1954, the Indochina phase of the Geneva Conference began and was attended by the United States, Great Britain, France, the Soviet Union, the People's Republic of China, Laos, Cambodia, the Democratic Republic of Vietnam (North Vietnam) and the State of Vietnam (South Vietnam).[cclxxix]

In late May 1954, Secretary of State John Foster Dulles transferred Colonel Lansdale to Vietnam hoping he could perform the same miracle there that he had performed in the Philippines.[cclxxx] Lansdale arrived in Saigon on June 1, 1954, and was assigned to Lt. General Mike O'Daniel's Military Advisory Assistance Group[cclxxxi] where he, as head of the U.S. intelligence mission in South Vietnam, assembled a twelve man (CIA) team that would grow to twenty members.[cclxxxii]

On June 4, 1954, the State of Vietnam and France initialed treaties, transferring complete sovereignty to the State of Vietnam; these treaties were ratified with signatures on December 29, 1954.[cclxxxiii] Independent of these treaties, the French Foreign Minister indicated in Geneva that the State of Vietnam was "fully and solely competent to commit" itself.[cclxxxiv] Exercising this independence the State of Vietnam made it known from the beginning that it would not be bound by any agreements made in Geneva, and it voiced the same position during and after the Conference.[cclxxxv]

Consistent with this position the State of Vietnam would elect not to sign the July agreement or join in the subsequent oral "Declaration" as it "believed to the end of the conference, that the French had brazenly and illegally sold [them] out"[cclxxxvi] because the settlement did not take into account "the unanimous will for national unity of the Vietnamese people."[cclxxxvii]

On June 16, 1954, shortly before the Geneva Conference concluded, Diem accepted Bao Dai's offer and assumed the position of premier.[cclxxxviii] At that time, however, he was virtually alone "(u)naided by Bao Dai, opposed by the French, and proffered by Americans mainly advice, criticism, and promises---but scant material assistance."[cclxxxix]

On June 24 and June 25, 1954, during the last great battle of the First Indochinese War, French, Cambodian and Korean soldiers were slaughtered by the Vietminh on Highway 19 in the Mang Yang

Pass.[ccxc] Fifteen years later I would convoy through the Mang Yang Pass on Highway 19.

After two and a half months of negotiations in Geneva, an "Agreement on the Cessation of Hostilities" was reached on July 20, 1954.[ccxci] This Agreement was only signed by the Commander-in-Chief of the French Union Forces in Indochina and by the North Vietnamese Commander-in-Chief of the People's Army of Vietnam.[ccxcii]

The center piece of the "Agreement" provided that the Democratic Republic of Vietnam (North Vietnam) and the State of Vietnam (South Vietnam) would be regrouped into two zones divided by a line near the 17th parallel[ccxciii] and that a general election regarding the unification of these zones would be held at some unspecified future time.[ccxciv]

In the "Final Declaration" entered into two days after the "Agreement" was signed Great Britain, France, the Soviet Union, the People's Republic of China and North Vietnam orally agreed, among other things, that the election called for in the "Agreement" would take place in two years.[ccxcv]

The United States proposed instead that elections, supervised by the United Nations, be held in Vietnam to reunify countries "now divided against their will…"[ccxcvi] The State of Vietnam also proposed that the United Nations take control of Vietnam and determine when the climate was such that free elections throughout the country could take place; however, it opposed a partition of the country.[ccxcvii]

While the State of Vietnam refused to sign the "Agreement" or to join in the "Final Declaration" (the Accords), it did say it would not use force to resist the cease-fire, and that it would "make and support every effort to re-establish a real and lasting peace in Vietnam."[ccxcviii]

56

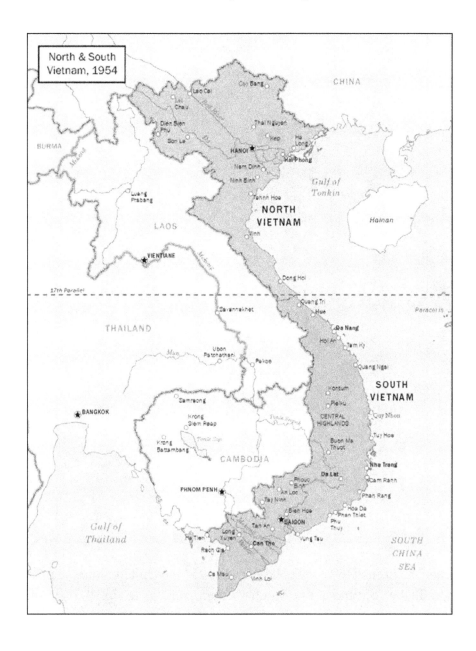

When the French left South Vietnam in 1954 the United States stepped in to fill the void and it, like South Vietnam, refused to sign the Geneva "Agreement" or join in the oral "Declaration." The United States did say, however, that it would also refrain from the use of force to disturb the Accords,[ccxcix] but added that any renewal of aggression by the other side would be viewed with "grave concern and as seriously threatening international peace and security."[ccc]

On September 8, 1954, Australia, France, New Zealand, Pakistan, the Philippines, Thailand, the United Kingdom, and the United States signed the Southeast Asia Collective Defense Treaty (the SEATO treaty). This mutual defense treaty also contained a protocol that provided for the protection of Laos, Cambodia and the territory of the free state of Vietnam if the protocol state or territory believed that an action endangered its peace and safety.[ccci] Each member country was to provide this protection in accordance with its own constitutional processes. (SEATO treaty Article IV and attached Protocol.)[cccii]

The United States and France sent a joint communiqué on September 29 to South Vietnam, Cambodia and Laos that reaffirmed their promise in the SEATO treaty to help them institute the principles of self-governance, independence, justice, and liberty and to continue to help them in their efforts to "safeguard their freedom."[ccciii]

On October 1, 1954, President Eisenhower sent a letter to Diem offering "to assist the Government of Viet-Nam in developing and maintaining a strong, viable state, capable of resisting attempted subversion or aggression through military means."[ccciv]

On January 1, 1955, Lieutenant General O'Daniel's Military Assistance Advisory Group was directed to begin assisting South Vietnam in the organization and training of its army.[cccv]

By the end of April, Bao Dai, unhappy with the way Diem was conducting the affairs of state, ordered him to return to France and turn the government over to a pro-French Army General.[cccvi] Diem refused to follow this order and called for an October referendum setting the stage for the people to choose between himself and Bao Dai. The next month, the U.S. Joint Chiefs sided with Diem concluding that he "shows the greatest promise of achieving the internal stability essential for the security of Vietnam."[cccvii]

In July 1955, the United States, as a tactic, urged Diem to consult with North Vietnam about the election called for in the "Declaration." As part of the tactic Diem was urged to insist that the election be conducted by secret ballot under strict supervision of the United Nations.[cccviii]

The U.S., in so urging, knew that a similar recommendation had been rejected on previous occasions by East Germany and by North Korea, and had just been rejected by the Democratic Republic of Vietnam (North Vietnam) at the Geneva Conventions. Therefore, reasoned the United States, these conditions would be rejected again, and would allow the State of Vietnam to "make a record" and argue, in good faith, that North Vietnam had unreasonably rejected the election provisions in the Accords.[cccix]

Diem, however, was not interested in "making a record" or in attempting to gain a tactical advantage under the Accords because, as far as he was concerned, the State of Vietnam was not bound by France's "sellout." Therefore, he rejected U.S. pressure to "negotiate" making his position perfectly clear, in July 1955 when he said:

> We did not sign the Geneva agreements. We are not bound in any way by these Agreements signed against the will of the Vietnamese people. ... We shall not miss an opportunity, which would permit the unification of our homeland in freedom, [i.e. free elections] but it is out of the question for us to consider any proposal from the Viet Minh if proof is not given that they put the superior interests of the national community above those of communism.[cccx]

On October 23, 1955, Diem defeated Bao Dai with 98% of the vote in the "October referendum."[cccxi]

Even though the United States had not signed the "Agreement" in Geneva or joined in the "Declaration" it had made a decision to abide by the "Accords" which, among other things, limited each party to the number of military advisors it had in Vietnam when the Accords were adopted.[cccxii]

At the time the Accords were adopted the United States, had 342[*] military advisors in Vietnam[cccxiii] and, faced with this limitation, the Joint Chiefs informed Eisenhower that even the risk of training the South Vietnamese Army was not worth the gamble; saying that:

> ...the United States should not participate in the training of Vietnamese forces in Indochina. However, if it is considered that political considerations are overriding, the Joint Chiefs of Staff would agree to the assignment of a training mission to MAAG Saigon, with safeguards against French interference with the US training effort.[cccxiv]

Lt. General J. Lawton Collins (Special Advisor in Vietnam with Ambassadorial rank) was not quite as pessimistic as the Joint Chiefs telling the National Security Council there was:

> ...at least an even chance that Vietnam (could) be saved from Communism if the present programs of its government are fully implemented... I cannot guarantee that Vietnam will remain free, even with our aid. But I know that without our aid Vietnam will surely be lost to Communism.[cccxv]

---

[*]As the Accords were amended the number of advisors incrementally increased to 692.

In the end, Eisenhower concluded that political considerations overrode military concerns, but made it clear that the advisor's purpose was just to put South Vietnam's army in fighting shape not to engage in combat. As the Korean War had just concluded American thinking was that the deployment of large U.S. forces to mainland Asia would never happen again.[cccxvi] (No more Koreas.)

On October 26, 1955, Diem decreed that in the future the State of Vietnam would be called the Republic of Vietnam.[cccxvii] And, this Republic began "in just about as total an organizational vacuum as [was] possible"[cccxviii] but it gained a president who was "untarred by the colonialist brush, a patriot with integrity, who opposed Communists, sects, and other narrow interest groups not for the sake of his own self-interest, but because of deep moral and religious beliefs."[cccxix]

Diem was South Vietnam's "first nationalist ruler [who] earned his legitimacy by having nothing to do with the occupying power [but] …a mandarin to whom the sharing of power outside the family was extremely awkward."[cccxx] Therefore, when he did away with Bao Dai's corrupt cabinet he kept most decisions, to himself and his brothers.[cccxxi]

One brother, Luyen, was assigned to France as Vietnam's liaison with Western diplomats, another brother, Can, was given control of the northern part of the Republic, [cccxxii] and the most influential brother, Nhu, became Diem's chief advisor and head of the Republic's secret police.[cccxxiii] A fourth brother, Ngo Dinh Thuc, was a leading cleric in the Catholic Community and later became Archbishop of Vietnam.[cccxxiv]

This autocratic rule was not understood or appreciated by some in the United States,[cccxxv] but Eisenhower's Secretary of State, John Foster Dulles, "dismissed the idea of broadening [Diem's] government."[cccxxvi] The Eisenhower administration, for example, recognized that Syngman Rhee of South Korea ran a "repressive regime," however, it had still entered into a bilateral treaty with him agreeing to keep U.S. troops in South Korea as long as it took to insure the country's safety. "This meant that the United States was defending an authoritarian [leader who] had little patience with, or interest in, democratic procedures. South Korea was what…[Rhee] not the Americans want(ed) it to be…"[cccxxvii]

While Vietnam was clearly on the Soviet Union's Cold War radar screen, a letter dated December 30, 1955, made it clear it was not the only country, undergoing decolonization, on their screen. In this letter Ivan Maiskyi, a Russian diplomat, advised Khrushchev that "the battle for the world supremacy of socialism would involve the liberation of colonial and semi-colonial nations from imperialist exploitation … At this time [he said] conditions for this struggle in Asia, Africa and Latin America …" were favorable. After reading this letter, Khrushchev agreed that "Africa and other territories undergoing decolonization [should] be a new front in the Cold War."[cccxxviii]

PHOTOGRAPHS FROM 1945 to 1957

During World War II the OSS enlisted Ho Chi Minh to send reports on weather and Japanese troop movements to U.S. intelligence operatives in China; in return, his Vietminh were supplied with weapons and training. Here an OSS officer watches on August 17, 1945, as Vietminh practice throwing hand grenades. (National Archives)

Ho Chi Minh in Paris in March 1946, during the signing of the Ho-Sainteny Agreement (or the Franco-Vietnamese Accords) making North Vietnam a free state in the French Union. (National Archives)

President Eisenhower bestowing a rare honor on President Ngo Dinh Diem by personally greeting him at Washington National Airport on May 5, 1957; behind Eisenhower is Secretary of State John Foster Dulles. (National Archives)

CHAPTER THREE
1956 to July 1964

On February 25, 1956, First Secretary Nikita Khrushchev gave a "secret" midnight speech denouncing the terrorism of Joseph Stalin. This denunciation so dismayed Mao Zedong, who was still a Stalinist disciple, that an ideological split (but not a break) developed between the two countries.[cccxxix]

In April 1956, Khrushchev proclaimed that the Soviet Union was committed to a policy of "peaceful co-existence."[cccxxx]

On July 7, 1956, President Diem promulgated a constitution that was modeled on U.S. and French precedents guaranteeing the freedom of press, speech and assembly unless suspended by the president during the first four years due to a state of emergency.[cccxxxi]

Frederick E. Nolting, after becoming Ambassador to Vietnam under President John F. Kennedy, said that Diem, while autocratic, was highly moral, deeply religious, and a conscientious leader who agonized over the decisions he had to make while endlessly weighing "the pros and cons usually from the moral point of view."[cccxxxii]

Nolting added that when Diem became president:

> It was difficult for anyone unfamiliar with the country to realize the jealousies, which existed among the more educated Vietnamese people and the differences from province to province, region to region. These differences were...partly a legacy of seventy-five years of French colonial rule. The greatest single problem of the Diem government was to bring about some degree of unity among the various non-Communist

elements in the country. One of the main goals of the Viet Cong[*] and [of] Hanoi was to prevent this. The more Diem succeeded in giving South Vietnam a single identity, the more his overthrow became the Communists' principal objective.[cccxxxiii]

In spite of these problems, Diem was able to strengthen both the government and the economy of South Vietnam in 1956 while defeating his enemies.[cccxxxiv] And, the year came to an end without the elections orally called for at the 1954 Geneva Convention, leaving the Republic of Vietnam and the Democratic Republic of Vietnam separated near the 17th parallel. The year also ended with Colonel Landsdale being reassigned to Washington, D.C., and when he departed he, in his opinion, left "a very popular Vietnamese leader running things, a man who was being very responsive to the needs of the people."[cccxxxv]

In early January 1957, Eisenhower committed to defend the Middle East against communist aggression, a commitment that later became known as the Eisenhower Doctrine.[cccxxxvi]

Also in January 1957,[cccxxxvii] the UN General Assembly "overwhelmingly voted for the admission of the R.S.V. [South Vietnam] as a member state of the United Nations."[cccxxxviii] The Soviet Union, alternatively, introduced a draft resolution that proposed admitting North and South Korea and North and South Vietnam into the UN or no one at all.[cccxxxix]

---

[*] South Vietnamese communists viewed Viet Cong as a derogatory term; therefore, when the abbreviation "VC" is used in this book it is an abbreviation for "Vietnamese Communist." However, references to Viet Cong, when found in quotes, are left unchanged.

During a debate on this proposal, the Soviet Representatives to the United Nations contended that the admission of these four states was appropriate because:

> [B]oth in Korea and Viet-Nam two separate States existed which differed from one another in political structure...

> [T]here were two states in Korea and two States in Viet-Nam...

> The realistic approach was to admit that there were two States with conflicting political systems in both Korea and Viet-Nam. In the circumstances, the only possible solution was the simultaneous admission of the four countries constituting Korea and Viet-Nam.

> [T]wo separate and independent States had been established in each of these countries [Korea and Vietnam] with different political, social and economic systems.[cccxl]

Here, according to the Pentagon Papers, the Soviets seemed ready "in the interests of 'peaceful coexistence,' to make a great power deal which would have lent permanency to the partition of Vietnam."[cccxli] This offer, however, was not accepted by the UN.

And, apparently not persuaded by Khrushchev's call for "peaceful coexistence," Eisenhower informed Congress in a special May message that his primary foreign policy concern was to get military assistance from other countries to help counter "Soviet-Chinese military power..." because, he said, "The communist goal of conquering the world has never changed." [cccxlii]

Also in May 1957, Diem went to the United States to address Congress and while there he was touted as "the man who had saved his country from communism," and honored with a tickertape parade through the streets of New York City.[cccxliii] Even so, the communist threat to South Vietnam remained ever-present, and on May 11, 1957, President Eisenhower and President Diem issued a joint statement noting 'the large buildup of Vietnamese communist military forces in North Vietnam;' and further noting:

> that the Republic of Viet-Nam is covered by Article IV of the Southeast Asia Collective Defense [SEATO] Treaty [where it was agreed] that aggression or subversion threatening the political independence of Viet-Nam would be considered as endangering [its] peace and stability.[cccxliv]

In October 1957, the Soviet Union got a leg up in the Cold War when it launched Sputnik, the first artificial satellite to orbit the earth.[cccxlv]

In November 1957, Ho Chi Minh and his deputy, Le Duane, not interested in a policy of "peaceful coexistence," traveled to Moscow to attend the "Conference of Communist and Workers Parties of Socialist Countries," and while there succeeded in getting the Conference to issue a declaration that provided for a nation's "non-peaceful transition to socialism" if non-peaceful means were necessary.[cccxlvi]

This declaration was deemed by Hanoi to be its "go ahead" from Moscow and Peking to forcibly pursue its objectives and it "has been cited repeatedly by both North and South Vietnamese communists as a strategic turning point in their modern history."[cccxlvii]

The French colony of Guinea became the independent Republic of Guinea on October 2, 1958, and the Kremlin saw this as its "first potential stronghold in Sub-Saharan Africa."[cccxlviii]

On March 13, 1959, Eisenhower, relying on the "Vandenberg Doctrine," told Congress there was a need to continue "Mutual Security Program(s)... for several reasons:"

> First, the United States and the entire free world are confronted by the military might of the Soviet Union, Communist China, and their satellites. These nations of the Communist Bloc [he said] now maintain well equipped standing armies totaling more than 6,500,000 men formed in some 400 divisions. They are deployed along the borders of our allies and friends from the northern shores of Europe in the Mediterranean Sea around through the Middle East and Far East to Korea. These forces are backed by an air fleet of 25,000 planes in operational units, and many more not in such units. They, in turn, are supported by nuclear weapons and missiles. On the seas around the land mass is a huge navy with several hundred submarines.

> Second, [he said] the world is in a great epoch of seething change...

*****

> Communism [he continued] exploits the opportunity to intensify world unrest by every possible means. At the same time Communism masquerades as the pattern of progress as the path to economic equality, as the way to freedom from what it calls "Western imperialism" as the wave of the future.

> For the free world there is the challenge to convince a billion people in the less developed areas that there is a way of life by which they can have bread and butter, a better livelihood and the right to choose the means of their livelihood, social change and social justice—progress and liberty. The dignity of man is at stake.

Communism is determined to win this contest, freedom must be just as dedicated or the struggle could finally go against us. Though no shot would have been fired freedom and democracy would have lost.

The battle is now joined. The next decade will forecast its outcome...[cccxlix]

On the same day Eisenhower was telling Congress why Mutual Security Programs were so necessary (March, 13, 1959) the communist party in North Vietnam was declaring that "the time ha(d) come to struggle heroically and perseveringly to smash the GVN (South Vietnamese Government) ..."[cccl]

In April 1960, Diem officially asked the Eisenhower administration to send Lansdale, by then a Brigadier General, back to Vietnam to help deal with "intensified Communist guerilla activity."[cccli] However, State and Defense Department officials objected.

In October 1960, the *New York Times* saluted Diem on his first five years in office.[ccclii] And, Eisenhower, as well, saluted him for a job well done in a letter dated October 25, 1960, saying:

DEAR MR. PRESIDENT:

My countrymen and I are proud to convey our good wishes to you and to the citizens of Viet-Nam on the fifth anniversary of the birth of the Republic of Viet-Nam.

We have watched the courage and daring with which you and the Vietnamese people attained independence in a situation so perilous that many thought it hopeless. We have admired the rapidity with which chaos yielded to order and progress replaced despair.

During the years of your independence, it has been refreshing for us to observe how clearly the Government and the citizens of Viet-Nam have faced the fact that the greatest danger to their independence was Communism. You and your countrymen have used your strength well in accepting the double challenge of building your country and resisting Communist imperialism. In five short years since the founding of the Republic, the Vietnamese people have developed their country in almost every sector. I was particularly impressed by one example. I am informed that last year over 1,200,000 Vietnamese children were able to go to elementary school; three times as many as were enrolled five years earlier. This is certainly a heartening development for Viet-Nam's future. At the same time Viet-Nam's ability to defend itself from the Communists has grown immeasurably since its successful struggle to become an independent Republic.

Viet-Nam's very success as well as its potential wealth and its strategic location have led the Communists of Hanoi, goaded by the bitterness of their failure to enslave all Viet-Nam, to use increasing violence in their attempts to destroy your country's freedom.

This grave threat, added to the strains and fatigues of the long struggle to achieve and strengthen independence, must be a burden that would cause moments of tension and concern in almost any human heart. Yet from long observation I sense how deeply the Vietnamese value their country's independence and strength and I know how well you used your boldness when you led your countrymen in winning it. I also know that your determination has been a vital factor in guarding that independence while steadily advancing the economic development of your country. I am confident that these same qualities of determination and boldness will meet the renewed threat as well as the needs and desires of your countrymen for further progress on all fronts.

Although the main responsibility for guarding that independence will always, as it has in the past, belong to the Vietnamese people and their government, I want to assure you that for so long as our strength can be useful, the United States will continue to assist Viet-Nam in the difficult yet hopeful struggle ahead.

Sincerely,

DWIGHT D. EISENHOWER[cccliii]

In November 1960, the objections to Landsdale's trip to Vietnam were withdrawn provided he would not contradict Ambassador Durbrow's position that Diem needed: (1) to send his brother Ngo Dinh Nhu abroad as an ambassador, (2) to add opposition politicians to his cabinet, and (3) to lift restrictions on the press.[cccliv]

On November 8, 1960, John F. Kennedy defeated Richard M. Nixon to become president-elect.

In December 1960, the communist party in North Vietnam, the Lao Dong Party, found it had perception problems operating as such in South Vietnam; therefore, on December 20, 1960, Hanoi changed its name in South Vietnam to the National Liberation Front of South Vietnam (the NLF).[ccclv]

In explaining this name change Hanoi said the "National Liberation Front" was a name that could be used:

… in public to appeal to the (local) population and … in our strategy to sow division and isolate Diem.[ccclvi]

A Communist Directive, further explaining the name change, said:

If the Party Chapter for South Vietnam openly kept its old name identifying it as a Party Chapter … under the leadership of the Party Central Committee in North Vietnam, then our enemies both domestic and foreign, could utilize that to spread distortions and accusations that North Vietnam was intervening to overthrow South Vietnam, and this would cause problems for North Vietnam in its struggle to gain support for South Vietnam from the standpoint of international legalities.[ccclvii]

But to make sure the Party faithful knew who really was in control, the directive went on to say:

Although the overt name (NLF) will be different than that used in North Vietnam, secretly internally and from an organizational standpoint, the *Party Chapter for South Vietnam* will still be part of the Vietnamese Labor Party and will be under the *Party Central Committee* headed by Ho Chi Minh.[ccclviii] (Emphasis mine)

On January 6, 1961, Khrushchev abandoned his "peaceful coexistence policy," and made it clear that the Soviet Union would support all "wars of national liberation" anywhere in the world.[ccclix]

The day before Kennedy was sworn in Eisenhower told him (through his Secretary of State) that Laos was being threatened by the Soviet Union and if it fell to communism the rest of Southeast Asia would fall too. Therefore, it was suggested that he get his SEATO allies to join in its defense and if they would not join it was further suggested that he do so unilaterally.[ccclx]

In his Inaugural Address on January 20, 1961, President Kennedy responded to Khrushchev's promise to support "wars of national liberation anywhere," saying the United States would always be there to defend freedom "at its hour of maximum danger."[ccclxi]

As Kennedy assumed the presidency it was observed   that "[t]hroughout the 1960s, the terrain of the Cold War became truly global, ranging from Europe to the Middle East, to Asia, to Africa and to Latin America with the possibility of nuclear war and the reality of guerrilla war, insurrection and subversion. Battles hot and cold were fought in Cuba, Berlin and Vietnam."[ccclxii]

Kennedy's first chance to defend freedom in the Cold War came in Cuba on April 17, 1961, when a group of CIA-directed Cuban exiles tried to retake control of Cuba from the communists, but this effort failed miserably in the Bay of Pigs.[ccclxiii]

Kennedy's second chance came in Laos when he tried to act through negotiation rather than by confrontation. In so doing, Kennedy met with Khrushchev in Vienna, Austria at a Summit on June 4, 1961,[ccclxiv] and there the two agreed on a plan to make Laos a neutral country.[ccclxv] The plan was finally consummated by the UN in Geneva with the Declaration on the Neutrality of Laos (The Geneva Accords of 1962).[ccclxvi] Here Kennedy would also fail, but it took longer.

Kennedy's third chance to defend freedom came at the same Vienna Summit. The threat arose when Khrushchev told Kennedy he was going to defy the terms of the Potsdam Declaration and take total control of West Berlin.[ccclxvii] In order to thwart this threat Kennedy went to Congress in July and asked for: an additional $3.2 billion dollars for the Armed Forces; an increase of over 200,000 active duty servicemen, and a doubling of the draft.[ccclxviii] Here Kennedy's efforts were successful.

Kennedy's fourth chance to defend freedom came in Africa, where the USSR's actions between 1956 and 1964 in West Africa (Ghana, Guinea and Mali) and in Central Africa (the Congo) were "considered part of a holistic [comprehensive] African strategy, a subtle and detailed Kremlin master plan to dominate Africa."[ccclxix] Here, Kennedy was also successful.[ccclxx]

Kennedy's fifth chance to defend freedom came in Vietnam, and to help him with this task Kennedy found a twelve-page report sitting on his desk when he took office. The report had been written by Brigadier General Edward Lansdale and recommended that the United States "select dedicated Americans with empathy for the Vietnamese and send them to advise the GVN (government of Vietnam) 'with sensitive understanding and wisdom.'... (and) give them total responsibility to match their total commitment, and free them from the encumbrances of the regular bureaucratic machinery (be it military or civilian) in order that they may operate effectively according to the situation."[ccclxxi]

To that end, Lansdale said:

> When there is an emergency the wise thing to do is to pick the best people you have, people who are experienced in dealing with the precise type of emergency, and send them to the spot with orders to remedy the situation. When you get the people in position and free them to work, you should then back them up in every practical way you can. The real decisions will be made in little daily actions in Vietnam, not in Washington. That's why the best are needed on the spot.

Our U.S. team in Vietnam should have a hard core of experienced Americans who know and really like Asia and the Asians, dedicated people who are willing to risk their lives for the ideals of freedom, and who will try to influence and guide the Vietnamese towards U.S. policy objectives with the warm friendships and affection which our close alliance deserves. We should break the rules of personnel assignment, if necessary, to get such U.S. military and civilians in Vietnam.[ccclxxii]

According to the Pentagon Papers, Lansdale was "a uniquely qualified professional military officer [who] ...worked closely in the Philippines with Ramon Magsaysay in [his] successful campaign against the Huk [communist] rebellion and [who] served later as head of the U.S. intelligence mission in South Vietnam in the mid-50s. [Someone who] knew President Diem well and was trusted by the GVN leader....His views on counterinsurgency command attention."[ccclxxiii]

The plan, coming from someone with Lansdale's unique background, so captured Kennedy's attention that seven days after he took office, he brought Lansdale to the White House to discuss it more fully.[ccclxxiv] After Lansdale's presentation Kennedy remained very interested, but there was a serious flaw in the plan in that it recommended freeing the people on the ground from the encumbrances of the bureaucratic machinery in Washington D.C., causing it to be torpedoed by that same bureaucratic machinery.[ccclxxv]

Put another way Lansdale's plan "succumbed to organizational principles with very deep [bureaucratic] roots."[ccclxxvi] However, even though Kennedy rejected this plan he remained dedicated to Vietnam's cause and on August 2, 1961, he made it clear, "the United States [was] determined that the Republic of Vietnam shall not be lost to

Communists for lack of any support that the United States can render."[ccclxxvii] This initial support, as it turned out, was in the form of 400 Green Berets that had previously been inserted into South Vietnam on May 11, 1961, to conduct covert operations.[ccclxxviii]

In a December 14, 1961, letter to President Diem, Kennedy personally promised to protect South Vietnam and preserve its independence.[ccclxxix] In furtherance of this promise, Kennedy (unlike Eisenhower) began to exceed the number of U.S. advisors allowed in Vietnam by the Geneva Accords something Kennedy deemed to be necessary because he thought the situation in Vietnam was becoming desperate.[ccclxxx]

By December 31, 1961, the U.S. had 3,205 advisors in Vietnam and during that year 11 were killed.[ccclxxxi]

At the beginning of 1962, the U.S. started defoliating the jungles with an herbicide, known as "Agent Orange" (so called because of the orange stripes on its canisters) to make it easier to locate the enemy.[ccclxxxii] While this herbicide was doing its job in the jungles, scientists warned as early as 1966 that it could also be harming people. DOD, however, disagreed, and the spraying continued.

As it turned out the scientists were right, and in 1991 Congress enacted legislation to compensate those harmed by the defoliant. As of 2015, over 1.3 million veterans had received $24 billion in Agent Orange disability compensation.[ccclxxxiii] My friend Jim McCartin was one of those who benefited from this legislation, until he died from cancer caused by Agent Orange.

In a February 1962, *Newsweek* article Major General Lansdale compared his experience in the Philippines to what was then happening in Vietnam pointing out that in the Philippines the communists:

> ...had analyzed the people's grievances and made the righting of these wrongs into slogans. And the change came when Ramon Magsaysay became Defense Minister. He was from the people, loved and trusted them. He and the army set about making the constitution a living document for the people. As they did so, they and the people emerged on the same side of the fight. The [communists] lost support and had to go on the defensive.[ccclxxxiv]

With this article Landsdale was presumably trying to rally the American public around him and his cause but, by this time, Kennedy had decided to go in a different direction.

In mid-1962 Diem, drawing on "a-tried-and-true pacification tactic that had worked for the British from the time of the Boer War at the turn of the century to the Malayan 'Emergency' in the 1950s...," developed a "Strategic Hamlet" pacification program to protect his rural population.[ccclxxxv] Under this program rural hamlets would be:

> ...surrounded by moats and barbed wire, and a hamlet militia would be armed to resist insurgent incursions. If the hamlet came under heavy attack, it would have a radio or field telephone to call for reinforcements from the Civil Guard, a regional militia that later became known as the Popular Forces, or from the Army of the Republic of Vietnam (ARVN). Inside the hamlets villagers would be able to elect their own leaders so that they would have greater legitimacy, reversing a decision Diem had made in 1956...." [Diem and his brother Nhu, the architect of the Program,] ... hoped that the hamlets would not only stymie the Communist advances but also

galvanize a new base of support for their regime among villagers allowing them to lessen their reliance on the United States and the urban Francophone [French speaking] elite, both of whom they distrusted.[ccclxxxvi]

By July 23, 1962, "present and future developments" on the ground in Vietnam had started to look so good to McNamara, that he began planning on the withdrawal of all U.S. forces from South Vietnam by 1965.[ccclxxxvii]

In October 1962, Diem made the "Strategic Hamlet Program the avowed focus of his counterinsurgent campaign,"[ccclxxxviii] and under this program Saigon gained "control over more than two-thirds of the rural population."[ccclxxxix]

On October 1, 1962, General Maxwell Taylor became Chairman of the Joint Chiefs of Staff and General Earle Wheeler became the Army Chief of Staff.[cccxc] From 1962 to 1963, according to historian Max Boot:

> the Saigon government was making real progress against the Vietcong while also encountering undeniable problems, yet most American journalists and policymakers could perceive nothing but the shortcomings of the Ngo Dinh Diem regime while simply taking it on faith that any alternative would be preferable. This one-sided outlook---too distrustful of the incumbent president, too trusting of his would-be successors— would ultimately prove fatal to Diem's chances of survival.[cccxci]

Meanwhile, Kennedy was forced to defend freedom once again when Russian ballistic missiles were discovered in Cuba in October 1962. In response, Kennedy "quarantined" Cuba with 180 ships and put the

Strategic Air Command, with sixty nuclear loaded B-52s, on high alert.[cccxcii]

But, instead of immediately confronting Russia militarily Kennedy entered into negotiations with Khrushchev who, in the end, agreed to remove his missiles from Cuba and, in return, Kennedy agreed: not to attack Castro again; to remove U.S. missiles from Turkey and Italy, and to allow Khrushchev to keep his 40,000 troops in Cuba.[cccxciii]

Here Kennedy, even with his concessions, was thought to have been successful. In fact, he was thought to have been so successful by Mao Zedong that another crack (but still not a break) in the Sino/Soviet bloc developed because Mao viewed the removal of the missiles from Cuba as "an unprecedented humiliation to socialist countries."[cccxciv]

On December 2, 1962, Senate Majority Leader Mike Mansfield (D) reversed his favorable opinion of Diem and became a critic because of Diem's autocratic government.[cccxcv]

At the end of 1962, there were 9,000 Americans in Vietnam. During that year, 31 were killed in action and 41 were wounded; at the same time 4,457 South Vietnamese were killed in action and 7,195 were wounded.[cccxcvi]

In March 1963, Ho Chi Minh and First Secretary, Le Duan openly sided with Communist China over Russia.[cccxcvii]

On May 8, 1963, Buddhists in Hue gathered to protest a decree that gave the Vietnamese flag precedence over all religious banners flown in public places. Authorities allowed the protest to continue, but when the protestors tried to take possession of the local radio station, the deputy province chief ordered them to leave.[cccxcviii] The demonstrators, however, refused to disperse at which time he (the deputy province chief) had them sprayed with fire hoses. When they still would not leave, he (ill-advisedly) ordered soldiers on the scene to shoot.[cccxcix] After the order was given shots were fired and nine people were killed.[cd]

The next day more than 10,000 people gathered to protest the May 8 incident in particular and the treatment of Buddhists by Diem's government in general.[cdi] In response to these protests Diem, on June 3, 1964, appointed an inter-ministerial committee headed by Vice President Nguyen Tho (a Buddhist) to address the Buddhists' concerns and demands.[cdii] Two weeks later the Diem government and the ruling Buddhist Monks published a joint communiqué settling their dispute.[cdiii]

But before the end of the month this settlement was set aside by a group of younger monks who had taken control of this dispute. According to the Pentagon Papers these younger monks:

> made intelligent and skillful political use of a rising tide of popular support. Carefully planned mass meetings and demonstrations were accompanied with an aggressive press campaign of opposition to the [Diem] regime. Seizing on the importance of American news media, they cultivated U.S. newsmen, tipped them off to demonstrations and rallies, and carefully timed their activities to get maximum press coverage.[cdiv]

On June 27, 1963, President Kennedy, in an attempt to obtain Republican support for the war, announced that his former political opponent, Henry Cabot Lodge, Jr.,* would succeed Ambassador Frederick Nolting.[cdv]

---

* Lodge, among other roles, had been a Republican Senator from Massachusetts (defeated by Kennedy) ambassador to the United Nations; vice presidential

On July 3, 1963, David Halberstam, Pulitzer Prize winning correspondent for *The New York Times* wrote an article in which he said that Americans wanted a new government in South Vietnam because of the way Diem was handling the Buddhist crisis.[cdvi]

Mark Moyer has opined that Halberstam's articles did "more harm to the interests of the United States than any other journalist in American History."[cdvii] General Hal D. McDowd concurred saying that, "We would have been all right in Vietnam if it hadn't been for people like Neil Halberstam."[cdviii] Ambassador Nolting, who also shared this view, said that shortly after Halberstam arrived in Vietnam he started "actively finding things to criticize about the Diem government and seldom, if ever, mention(ed) the good things it was doing."[cdix] "Beginning like drops of acid," he said, Halberstam's "reports steadily conditioned the climate of American opinion."[cdx]

On August 21, 1963, the Diem administration removed militant Buddhists from thirty of the nation's five thousand pagodas and martial law was declared at the request of the army generals. These actions, said the Canadian representative of the International Control Commission, were "justified in light of the warlike preparations in the pagodas and the clear intent of the Buddhist leadership to go on with political agitation until the government was overthrown."[cdxi]

The next day Lodge arrived in Saigon at 9:30 P.M.[cdxii] On August 24, 1963, the State Department, with the concurrence of President Kennedy, informed Lodge: (1) that he needed to tell Diem to remove his brother, Nhu, from power, and (2) that if Diem was unable or unwilling to do so he (Lodge) should contact Diem's generals and tell

---

candidate on the 1960 Nixon ticket (again defeated by Kennedy), and was a major general in the Army Reserve.

them the U.S. was prepared to cut off economic aid to South Vietnam and support a coup.[cdxiii]

Lodge, however, decided not to tell Diem to remove Nhu because he thought it would be unproductive and "would merely tip off the palace to the impending military action."[cdxiv] Therefore, instead of approaching Diem as instructed, Lodge, on August 26, 1963, informed "the generals," through CIA operative Lt. Col. Lucien Conein, that the United States had decided Nhu must go and that they ("the generals") needed to remove him and to decide whether to retain or remove Diem.[cdxv]

On September 6, 1963, the White House sent Major General Victor H. Krulak, USMC, and State Department representative Joseph Mendenhall to South Vietnam on a fact-finding mission.[cdxvi] After a whirlwind four-day trip Krulak and Mendenhall jointly briefed Kennedy on their mission and during this briefing Krulak told the president that even though there was "some dissatisfaction in the military" Diem was winning the war, and that a continuation of his policies would result in victory. Mendenhall, on the other hand, told Kennedy that as long as Diem was in power the war could not be won. Upon receiving these two divergent reports Kennedy rhetorically asked, "You two did visit the same country, didn't you?" [cdxvii]

Four days later Rufus Phillips, head of the Rural Affairs Office of the United States Agency for International Development (USAID) in Saigon, told Kennedy that General Landsdale needed to be reassigned to Vietnam.[cdxviii] This proposal, however, was opposed by Secretary McNamara.[cdxix]

Less than three weeks after arriving in Vietnam, Lodge sent an "Eyes Only" telegram to the Secretary of State, (with a copy to the White House) saying that, "the time has arrived for the US to use what effective sanctions it has to bring about the fall of the existing government and the installation of another."[cdxx]

The next day Senator Frank Church (D), with the president's approval, introduced a resolution that condemned Diem for repressing the Buddhists and called for the end of U.S. aid until the repression ceased.[cdxxi] Following the resolution and consistent with Lodge's recommendation, a critical $18.5 million aid package was deferred,[cdxxii] and, this deferral would work to pressure "the generals" into action.[cdxxiii]

President Kennedy, in view of the different reports from Krulak and Mendenhall, decided, on September 17, 1963, to send Secretary McNamara and General Taylor to Saigon on a second fact-finding mission.[cdxxiv]

A week later, Roger Hilsman, Assistant Secretary of State for Far Eastern Affairs, sent a hand-carried letter to Lodge that read:

Dear Cabot:

I am taking advantage of Mike Forrestal's safe hands to deliver this message.

… I have the feeling that more and more of the town is coming around to our view [i.e., that Diem must be removed by a coup] and that if you in Saigon and we in the Department stick to our guns the rest will also come around. As Mike will tell you a determined group here will back you all the way…[cdxxv] (Brackets in original.)

On October 2, 1963, McNamara and Taylor reported back to Kennedy on their follow-up trip saying, in summary, that:

1. The (overall) military campaign had made great progress and continues to progress.

2. There are serious political tensions in Saigon (and perhaps elsewhere in South Vietnam) where the Diem-Nhu government is becoming increasingly unpopular.

3. There is no solid evidence of the possibility of a successful coup, although assassination of Diem or Nhu is always possible. Although some, and perhaps an increasing number, of GVN military officers are becoming hostile to the government, they are more hostile to the Viet Cong than to the government and at least for the near future they will continue to perform their military duties.

4. Further repressive actions by Diem and Nhu could change the present favorable military trends. On the other hand, a return to more moderate methods of control and administration, unlikely though it may be, would substantially mitigate the political crisis.

5. It is not clear that pressures exerted by the U.S. will move Diem and Nhu toward moderation. Indeed, pressures may increase their obduracy. But unless such pressures are exerted, they are almost certain to continue past patterns of behavior.[cdxxvi]

With regard to the possibility of a spontaneous military coup McNamara and Taylor informed Kennedy that the chances were not high and that the U.S. should not organize one at that time.[cdxxvii]

However, just three days later CIA agent Conien, at Lodge's direction, met with General (Big) Minh (whose brother was a VC general)[cdxxviii] to see if "the generals" were planning an imminent coup. During this meeting Minh advised that three different plans were under consideration, one of which involved assassinations of Nhu and his wife but, according to Minh, not Diem; Conien remained noncommittal.[cdxxix] On October 23, 1963, Conein, at the direction of Lodge, advised "the generals" that the U.S. would not thwart a coup or deny economic or military aid to a new regime.[cdxxx]

On October 24, 1963, President Diem invited Ambassador Lodge and his wife to join him on the 27th at his house in Dalat to discuss the overall situation in Vietnam.[cdxxxi] Three days later Lodge met with Diem in Dalat, but afterward told Vietnamese Secretary of State Thauan that no progress had been made. However, Thauan, in response, told Lodge to be patient because, he said, Diem had taken the first step which meant "The Americans should be hearing from [him] again." [cdxxxii] That same evening (October 27th) Conein was advised by General Don that "the generals" coup would begin sometime between October 30 and November 2.[cdxxxiii]

The next day Lodge advised Washington a coup was imminent.[cdxxxiv] And, on the same day, (October 28th) an eight-member Congressional delegation that had recently returned from Vietnam released the following findings:

a. Diem with all his faults, his autocracy, his tolerance of venality and brutality is durable and has been winning. There is no visible substitute for Diem – at least none which guarantees improvement; thus, actions by U.S. representatives to join with coup plotters, as was apparently true in August, is harmful.

b. The conduct of the resident U.S. press is a grave reflection upon their entire profession. They are arrogant, emotional, unobjective and ill-informed. The case against them is best expressed by their having been repudiated by the responsible press.[cdxxxv]

As of October 29, 1963, General Harkins, the military commander in Vietnam, had been kept in the dark about the pending coup. However, since Lodge was scheduled to return to Washington on November 1, the NSC ordered him to inform Harkins of the plot as he (Harkins) would become the acting ambassador.[cdxxxvi] Upon being informed of the planned coup, Harkins sent several cables to General Maxwell Taylor, Chairman of the JCS, expressing his anger about Lodge's plotting with the South Vietnamese generals behind his back and, he added:

The Ambassador feels that …a change of government is desired and feels … that the only way to bring about such a change is by a coup.

I'm not opposed to a change in government, no indeed, but I'm inclined to feel that at this time the change should be in methods of governing rather than complete change of personnel. I have seen no batting order proposed by any of the coup groups. I think we should take a hard look at any proposed list before we make any decisions. In my contacts here I have seen no one with the strength of character of Diem, at least in fighting communists. Certainly, there are no Generals qualified to take over in my opinion.

I am not a Diem man *per se*. I certainly see the faults in his character. I am here to back 14 million SVN people in their leader at this time.

*****

I would suggest we not try to change horses too quickly. That we continue to take persuasive actions that will make the horses change their course and methods of action. That we win the military effort as quickly as possible, then let them make any and all the changes they want.

After all, rightly or wrongly, we have backed Diem for eight long hard years. To me it seems incongruous now to get him down, kick him around, and get rid of him. The U.S. has been his mother superior and father confessor since he's been in office and he has leaned on us heavily.[cdxxxvii]

On October 31, 1963, Lodge (who knew a coup was imminent, but not the exact time) delayed his scheduled trip to Washington.[cdxxxviii]

At 10 A.M. on November 1, 1963, (Saigon time) Diem told Lodge that he thought an attempted coup was imminent but did not know who was going to attempt it. Lodge, in response, (falsely) told Diem that he "didn't think there (was) anything to worry about."[cdxxxix] Thinking that Lodge was returning to Washington, Diem then asked Lodge to please tell President Kennedy he was a good ally and that he (Diem) would carry out his requests.[cdxl]

At approximately 1 P.M. on November 1, 1963, (Saigon time) the coup began.[cdxli] Seven and a half hours *after* the coup began, Lodge sent Kennedy a cable that arrived at the White House at 9:30 A.M. November 1 (Washington time).[cdxlii] In this cable Lodge quoted Diem as having said:

Please tell President Kennedy that I am a good and frank ally, that I would rather be frank and settle questions now than talk about them after we have lost everything…. Tell President

Kennedy that I take all his suggestions very seriously and wish to carry them out but it is a question of timing.[cdxliii]

And, Lodge added,

> I feel this is another step in the dialogue, which Diem had begun at our meeting in Dalat on Sunday [October 27]. If U.S. wants to make a package deal, I would think we are in a position to do it…In effect he [Diem] said: "Tell us what you want and we'll do it. Hope to discuss this in Washington."[cdxliv]

When the Palace was breached by the coup plotters on November 2, 1963, Diem phoned Lodge and asked for safe transport to the American embassy; this request, however, was denied. Diem, who had taken secret refuge in a church, then contacted General Don and was assured that if he and his brother surrendered, they would be given safe passage out of the county. Upon receiving this assurance Diem and Nhu surrendered unconditionally but, instead of being given safe transport out of the country, they were each shot in the back numerous times with a submachinegun and, for good measure, repeatedly stabbed.[cdxlv] Their deaths were then described by "the generals" as accidental suicides.[cdxlvi]

General "Big" Minh, who ordered the murders,[cdxlvii] explained that Diem "could not be allowed to live because he was too much respected by the simple gullible people in the countryside especially the Catholics and the refugees."[cdxlviii] And, Lodge later said to Halberstam, "What would we have done with them if they had lived? Every Colonel Blimp in the world would have made use of them."[cdxlix]

During the nine years Diem was in office less than 150 Americans died in Vietnam,[cdl] but after Diem's death things changed for the U.S. and for the "simple gullible people of the countryside" who saw their Strategic Hamlet Program die with Diem.[cdli]

With this coup, according to the Pentagon Papers:

> the nine-year rule of Ngo Dinh Diem came to a bloody and permanent end, and U.S. policy in Vietnam plunged into the unknown; *our complicity in the coup only heightening our responsibilities and our commitment in this struggling leaderless land.*[cdlii] (Emphasis mine)

On November 5, 1963, a new government was formed under General "Big" Minh who named himself President and Chief of the Military Committee.[cdliii]

Four days after the coup President Kennedy, who was said to have been shocked and horrified by Diem's murder, sent a cable to Lodge extending his appreciation for the fine job he was doing.[cdliv]

By the end of the next week, the U.S. announced it would begin withdrawing 1,000, of its 16,000 advisors in less than a month.[cdlv]

Exactly one week after the withdrawal announcement President Kennedy was tragically assassinated and on the same day Lyndon B. Johnson was sworn in as the 36th president of the United States.[cdlvi]

Robert McNamara later summed up the difference between Vietnam in early 1963 and the Vietnam after Diem's overthrow saying:

> …In early 1963, President Kennedy was able to report to the nation that "the spearpoint of aggression has been blunted in South Vietnam. It was evident that the Government had seized the initiative in most areas from the insurgents. But this progress was interrupted in 1963 by the political crisis arising

from troubles between the Government, and the Buddhists and students and other non-Communist oppositionists. (And, after Diem's overthrow,) … (t)here were two changes of government within three months. The fabric of government was torn. The political structure extending from Saigon down into the hamlets virtually disappeared. Of the 41 incumbent province chiefs on November 1, [1963], thirty-five were replaced. Nine provinces had three chiefs in three months; one province had four. Scores of lesser officials were replaced. Almost all major military commands changed hands twice. The confidence of the peasants was inevitability shaken by loss of leadership and the loss of physical security….[cdlvii]

On December 21, 1963, two months after Diem's murder, McNamara informed President Johnson that:

The situation [in Vietnam was] very disturbing. Current trends [he said] unless reversed in the next 2-3 months, will lead to neutralization at best and more likely to a communist controlled state.[cdlviii]

At the end of 1963, there were 16,300 Americans in Vietnam and during that year 78 were killed in action and 218 were wounded; during the same year 5,665 South Vietnamese were killed in action and 11,488 were wounded.[cdlix]

On January 6, 1964, General Minh removed everyone in the government formed on November 5, 1963, and entered a decree placing himself, General Don, and General Kim in control of the Military Revolutionary Council.[cdlx] Three weeks later General Nguyen Khanh, in a bloodless coup, removed Minh and put himself in charge of the Military Revolutionary Council.[cdlxi]

At the beginning of February, the Military Assistance Command of Vietnam (MACV) released an assessment concluding that political instability caused by Diem's ouster was the main reason for South Vietnam's military failures and for the rise in enemy activity during the previous three months.[cdlxii]

On June 7, 1964, approximately 35,000 Roman Catholics gathered in Saigon to protest the government's favoritism of Buddhists.[cdlxiii]

The White House announced on June 23, 1964, that General Taylor, then Chairman of the Joint Chiefs of Staff, would be replacing Ambassador Lodge who was returning to the U.S. to take part in Republican political activity.[cdlxiv]

At the end of June, Admiral Ulysses S. Grant Sharp became commander-in-chief-Pacific (CINCPAC) replacing Harold Donald Felt, who had been the CINCPAC since 1958.[cdlxv]

In early July, General Earle Wheeler, the Army Chief of Staff, replaced General Maxwell Taylor as Chairman of the Joint Chiefs of Staff and he, in turn, was replaced by General Harold K. Johnson.[cdlxvi]

Ambassador Taylor arrived in Vietnam on July 7, 1964.[cdlxvii]

SUMMARY

In October 1960, *The New York Times* validated Eisenhower's 1954 decision to stay and help the South Vietnamese when it saluted Diem saying:

> A five-year miracle, not a 'plan,' has been carried out. Vietnam is free and is becoming stronger in defense of its freedom and of ours. There is reason today to salute President Ngo Dinh Diem.[cdlxviii]

In his October 25 letter to Diem, Eisenhower echoed this approval saying that he, along with his countrymen, had:

> watched the courage and daring with which [he] and the Vietnamese people attained independence in a situation so perilous that many thought it hopeless. We have admired [Eisenhower told him] the rapidity with which chaos yielded to order and progress replaced despair.

According to the Pentagon Papers, Diem, while with faults:

> ... really did accomplish miracles... He took power in 1954 amid political chaos, and within ten months surmounted attempted coups d'etat from within his army and rebellions by disparate irregulars. He consolidated his regime while providing credibility for an influx of nearly one million destitute refugees from North Vietnam; and he did all of this despite active French opposition and vacillating American support. Under his leadership South Vietnam became well established as a sovereign state, by 1955 recognized de jure by 36 other nations. Moreover, by mid-1955 Diem secured the strong backing of the U.S. He conducted a plebiscite in late

1955, in which an overwhelming vote was recorded for him in preference to Bao Dai; during 1956, he installed a government - - - representative in form, at least - - - drafted a new constitution, and extended GVN (Government of South Vietnam) control to regions that had been under sect or Viet Minh rule for a decade; and he pledged to initiate extensive reforms in land holding, public health, and education. With American help, he established a truly national, modern army, and formed rural security forces to police the countryside. In accomplishing all the foregoing, he confounded those Vietnamese of North and South, and those French, who had looked for his imminent downfall.

While it is true that his reforms entailed oppressive measures--e.g., his "political reeducation centers" were in fact little more than concentration camps for potential foes of the government--his regime compared favorably with other Asian governments of the same period in its respect for the person and property of citizens. There is much that can be offered in mitigation of Diem's authoritarianism. He began as the most singularly disadvantaged head of state of his era. His political legacy was endemic violence and virulent anti-colonialism.

He took office at a time when the government of Vietnam controlled only a few blocks of downtown Saigon; the rest of the capital was the feudal fief of the Binh Xuyen gangster fraternity. Beyond the environs of Saigon, South Vietnam lay divided among the Viet Minh enclaves and the theocratic dominions of the Cao Dai and the Hoa Hao sects. All these powers would have opposed any Saigon government, whatever its composition; in fact, their existence accounts for much of the confidence the DRV [the North] then exhibited toward the outcome of the Geneva Settlement. For Diem to have erected any central government in South Vietnam without reckoning resolutely with their several armed forces and clandestine organizations would have been impossible: they were the very stuff of South Vietnam's politics.

Diem's initial political tests reinforced his propensity to inflexibility. The lessons of his first 10 months of rule must have underscored to Diem the value of swift, tough action against dissent, and of demanding absolute personal loyalty of top officials.[cdlxix]

To combat the "miracles" being worked by Diem Hanoi infiltrated approximately 23,000 North Vietnamese cadre into South Vietnam during 1961 and 1962.[cdlxx] In response, Diem initiated the "Strategic Hamlet Program" in February 1962 to counter Hanoi's stepped-up aggression; at the end of 1963 this program was thriving.

In spite of his gains in the countryside Diem had fallen out of favor with Kennedy, many in his administration and much of the U.S. press in Saigon because he was "too autocratic" or not "responsive enough to Washington." Therefore, in August 1963 the Kennedy administration, utilizing the "Buddhist crisis" as a reason, began orchestrating plans to remove Diem from office.

This was true even though Diem was probably less autocratic than present, former or future allies like Syngman Rhee in South Korea, Fulgencio Batista in Cuba, Anastasio Somoza in Nicaragua, Mobutu Seko in Zaire, Mohammed Shah in Iran, and Chiang Kai-Shek in Taiwan.[cdlxxi] So, why Diem?

Jeanne Kirkpatrick, U.S. ambassador to the United Nations under Ronald Reagan, later observed that:

> Beyond 'reasonable' doubt ... the communist governments of Vietnam, Cambodia and Laos [after 1975] were much more repressive than those of 'despised previous rulers.' The government of the People's Republic of China was more repressive than that of Taiwan; North Korea was more repressive than South Korea. 'Traditional autocrats,' she wrote, 'tolerate social inequities, brutality, and poverty, whereas revolutionary autocracies create them.'"[cdlxxii]

And Diem was not even "a despised ruler," at least by the people of his countryside. But the Kennedy administration saw things differently and since Diem would not respond to Washington's satisfaction Kennedy and Lodge caused a coup to be orchestrated by withholding aid to South Vietnam.

The coup took place on the watch of Ambassador Henry Cabot Lodge, on November 1, 1963. And, when Diem was murdered, the leader of the National Liberation Front said that his death was viewed as a "gift from heaven."[cdlxxiii]

The decision by the United States to use the Buddhist incident to forcibly remove Diem from office by coup was a horrible decision for several reasons.

First, after Diem's death, the UN commission, that had been impaneled to investigate the allegations of systematic Buddhist repression, determined there was no such systematic repression by Diem's government.[cdlxxiv] Second, Diem had been premier and then president for the nine years prior to his murder during which time he was said to have worked magic. Third, to counter the North's insurgency in the South, Diem initiated a Strategic Hamlet program in early 1962, a program that had given him so much respect from the people "in the countryside" that he was murdered to prevent those "gullible people" from rallying around him in the future. Unfortunately, when Diem died the success of his Strategic Hamlet program died with him. Fourth, Diem's death left a vacuum in South Vietnam that led to eight different governments within the time span of two years to the detriment of the South's military effort against the North, and Fifth, less than 150 Americans died in South Vietnam during the nine years Diem was chief of state (1954-1963) during the next ten years, however, over 58,000 more Americans would be killed there and over a hundred and fifty thousand more would be wounded.

According to historian Mark Moyer:

> …South Vietnam's President was ousted and killed by certain of his countrymen [however] ultimate responsibility for his fate belonged to Henry Cabot Lodge, to the President who appointed and refused to fire Lodge, and to the individuals who were giving Lodge information and advice on the political situation--a few State Department officials in Saigon and Washington and a handful of resident journalists…[cdlxxv]

Barbara Tuchman, Pulitzer Prize winning author, and a critic of the Vietnam War, chided the Kennedy administration saying that even though this coup:

> …violated a basic principle of foreign relations [it] did not bother the realists of the Kennedy school. That it made nonsense of the reiterated American insistence that Vietnam's conflict was 'their' war does not seem to have been considered… If it was their war [she said] it was also their government and their policies. For the defenders of democracy to conspire with plotters of a coup d' etat, no matter how cogent the reasons, could not be hailed in the history books as the American way.[cdlxxvi]

America did more than conspire with the coup plotters, it hatched and encouraged the plan for reasons that were not close to being cogent. Whether Kennedy would have stayed in Vietnam (as is often debated) remains to be seen. But, had he withdrawn, after his coup had "only heighten[ed] our responsibilities and our commitment in this struggling leaderless land,"[cdlxxvii] such a withdrawal certainly would not have been hailed in the history books as the American way either.

PHOTOGRAPHS FROM 1960-1963

Volunteers in the People's Self-Defense Force (formed in 1960) patrolling the Kien Dien hamlet perimeter, 50 kilometers north of Saigon. (National Archives)

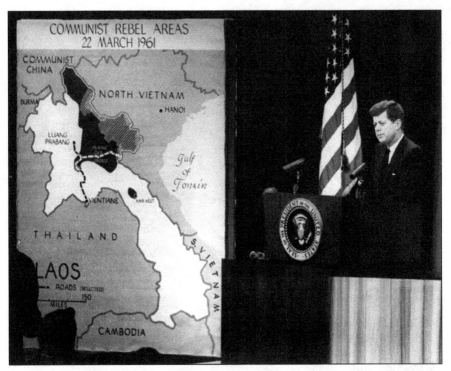

President Kennedy at the State Department on March 22, 1961, explaining his position on Laos. (National Archives)

VIET NAM 2

THE WHITE HOUSE
WASHINGTON

~~SECRET~~   February 1, 1963

MEMORANDUM FOR

THE PRESIDENT

South Vietnam

You are meeting this afternoon at 4:30 p.m. with
Secretary Rusk, Secretary McNamara, Mr. Gilpatric,
General Taylor, General Wheeler, Governor Harriman,
Director McCone, Mr. David Bell and Mr. William Bundy.
The announced purpose of the meeting is to give you an oppor-
tunity to hear General Wheeler's report on his trip to South
Vietnam.

As a means of stimulating action, you may wish to put
some of the following questions:

1.   Should General Harkins report directly to the JCS instead
of CinCPac?

2.   In view of Ambassador Nolting's completion of his two-year
extension in South Vietnam in mid-April, should we consider a new
appointment?

3.   Have we been as firm as we should with the GVN in putting
our views across on our military, domestic and foreign policy?

4.   Is U.S. air power ("Farm Gate") being used effectively to
support our guerrilla war strategy, i.e.:

(a) Is enough emphasis being placed on close air support
and liaison capabilities as against air strikes and interdiction?

~~SECRET~~

CONFIDENTIAL
E.O. 11852, Sec. 3(E) and 3(D)
Archivist of U.S.
by MFD.... NARS Date 10/14/76
(NLK-76-157)

**Talking points for a February 1, 1963, meeting with President Kennedy
prepared by MV Forrestal. (National Archives)**

On October 2, 1963, General Maxwell Taylor and Secretary McNamara submit a fact-finding report to the President made necessary because two prior reports were so inconsistent Kennedy had (rhetorically) asked the authors if they had visited the same country. (National Archives)

CHAPTER FOUR
August 1964 – March 1965

On August 2, 1964, the USS *Maddox*, was attacked by North Vietnamese torpedo boats in the Gulf of Tonkin twenty-eight miles off the coast while in international waters.[cdlxxviii] It was initially thought that the *C. Turner Joy* was also attacked in international waters two nights later, but further reconnaissance in daylight hours casts doubt on such an attack.[cdlxxix]

In response to the attack on the *Maddox*; the possible attack on the *C. Turner Joy* and other hostile North Vietnamese activity Senator J.W. Fulbright (D) and Representative Thomas E. Morgan (D) sponsored Public Law 88-408, the Southeast Asia (Gulf of Tonkin) Resolution, on August 6 before their respective chambers.[cdlxxx]

The next day Congress passed the Southeast Asia Resolution by votes of 414 to 0 in the House and 88 to 2 in the Senate. Senator Wayne Morse (D) and Senator Ernest Gruening (D) were opposed.[cdlxxxi] The resolution gave the president authority to take all necessary steps, including the use of armed forces, to assist any member of the Southeast Asia Collective Defense Treaty requesting assistance in defense of its freedom. And Congress, to show its support, instead of appropriating the $125 million requested by President Johnson, appropriated $400 million to begin the combat effort in South Vietnam.

Premier Souvanna Phouma of Laos simultaneously supported the U.S. response to the torpedo boat attack(s).[cdlxxxii]

On August 18, 1964, Ambassador Taylor advised Washington that he did not think the Saigon government could defeat the opposition simply by fighting "a counter guerilla war confined to South Vietnam." He, therefore, recommended "a carefully orchestrated bombing attack on North Vietnam" to prevent "a complete collapse of national moral" in Saigon.[cdlxxxiii]

The next week Senator Barry Goldwater (R) suggested that negotiations with Communist China would be the best way to end the Vietnam War.[cdlxxxiv]

President Johnson announced to the American people on August 29 that the U.S. would continue to assist the South Vietnamese with their struggle but would not fight their war.[cdlxxxv]

Despite polls showing that most Americans backed the Vietnam War, college students and faculty at the University of California (Berkley) staged the first major demonstration against it on September 30.[cdlxxxvi]

In a statement released on October 10, 1964, Saigon said that some 16,000 soldiers or agents had come from the North to the South under the Chieu Hoi (amnesty) program during the prior 20 months.[cdlxxxvii]

Nikita Khrushchev was overthrown on October 14 by Leonid Brezhnev who immediately began supplying the North Vietnamese with more military aid and quit trying to convince them to reach a negotiated settlement.[cdlxxxviii] Brezhnev also began building up the Soviet military which, by January 1969, almost had the same number of land-based intercontinental ballistic missiles as did the United States military.[cdlxxxix]

A U.S. government assessment taken one year after Ngo Dinh Diem was overthrown and assassinated, revealed that South Vietnam had deteriorated both militarily and politically.[cdxc]

On November 27, 1964, Ambassador Taylor returned to Washington[cdxci] and reported a continued deterioration of the pacification program and a continued weakening of the central government.[cdxcii] In this report he made it clear that in order for South Vietnam to succeed it must, among other things, establish an adequate government."[cdxciii] Specifically, he wrote:

> ...it is hard to visualize our being willing to make added outlays of resources and to run increasing political risks without an allied government which, at least, can speak for and to its people, can maintain law and order in the principal cities, can provide local protection for the vital military bases and installations, can raise and support Armed Forces, and can gear its efforts to those of the United States. Anything less than this would hardly be a government at all, and under such circumstances, the United States Government might do better to carry forward the war on a purely unilateral basis.[cdxciv]

At the end of 1964, there were 23,300 Americans in Vietnam; during that year 147 were killed in action and 522 were wounded. South Vietnam had 7,457 killed in action and 17,017 wounded.[cdxcv]

On January 6, 1965, Ambassador Taylor, arguing for permission to bomb North Vietnam, told President Johnson that, "Until the fall of Diem and the experience gained from the following months I doubt that anyone appreciated the magnitude of the centrifugal political forces which had been kept under control by his iron rule..." and, he said, since "there is no adequate replacement for Diem in sight" it might be too late for South Vietnam if the U.S. continued to wait for a good government in Saigon before bombing the North.[cdxcvi]

Japan's Prime Minister, Eisaku Sato, speaking to the National Press Club in Washington, D.C. suggested that the problems in Vietnam could not be solved by the "rational approach" of the West but should be left to the Asians themselves.[cdxcvii] This advice should have been given before Diem's ouster, but even if it had been given it probably would have fallen on deaf ears in Washington.

Soviet Premier Aleksi Kosygin arrived in Hanoi on February 6, 1965, to discuss potential political solutions to the war; however, a meeting of the minds could not be reached, causing one of the participants to later describe the North Vietnamese as "a bunch of stubborn bastards."[cdxcviii] And, the same day Kosygin arrived in Hanoi, National Security Advisor McGeorge Bundy arrived in Saigon to confer with Ambassador Taylor about possible political solutions to the war.[cdxcix]

The next day (February 7) the VC attacked Camp Holloway in the central highlands killing eight Americans and wounding over a hundred more.[d] As a result of the attack McNamara and Taylor strongly urged the immediate implementation of a sustained bombing policy and Bundy, upon visiting the site of the attack, phoned the president and told him that "without new U.S. action defeat appear(ed) inevitable—probably not in a matter of weeks, or perhaps even months, but within the next year or so."[di]

In response to this raid Johnson called his top advisors together and informed them that he would be answering the attack with retaliatory air raids (which would come to be known as Rolling Thunder).[dii] Everyone present, with the exception of Vice President Hubert Humphrey and Senator Mike Mansfield (D) agreed.[diii]

On February 10, the VC blew up U.S. quarters at Quinhon, 75 miles east of Pleiku, killing twenty-three Americans.[div] Due to this increased enemy activity General Westmoreland advised on February 22nd that the air base in Da Nang needed to be protected by U.S. combat troops and he recommended bringing in two battalions of Marines to set up a perimeter defense.[dv] This request was opposed by Ambassador Taylor in a February 22, 1965, cable to the State Department in which he said that the deployment would be the first step in the assumption of a ground war in which a "White-faced soldier armed, equipped and trained as he is [is] not [a] suitable guerrilla fighter for Asian forests and jungles. French tried to adapt their forces to this mission and failed; I doubt that US forces could do much better."[dvi]

About a month later General Nguyen Van Thieu requested, on behalf of South Vietnam, the insertion of U.S. Marines but asked that the insertion be made in the most inconspicuous way possible.[dvii]

On March 6, the Pentagon issued the following news Release:

> TWO U.S. MARINE BATTALIONS TO BE DEPLOYED IN VIETNAM. After consultation between the governments of South Vietnam and the United States, the United States Government has agreed to the request of the Government of Vietnam to station two United States Marine Corps Battalions in the Da Nang area to strengthen the greater security of the Da Nang Air Base complex.
>
> The limited mission of the Marines will be to relieve Government of South Vietnam forces now engaged in security duties for action in the pacification program and in offensive roles against Communist guerrilla forces.[dviii]

Two days later combat Marines began landing in Vietnam and on April 6, 1965, the president promulgated National Security Action Memorandum (NSAM) 328, changing the Marine mission "from one of advice and static defense to one of active combat operations…"[dix]

It has been opined that NASM 328 was a "pivotal document" because it marked "the acceptance [by] the president of the United States…that

U.S. troops would engage in offensive ground operations against Asian insurgents."[dx.]

On April 28, CIA Director John A. McCone resigned and sent a memorandum to the president opposing a ground force build-up in South Vietnam unless it was accompanied by a greatly intensified air campaign against North Vietnam.[dxi] At about this time much of academia and many students in America began taking the position the United States was now illegally involved in another country's civil war.

SUMMARY

As military activity increased in the mid-1960s many in academia began to argue that the United States was illegally involved in a civil war between North and South Vietnam.

In rebuttal, Eugene V. Rostow, National Security Advisor under President Johnson, succinctly said:

> Since Truman's time ….the United States has taken the view that two states [North and South Vietnam] emerged in Vietnam within the meaning of international law, two states exercising authority within their respective jurisdictions, and protected against external attack by the principals of the [United Nations] Charter, endowed that is with the right of self-defense and a right to ask other states to assist them in the exercise of that right.[dxii]

This position is supported by the facts. Vietnam was divided at the 16th parallel during the Potsdam Conference in 1945. By mid-1955, it (the state of Vietnam) was recognized by approximately 35 nations; in 1957 the Soviet Union conceded in the UN that there were "two states in Vietnam,"[dxiii] and as of mid-1966 South Vietnam was recognized by some 60 nations.[dxiv]

As a separate internationally known entity, South Vietnam was endowed by the principals of the United Nations Charter with the right to defend itself and the right to ask others to help them in their defense (the right of collective self-defense).

In addition, South Vietnam's right of collective self-defense was strengthened by the Southeast Asia Collective Defense Treaty (SEATO) signed on September 4, 1954, by Australia, France, New

Zealand, Pakistan, Philippines, Thailand, the United Kingdom and the United States.

Article IV of this treaty and its attached Protocol provides that an armed attack against any party or against the states of Cambodia and Laos or against "the territory under the jurisdiction of the state of Vietnam" would endanger its own peace and safety. Accordingly, the parties to the treaty were to meet this danger in accordance with their own constitutional procedures.[dxv]

In 1957, when North Vietnam began to build up its forces, President Eisenhower and President Diem issued a joint statement making it clear that South Vietnam was:

> covered by Article IV of the Southeast Asia Collective Defense Treaty [and] that aggression or subversion threatening the political independence of [South Vietnam] would be considered as endangering peace and stability.[dxvi]

When North Vietnam continued to "endanger peace and stability" by infiltrating men into South Vietnam,[dxvii] President Kennedy warned on August 2, 1961, that "the United States [was] determined that [South Vietnam] shall not be lost to the Communists for lack of any support which the United States can render."[dxviii]

This warning, however, did not deter North Vietnam and by December 1961 it had infiltrated an estimated 10,000 men into South Vietnam.[dxix] This caused President Diem to ask for help and President Kennedy replied by telling him that the United States was "prepared to help [South Vietnam] to protect its people and to preserve its independence."[dxx]

Still not deterred, North Vietnam infiltrated an estimated 13,000 more personnel into South Vietnam in 1962, and by the end of 1964 the

North was thought to have moved over 40,000 guerrillas into the South.[dxxi]

In addition, between 1961 and 1964, the Hanoi directed National Liberation Front (NLF) had: instigated around 44,000 military attacks; engaged in some 18,000 kidnappings, and assassinated about 3,000 people in South Vietnam,[dxxii] and this activity had not escaped Washington's attention. Therefore, when the USS *Maddox* was attacked in international waters on August 2, 1964, Congress was prepared to, and did, enact the Southeast Asia Resolution (Public Law 88-408) five days later.

In this Resolution it was noted that the attack on the *Maddox* was "part of a deliberate and systematic campaign of aggression that the Communist regime in North Vietnam has been waging against its neighbors and the nations joined with them…" Congress went on to decree that "Consonant with the Constitution of the United States, and with the Charter of the United Nations and in accordance with its obligations under the Southeast Asia Collective Defense Treaty the United States is, therefore, prepared, as the president determines to take all necessary steps, including the use of armed force to assist any member or protocol state [Cambodia, Laos or the state of Vietnam] requesting assistance in defense of its freedom."[dxxiii]

Therefore, in 1965 when the South Vietnamese asked the United States for help in repelling North Vietnam's aggression the requested assistance was given pursuant to: the provisions of the United Nations Charter; the provisions of the SEATO treaty, and the provisions of the Southeast Asia Resolution.

It should be noted Vietnam was not the only place international boundaries created at Potsdam were challenged. Such boundaries were also challenged in 1950 when North Korea crossed the 38th parallel and attacked South Korea. At that time Truman (alone) committed troops to a three-year war in defense of South Korea.

The Potsdam boundaries were also challenged in Berlin. They were first challenged in 1948 when the Soviet Union attempted to take control of West Berlin with 40 army divisions. At that time Truman countered by blockading East Berlin and by strategically placing bombers in Great Britain making it clear that the allies considered the boundaries created at the Potsdam Conference binding under international law. After a tense yearlong standoff, the Soviet Union finally backed down. The allies' defense of these boundaries, then, "became a symbol of [their] willingness to oppose further Soviet expansion..."

The Potsdam boundaries in Berlin were once again challenged by Premier Nikita Khrushchev in June 1961. The following month President Kennedy in a report to the nation on "the Berlin Crisis" said:

> Seven weeks ago tonight I returned from Europe to report on my meeting with Premier Khrushchev and the others... In Berlin, as you recall, he intends to bring to an end, through a stroke of the pen, first our legal rights to be in West Berlin-and secondly our ability to make good on our commitment to the two million free people of that city. That we cannot permit.
>
> *****
>
> We are there as a result of our victory over Nazi Germany--and our basic rights to be there, deriving from that victory, include both our presence in West Berlin and the enjoyment of access across East Germany... Berlin is not a part of East Germany, but a separate territory [created at the Potsdam Conference]

under the control of the allied powers. Thus, our rights there are clear and deep rooted…[dxxiv]

Kennedy responded to the Soviet threat by: doubling the draft; calling on Congress to increase the armed services by over 200,000 men, and by asking for a $3.2 billion increase in the defense budget. The Soviets, recognizing Kennedy's determination to defend West Berlin's boundaries at all costs, built a wall instead of going to war.

Even though the president acted unilaterally in Korea and two times in Berlin, without the benefit of Congressional action, academia never contended the United States was acting illegally. But when it came to Vietnam it was a different story. It was a different story even though the United States went to South Vietnam's assistance pursuant to the Southeast Asia Resolution and the SEATO treaty, both of which were passed with the advice and consent of the Senate.

Contrary to what many in academia argued at the time, the United States was legally assisting South Vietnam with its self-defense. Recognizing this fact, others in academia proffered a second argument in support of their "illegal civil war theory." Under this theory it was argued that the United States was illegally engaged in a civil war *within* South Vietnam "to determine who was going to govern South Vietnam."[dxxv]

This would have been the better argument if it was supported by the facts, but it was not. As noted in the Pentagon Papers, even if:

> the rebellion against Diem in South Vietnam proceeded independently of, or even contrary to directions from Hanoi through 1958, Hanoi moved thereafter to capture the revolution.[dxxvi]

Hanoi began to capture the revolution by infiltrating guerillas into the South and by controlling attacks in the South through the Lao Dong Party which, due to perception problems, changed its name to the National Liberation Front of South Vietnam (the NLF) on December 20, 1960.[dxxvii]

In explaining this name change, Hanoi issued a directive explaining that the "National Liberation Front" was a name that could be used:

> … in public to appeal to the (local) population and … in our strategy to sow division and isolate Diem.[dxxviii]

But to make sure the Party faithful knew who was really in control Hanoi went on to say:

> Although the overt name [NLF] will be different than that used in North Vietnam, secretly internally and from an organizational standpoint, the Party Chapter for South Vietnam will still be part of the Vietnamese Labor Party and will be under the Party Central Committee headed by Ho Chi Minh.[dxxix]

It is clear from the beginning, therefore, that this war was not a civil war among the South Vietnamese for control of South Vietnam. But, the ultimate proof that this was not an internal civil war was how the war ended: with Hanoi's tanks knocking down the gates of the Presidential palace in Saigon and with South Vietnam's acting president, Duong Van (Big) Minh, surrendering to North Vietnam's commander, Colonel Bui Tin.

After this surrender, "[t]he North Vietnamese swept aside the People's Revolutionary Government [the political organ of the NLF] and…unified North and South Vietnam as the Socialist Republic of Vietnam."[dxxx]

This war was not a war among the South Vietnamese to determine who would govern South Vietnam; to the contrary, it was an attempt by Hanoi to take control of the territory governed by Saigon, and Hanoi eventually prevailed.

In spite of the law and the facts, 3,000 faculty members and students at the University of Michigan organized the first "teach in" in opposition to the war in March 1965 and this opposition, thereafter, spread from coast to coast. At the University of California, Berkley, for example, 26 faculty members joined in a letter stating that, "The United States Government [was] committing a major crime in Vietnam," and expressed their shame and anger that this blood bath was happening in their name.

Then, relying on academia's (erroneous) claim that the U.S. was illegally participating in a "civil war," students around the country started taking their protests to the streets with such chants as, "Hell no we won't go," "Hup, two, three, four we don't want your f------ war," "Make love, not war," "Hey, Hey, LBJ how many babies did you kill today"? and, "I don't give a damn for Uncle Sam; I ain't going to Viet Nam."

According to war critic Tuchman, all of this protesting:

> was denounced [by the U.S.] as aiding the enemy by encouraging them to hold out, which was true, and as unpatriotic, which was also true, for the saddest consequence [of this protesting] was loss of a valuable feeling by the young, who laughed at patriotism.[dxxxi]

But, nobody laughed louder than Ho Chi Minh who planned on defeating the United States the same way he defeated France: by creating enough dissension from within that it would divide the country and eventually cause it to crack, which it did in 1975.

PHOTOGRAPHS FROM 1964 to 1965

A fleeing North Vietnamese torpedo Boat just after it attacked the USS Maddox in the Gulf of Tonkin on August 2, 1964. The Maddox, while hit by a shell from a deck gun, was never hit by a torpedo. (National Archives)

The USS Ticonderoga whose planes helped drive off the North Vietnamese P-4 torpedo boat(s) that attacked the USS Maddox on August 2, 1964. (National Archives)

On March 8, 1965, U.S. Marines land at Da Nang. South Vietnam's future Ambassador to the United States, Bui Dem, later commented that, "For the United States this event signaled the start of a new American land war in Asia. For the South Vietnamese it meant the presence once again of foreign soldiers on our own territory." (National Archives)

VC under fire south of Saigon in 1965. (National Archives)

CHAPTER FIVE
May 1965-October 1966

By May 1965, there were differences of opinion between General Westmoreland and the Marine Corps generals about how to best proceed in Vietnam. The Marine Corps generals preferred the "enclave-defense pacification" approach (Diem's approach). Westmoreland, on the other hand, preferred the "search and destroy" approach, and since he was the commander of MACV, his approach, of course, prevailed.[dxxxii]

On June 19, almost two years and eight governments after Diem's murder, Air-Marshall Ky, who was nominally a Buddhist,[dxxxiii] became Prime Minister of South Vietnam declaring that he would "rule with an iron hand" [dxxxiv] and, by this time, the United States was more than willing to accept an autocratic ruler. In fact, at about the same time Ky took charge, President Johnson was lamenting that, "The worst mistake we ever made was getting rid of Diem."[dxxxv]

Within a week of Ky's ascension to power, General Westmoreland deemed it necessary to strengthen the position of the South Vietnamese government, and was formally given authority to commit U.S. troops to battle.[dxxxvi] Thereafter, the first army search and destroy mission took place on June 28.[dxxxvii]

Just one week after that search and destroy mission, Maxwell Taylor announced his plans to resign his post as Ambassador. And, by this time, he had come to accept Westmoreland's view that it was necessary to employ U.S. combat troops in Vietnam.[dxxxviii]

By July 15, the III Marine Amphibious Force (III MAF), operating out of Chu Lai with the 1st and 2d Battalion 4th Marine Regiment (4th

Marines) and 3d Battalion 3d Marine Regiment (3d Marines), had established enclaves protecting air bases at Chu Lai, Da Nang, Phu Bai and Qui Nhon.[dxxxix]

Major General Lewis W. Walt, Commanding General of the III Marine Amphibious Force, received orders on August 6 to undertake the first large-scale Marine Corps action against the enemy.[dxl] This order resulted in the planning of Operation Starlite[*] which would pit Marine Corps Regimental Landing Team 7 (RLT-7) against the 1st Vietcong Regiment located near the village of Van Toung. This would be the first meeting between the Marines and VC "in open battle in regimental-sized formations," and the plan was to conduct a surprise "hammer and anvil operation," that would drive the enemy into the sea.

Meanwhile back in the states during an August 9 interview on national television, Harry Reasoner asked Secretary McNamara and the Secretary of State, Dean Rusk, to explain "… how our honor [was] involved in Viet-Nam? And "how our security [was] involved in those rice paddies and remote villages?"

Consistent with the "Vandenberg Doctrine" Secretary Rusk noted that America's security depends on its world-wide Mutual Security commitments, and added that:

> …there is no need to parse these commitments in great detail. The fact is we know we have a commitment. The South Vietnamese know we have a commitment. The communist world knows we have a commitment. The rest of the world knows it.

---

[*] Originally dubbed "Operation Satellite," but the clerk preparing the final order misread the draft in the dim light and typed "Starlite instead."

Now this means that the integrity of the American commitment is at the heart of the problem. I believe the integrity of the American commitment is the principal of peace throughout the world. We have 42 allies [created by mutual security agreements]. Those alliances were approved by overwhelming votes of our Senate. We didn't go into those alliances through some sense of amiability or some philanthropic attitude toward other nations. We went into them because we consider these alliances utterly essential for the security of our own nation.

Now, if these allies, or more particularly, if our adversaries should discover that the American commitment is not worth anything. Then the world would face dangers of which we have not yet dreamed. And it is important for us to make good on that American commitment to South Viet-Nam.[dxli]

Making good on that commitment, of course, was a difficult task as evidenced on the ground in battles like Operation Starlite. This battle commenced a week after the Reasoner interview in the late afternoon of 17 August 1965 when Company M, 3d battalion, 3d Marines established a blocking position in the north to prevent the 1st VC Regiment from escaping. The operation continued early the next morning with amphibious landings on Green Beach by Companies I, K and L, of 3d battalion, 3d Marines and with the insertion of Companies G, E and H of 2d battalion, 4th Marines by helicopter from the west. The 3d battalion, 7th Marines arrived later that morning and became the operation's Floating Reserve.[dxlii]

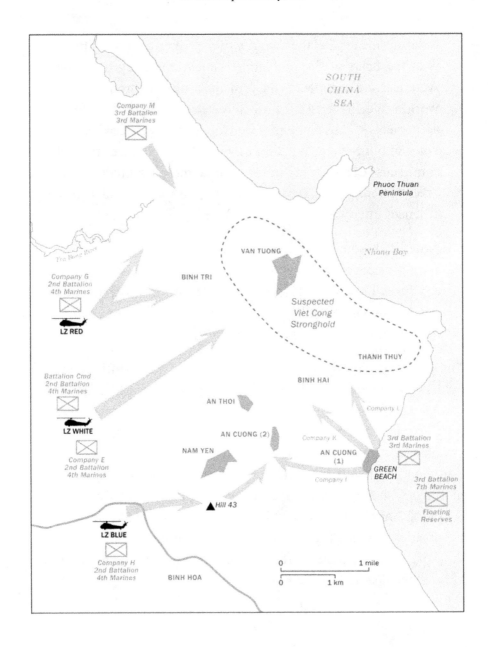

At approximately 0930 on 18 August Second Lieutenant Tommy Benton (a fraternity brother a year ahead of me at the University of Richmond) approached Green Beach on the USS Iwo Jima.[dxliii] Benton, who was a platoon commander in India Company (Company I), later described this Operation as it got underway in a letter to his father saying:

Dear Dad:

> …We left the ship [in an amtrac - - amphibious tractor] at 0500 approaching an area militarily designated 'Green Beach,' 20 miles south of Chu Lai. The VC had planted electrical charges in the water and on the beach. The fear and helplessness of being locked inside that stuffy Am Tract heading for the beach, and hearing and seeing the explosions going off all around us, had my heart in my throat and my kidneys wanting relief.[dxliv]

The operation continued to unfold when the explosive charges on the beach failed to slow down Company I making it possible for it:

> to secure its first objective, the southern half of the village of An Cuong (1), and move on to its next objective; a streambed two kilometers west of the village. As the Company continued to advance, its commander, Captain Bruce D. Webb, noticed that Company H, 2d Battalion, 4th Marines, had been inserted next to him into the midst of an enemy battalion, and was receiving heavy fire from multiple directions. Webb, therefore, asked for and received permission to cross into 2d Battalion's zone of action to provide relief and to help secure the village of An Cuong (2).[dxlv]

> An Cuong (2), was a wooded village fronted by a streambed which enabled the enemy to provide stiff resistance as

Company I approached. Due to its well defended location the only way Company I could take the village was by a frontal assault which it undertook along with three tanks that had joined the unit along the way. After a fierce pitched battle, the company secured the village but, in the process, lost its C.O. when an enemy soldier, pretending to be dead, tossed a grenade into the company command group. The battalion commander, Lieutenant Colonel Joseph Muir, upon being informed of the situation, ordered the new C.O., the company's executive officer, to catch up with the left flank of Company K.[dxlvi]

By early afternoon Companies K and L of 3d battalion, 3d Marines had reached their original objectives, and Company I had caught up with the left flank of Company K. With the 3d battalion, 3d Marines, now intact, it began moving north toward its next objective.[dxlvii] However, Company I's progress was slowed once again when a resupply convoy bringing it "badly needed water and ammunition" got lost and ran into an ambush. This ambush started with a barrage of incoming mortar rounds and fire from 57mm recoilless rifles, and ended with the convoy being attacked by over 300 enemy soldiers.[dxlviii]

When Muir was alerted to this attack and told that the resupply convoy was now lost, he ordered Company I to return to the battalion command post[dxlix] and join a relief column headed by the battalion executive officer. The mission of the relief column was to locate and extract the "lost convoy" thought to be somewhere near the village of An Cuong (2).[dl]

The relief column set out at 1300 hours with a tank, two Ontos (anti-tank vehicles) and four amtracs, with the bulk of Company I riding in, or on, the vehicles. The initial plan was to locate the resupply convoy and overwhelm its attackers with a sudden assault. However, shortly after getting underway the lead tank and the other armored vehicles were hit with heavy enemy fire causing the column to back up and come to a halt.[dli]

At this point, Company I dismounted and continued the search on foot and, in the process, ran into heavy resistance around An Cuong (2) which, even though secured that morning, had been re-infiltrated by the enemy through its camouflaged fighting holes and tunnel networks.[dlii] As a result, Company I once again found itself in heavy fighting among the hedgerows and trenches around An Cuong (2), and was only able to re-enter the village after an air strike was called in to clear the way. This would not be the last time U.S. forces in Vietnam would have to retake an area previously secured.[dliii]

When Company I failed to locate the "lost convoy" at An Cuong (2), the search continued, but as the evening wore on the Company became battered and separated into smaller units. Therefore, sometime during the night of 18 August, while it was still searching for the "lost convoy," Company I was ordered to reunite and return to the battalion command post to stand down.[dliv]

This night withdrawal, too, proved to be difficult because the battlefield was constantly illuminated with flares to help detect enemy movement. While this illumination was helpful to the Marines dug in for the night, it seriously impeded the withdrawal of Company I because every time a flare went up the Company became exposed and had to hit the ground to avoid becoming a target. On the other hand, when the battlefield was not illuminated there was a possibility the Company might unintentionally intermix with the VC or be ambushed in the darkness, both of which happened. In spite of these obstacles, and after having fought nonstop for nearly 24 hours, what was left of Company I finally made it back to the command post around 0430.[dlv]

During the 24 hours of fighting almost half of the 165 men in Company I were killed or wounded; with 19 dead and 63 wounded. Lieutenant Benton, whose platoon had faced some of the heaviest fighting, finished the 24-hour battle with only 19 men; having had 17 of his 36-man platoon killed or wounded.[dlvi]

At 1000 hours the next morning (19 August) the 3d Battalion, 7th Marines (which had been called in from their Floating Reserve position) located the 10 remaining men of the 30-man lost convoy "buttoned up in several amtracs."[dlvii]

While Benton lost the heel on one of his boots to an enemy bullet,[dlviii] he was not physically wounded during Operation Starlite, but it was during this operation that he began having second thoughts about the new U.S. role in Vietnam.

Explaining this change of thought Benton said:

When we were guarding villages so our medics could provide help to those in need and when we distributed food to those who were starving, I was proud of our involvement. But going on search and destroy missions every day, knowing someone in my platoon will likely be shot by an unseen enemy before we could get across a rice paddy has left me frazzled...

There has to be a better way. There *has* to be.[dlix] (Emphasis Benton's)

In view of the 614 confirmed, and the many estimated, enemy dead, as compared to the 45 Marines killed in action,[dlx] it was felt that the U.S. had "inflicted a decisive defeat on the enemy" during Operation Starlite even though Company I of 3d battalion, 3d Marines and Company H of 2d battalion, 4th Marines suffered heavy losses.

Two days after the operation, the commanding general of the III Marine Amphibious Force sent a congratulatory telegram to those who fought in the battle in which he said:

TWO DAYS AGO A VC REGIMENT WAS DECIMITAED AT VAN TUONG BY A SURPRISE AMPHIBOUS/HELICOPTER ASSAULT. THIS SIGNIFICANT DEFEAT OF A TOUGH, WELL-ARMED, AND FANATICAL ENEMY IS A TRIBUTE TO THE PROFFESSIONAL SKILL, CONSUMATE COURAGE, AND TEAM WORK OF ALL WHO PARTICIPATED, AND IS A BRIGHT NEW CHAPTER IN THE ANNALS OF OUR COUNTRY'S HARD WON BATTLES AGAINST THE ENEMIES OF FREEDOM.

WHILE WE HAVE HAD FRIENDS AND COMRADES FALL IN THIS BATTLE THEY DIED IN A GREAT CAUSE... THE PRESERVATION OF FREEDOM IN THIS WORLD. THERE IS NO BETTER CAUSE. WELL DONE TO ALL WHO PARTICIPATED.

GENERAL LEWIS W. WALT[dlxi]

Tommy (who now goes by Tomas) Benton like many Vietnam Combat Veterans returned home looking, but not feeling, the same, and not understanding why. His problem was finally diagnosed in 1989 by a Veterans Administration psychiatrist who almost immediately identified him as a "poster boy for PTSD (Post Traumatic Stress Disorder)."[dlxii]

When I wrote my old fraternity brother to ask if I could use his Vietnam experience in this book he replied by telling me not to take offense but that he could not remember me or much about his days at the University of Richmond. He then said that when he started reading the foregoing pages in this chapter "too many horrible memories reappeared," so, without reading further, he granted me permission to use his material.

Benton was not the only fraternity brother who went through the Marine Corp's Platoon Leaders Course in the summer of 1963, so did Bill Strickland and "Bud" Baker, but when they completed their tours, their careers went in different directions.

Strickland returned to law school and then spent 40 years at McGuire, Woods, a 186-year-old world-wide law firm, where he was the Managing Partner from 1995 to 2008. Baker also returned to graduate school and, after earning an MBA, spent 34 years with Wachovia Bank (then the 4th largest bank in the United States) where he became its president and chief executive officer. Benton, rather than having a career with one employer made his living in a number of ways including: college professor, author, Island Administrator, and Roustabout with the Clyde Beatty/Cole Brothers Circus.[dlxiii] But, not surprisingly, he said "the watershed [moment] in [his] life" occurred in Vietnam [dlxiv] during the first major Marine Corps battle of the Vietnam War. More about Benton's interesting life can be found in *Pieces of my Puzzle.*[dlxv]

Major Donald G. Radcliff, of the Army's First Calvary Division (Air Mobile) became "the Cav's" first combat casualty while piloting a gunship in support of Operation Starlite,[dlxvi] and the Cav's base camp in the central highlands was subsequently named in his honor. Four years later I would spend the last six months of my tour at Camp Radcliff.

On August 26, 1965, Henry Cabot Lodge returned to Vietnam and reassumed his post as Ambassador [dlxvii] while Maxwell Taylor returned to Washington and became special advisor to the president.

Three months after Lodge's return Secretary McNamara told the president that South Vietnam only controlled 25% of the countryside and that more than 200,000 additional troops would be needed to compete with the enemy buildup. However, before inserting additional troops, McNamara recommended a four-week bombing pause "to give NVN a face-saving chance to stop the aggression." [dlxviii] The Joint Chiefs disagreed with the proposed bombing pause.[dlxix]

By the end of 1965, there were 194,300 Americans in Vietnam and during that year 1,369 were killed in action and 3,308 were wounded. During the same period 11,249 South Vietnamese were killed in action and 23,118 were wounded.[dlxx]

On January 8, 1966, Senate Majority Leader Mike Mansfield (D), who had recently returned from Vietnam, told the Senate Foreign Relations Committee that the military situation was no better then than it had been "at the outset."[dlxxi]

As March 1966 drew to a close, the Buddhist problem Lodge thought he had solved during his first term resurfaced when ten thousand Buddhists gathered to protest Premier Ky's failure to hold elections as he had promised. During these protests Buddhists burned themselves alive even more frequently than they had during Diem's presidency.[dlxxii]

Premier Ky and his Chief of Staff, General Nguyen Van Thieu, attempted to satisfy the Buddhist's complaints on April 14, 1966, by promising he would dissolve the present government and replace it with an elected legislative assembly. This promise was momentarily satisfactory and an uneasy truce began[dlxxiii] but, seeing no movement toward elections, the Buddhists warned on May 8, 1966, that their protests would be renewed if elections were not held as promised.[dlxxiv]

In a preemptive move, Premier Ky, who had promised to rule with an iron hand, sent troops to Da Nang a week later to quell this unrest and "[a]ided by U.S. Marines (they) brutally crushed the Buddhists and their supporters."[dlxxv]

SUMMARY

This was a crucial time in the war. Maxwell Taylor, a highly decorated four star general and former Chairman of the Joint Chiefs, initially recommended against inserting combat troops into Vietnam, but soon reversed his position and agreed with Westmoreland's recommendation to do so.

While the Marine Corps Generals thought that having the ability to engage in combat operations when necessary was a positive step, they also thought the Marines, as a general rule, could be better used to secure villages. That is to say, when possible, they seemed to prefer the pacification approach started by Diem's Strategic Hamlet Program. So did Lt. Benton, a Marine on the frontlines, who echoed those sentiments saying that he was proud of his efforts when guarding villages so medics could provide help to those in need and when distributing food to those who were starving. But, when it came to search and destroy missions, he believed that, "There *has* got to be a better way."

However, General Westmoreland, the MACV commander, thought the search and destroy approach was the future of the war, so that was the approach taken. Even though the Marine Corps Generals may not have thought search and destroy missions were the best way to wage the war they were carried out in a superb manner, as in Operation Starlite.

The problem with Westmorland's approach, however, was that Hanoi was willing to lose as many men as it took to prevail. So, in hindsight, the pacification approach advocated by the Marine Corps, Diem (and later by General Abrams) was probably the best way to have pursued this war from start to finish. Hindsight has also confirmed that removing Diem on the basis of the 1963 Buddhist unrest was not in the best interest of the United States or in the best interest of South Vietnam. Despite Diem's departure from the scene Buddhist unrest remained and when the Buddhists rebelled a second time, the rebellion was handled differently by everybody including Lodge on his second tour as Ambassador. This time, instead of negotiating with the Buddhists, Premier Ky sent a thousand South Vietnamese Marines into Da Nang to suppress the rebellion. And, the United States was said to be "relieved and more than satisfied with the outcome."[dlxxvi]

Instead of condemning the South Vietnamese government, as he did in 1963, Lodge not only approved of the action taken he joined in because he thought a stable South Vietnam was absolutely necessary. As he explained in his memoir:

> ...when I returned for a second tour in the summer of 1965, I found the Saigon government in a state of grave instability and turmoil. The changes of prime minister could only be described as kaleidoscopic. Every time there was such a change, the enemy would infiltrate the government. Without stability, the government would soon be subverted from within.[dlxxvii]

He went on to say that:

> Until there was stability, no effort to ward off the Northern aggression could even get started–let alone succeed. Without stability no social progress would be possible. No wonder that, in the United States, both press and politicians clamored for stability in Vietnam. My experience with coups in my first term—and Ambassador Taylor's experiences—led to the inevitable conclusion that the South Vietnamese should give a high priority to establishing a stable and orderly government. [*Say what?*] South Vietnam seemed to face three choices: to

continue the then existing madhouse with results which would in the not-so-long run turn the government of South Vietnam over to Hanoi; to turn the government over to Hanoi immediately; or to try to establish a government under a constitution. (Comment in brackets mine.)

… The aim was not to create a constitution which would bring democracy— clearly an impossible task—but to create something which would start the few politically active people thinking in terms of settling their differences by voting rather than by coups. The mere decision in the summer of 1965 to make a constitution brought with it more orderly processes of government and began to substitute certain legitimacy to the hurly-burly of unending coups. Of course, the constitution did not change the basic nature of Vietnamese society: South Vietnam still retained feudal and Confucianist traits.

Continuing, Lodge said:

The most dangerous situation during my second tour was the so-called Struggle Movement which at its zenith in the spring of 1966, had taken over control of Hue and Da-Nang and was a threat in other cities of South Vietnam…The Struggle Movement manifestly helped the Viet Cong, but we believed that the Viet Cong neither started nor ran it. It was operated by certain Buddhist sects and the political machine of an angry political general, General Thi. It was a hard-hitting grab for power and secession based on the ever-present spirit of Central Vietnamese localism.

The irrelevance of modern Western military force to the Struggle Movement in Danang and Hue was illustrated by the way in which the Strugglers took over the city of Danang. A small group of Strugglers came from Hue, called on the chief of police, told him that they intended to take over Danang and the first step was to take over the police force. They therefore instructed the chief to turn the police over to them by 6 P.M. that evening or his wife and children would be kidnapped, his house would be burned down, and he himself would be assassinated. The result of these terrorist measures was that the Struggle committee took over the city.

The III Marine Amphibious Force was a large American military force, based a few miles outside of Danang and able to take on any unit of equivalent size. But it was completely out of its game as far as the Struggle Movement was concerned, and had been instructed not to get involved...

[Therefore until] Prime Minister Ky moved in with the Vietnamese police and special troops in June, our side did not have the fine-mesh net with which to catch the small but deadly fish of terrorism.

By police methods, by waiting for the right time, by moving by stealth at night and thus achieving surprise, Prime Minister Ky skillfully reestablished the authority of the government with few causalities.

Surely, there was a lesson to be learned from this: that if major stress were placed in a timely way on police and territorial force techniques, the aggression might, eventually, be liquidated without growing into a conventional war and with virtually no loss of American life, no disruption of Vietnamese civilian life, and much smaller Vietnamese uniformed causalities....[dlxxviii]

In September, the Ky/Thieu government provided for the election of a Constituent Assembly;[dlxxix] however, Buddhists, connected with the Buddhist rebellion, were excluded from participating.[dlxxx]

And, Ambassador Lodge "unreservedly backed" this *autocratic* decision to exclude rebelling Buddhists because, in his view, the government "should not be discouraged from taking moderate measures to prevent elections from being used as a vehicle for a Communist takeover of the country."[dlxxxi]

Is this the same Henry Cabot Lodge who arrived in South Vietnam in 1963 and immediately began condemning President Diem who had a Buddhist vice president; an eighteen-member cabinet comprised of eight Buddhists, five Catholics, and five Confucians; thirty-eight province chiefs comprised of twenty-six Buddhists or Confucians; twelve Catholics; and a military with only three Catholics among its top nineteen officers?[dlxxxii]

Is this Henry Cabot Lodge, who wanted people to start "thinking in terms of settling their differences by voting rather than by coups," the same Henry Cabot Lodge who, when he arrived in Vietnam in August 1963, immediately began engineering a coup against an elected president who had successfully run the country for nine years?

It seems ironic that this "re-born" Lodge commended the special police activity for restoring government authority and preventing Buddhist aggression from growing in 1966 when he condemned such tactics in 1963.

It was unfortunate that Lodge did not know in 1963, as he seemed to have learned by 1966, that even with a constitution South Vietnam would retain its "feudal and Confucianist traits," and it was even more unfortunate that Lodge had not taken the time in 1963 to learn that

Diem, who was "steeped" in Confucianism, had the "political machine" (and constitution) in place to deal with Buddhist aggression.

It was unfortunate Lodge, Kennedy and the United States Department of State did not recognize in 1963, as Lodge did in 1966, that it was "clearly an impossible task" for any constitution (including Diem's constitution) to create a "democracy" as we know it under the conditions existing in South Vietnam.

As previously discussed, it was unfortunate that Lodge, Kennedy and the United States Department of State were unable to wait for the UN Commission to finish its investigation into claims that Diem's government had pursued a policy of discrimination against Buddhists. If they had they would have learned that Diem's government *had not* pursued such a policy.[dlxxxiii]

It was unfortunate that Lodge did not recognize in 1963 that "militant Buddhists" in South Vietnam were attempting to overthrow the government as he came to understand in 1966.

And finally, it was unfortunate that in 1963 Lodge had waited until after the coup against Diem had begun to inform President Kennedy that Diem appeared ready to make a package deal they could talk about when he got back to Washington[dlxxxiv] which, of course, never happened because Diem was long dead by the time Lodge arrived in Washington.

The removal of Diem in 1963, with Lodge's complicity (over the strong objection of Commanding General Harkins and former Ambassador Nolting) was unfortunate indeed. And it is ironic that Ambassador Lodge returned three years later praising Premier Ky who was then ruling South Vietnam "with an iron hand," when he removed Diem because he was "too autocratic."

If the United States did not owe the South Vietnamese loyalty before it destroyed their government in 1963 it certainly did afterward. As the authors of the Pentagon papers put it, "Our complicity in [Diem's] overthrow heightened our responsibilities and our commitment in an essentially leaderless Vietnam."[dlxxxv]

And, unfortunately, after the coup Vietnam continued as a leaderless land for over two years while "the generals," who supposedly wanted nothing for themselves, took turns trying to gain control of the government in Saigon rather than fight communist aggression.

However, at least the latest leader, Ky, seemed focused on winning the war again.

PHOTOGRAPHS BETWEEN 1964 AND 1965

A crew on the USS Enterprise gets an F-4B Phantom ready for night operations on April 5, 1965. (National Archives)

A Marine Corps MP, with helpers, at Da Nang's Check Point Charlie on July 28, 1965. (National Archives)

Former Secretary of State Dean Acheson, one of Johnson's "wise-men," at the White House on July 8, 1965. (National Archives)

The First Calvary Division (Air Mobile) landing at Qui Nhon on September 14, 1965, on its way inland to An Khe. (National Archives)

Bob Hope and friends trying out a new dance step in December 1965 on the USS Ticonderoga. (National Archives)

Two members of the 173rd Airborne Brigade in Long Khanh Province await a helicopter coming to evacuate their fallen comrade in 1966. (National Archives)

Three F-105 Thunderchiefs being refuled by a KC-135 Stratotanker while on a January 1, 1966, bombing mission. (National Archives)

Part of a 1,200-man Marine Corps amphibious assault operation that took place 35 miles outside of Saigon on March 26, 1966. (National Archives)

A Navy gunner manning his 50 caliber machine gun on March 26, 1966, as his utility Boat patrols the Rung Sat zone during Operation Jackstay southeast of Saigon. (National Achieves)

On March 27, 1966, elements of the First Calvary Division (Air Mobile) sweep an area south of Pleiku during Operation Lincoln. (From the VA029834 Robert Lafoon Photograph Collection, courtesy of the Vietnam Center and Sam Johnson Vietnam Archive, Texas Tech University.)

Elements of the First Infantry Division on a sweep near the village of Xa Cam My, 40 miles from Saigon, on April 2, 1966, during Operation Abilene. (National Archives)

On May 16, 1966, members of the 25th Infantry Division head to a new staging area during a search and destroy mission northeast of Cu Chi. (National Archives)

On September 8, 1966, South Vietnamese Marines are dropped off on an unknown LZ. (National Archives)

CHAPTER SIX
October 1966-December 1968

Secretary McNamara appeared to have reached a turning point toward the use of force in Vietnam on October 14, 1966, when he recommended: (1) that bombing be capped at then current levels, and (2) that only 40,000 more troops be sent to Vietnam.[dlxxxvi] The Joint Chiefs strongly disagreed with this recommendation saying it was time to apply all-out pressure on the enemy, adding that they believed the decisions made during the next sixty days could well determine the war's outcome.[dlxxxvii]

Just over a month later Secretary McNamara sent a secret report to the president telling him that according to Pentagon calculations the additional troops given to General Westmoreland had not resulted in the predicted increase in enemy causalities; therefore, he recommended against any large increases in future troop deployments. The president rejected this secret assessment.[dlxxxviii]

In December 1966, Admiral Sharp, Commander in Chief in the Pacific, told Washington that "only civilian imposed restraints on targets had prevented the bombing from bringing the Democratic Republic of Vietnam to its knees and [to] its senses about its aggression in the South."[dlxxxix]

At Christmas time in 1966, Cardinal Francis Spellman, the Roman Catholic Bishop of New York and Roman Catholic vicar of the armed forces, told U.S. servicemen in Saigon that the Vietnam War was "a war for civilization—certainly [he said] it is not a war of our seeking. It is a war thrust upon us—we cannot yield to tyranny." And, he added, "Anything less than victory is inconceivable."[dxc]

By the end of 1966, there were 194,300 Americans in Vietnam. During that year 5,008 were killed in action and 16,526 were wounded; during the same year, 11,953 South Vietnamese soldiers were killed in action and 20,975 were wounded.[dxci]

While the administration was internally debating the best way to fight the Vietnam War those against it were unified in their opposition and their voices were growing louder. On March 25, 1967, for example, the Reverend Martin Luther King, Jr. told 5,000 anti-war demonstrators in Chicago that the Vietnam War was, "a blasphemy against all that America stands for."[dxcii]

On April 15, 1967, over 100,000 war protestors gathered in New York City's Central Park to listen to protest speeches and burn draft cards prior to beginning a protest march through the city, and 20,000 like-minded people engaged in another protest march through the streets of San Francisco.[dxciii]

General Westmoreland, in an attempt to convince his civilian bosses there was a path to victory, returned to Washington on April 24 and over the next three days tried to explain that the best (and maybe the only) way to win the war would be to station 200,000 troops at the 17th parallel in Laos along the Ho Chi Minh Trail. By doing this he said he could stop the infiltration of NVA troops and equipment into South Vietnam. This plan was backed by Johnson's National Security Advisor, Walter Rostow, but opposed by Secretary Rusk and Secretary McNamara. In the end, the president followed Rusk and McNamara's advice and refused to authorize the plan.[dxciv]

While on this trip to Washington, Westmoreland also noted that the GIs in Vietnam were "dismayed and so [was he] by recent unpatriotic acts at home" because, he said, this conduct provided the enemy with "support in the United States that gives him hope that he can win politically that which he cannot win militarily." But, Westmoreland added, "(b)ased on what [he] heard and saw, 95 percent of the people are behind the United States' effort in Vietnam" and, if "(b)acked at home by resolve, confidence, patience and continued support, we will prevail in Vietnam over the communist aggressor."[dxcv]

I think, however, it is safe to say that far less than 95 percent of the people were behind the U.S. effort at home. In fact, backing at home was even beginning to waiver in high places. On May 4, 1967, for example, former National Security Advisor McGeorge Bundy sent a letter to the president in which he said: that a ceiling should be put on the U.S. effort in Vietnam; that the air war should not be escalated, and that Haiphong harbor should not be mined.[dxcvi] This is the same McGeorge Bundy who, after viewing the attacks at Camp Holloway just two years earlier, had called President Johnson from Vietnam and urged him to implement a policy of sustained reprisal against North Vietnam.

Secretary McNamara, too, was having second thoughts as evidenced by a memorandum in which he "crystalized (his) growing doubts about the trend of events" and sent to the president on May 19. In this memorandum he recommended that bombing of the North be restricted to the infiltration 'funnel' below the twentieth parallel; that additional deployments, if any, be limited to 30,000 (as opposed to the 200,000 requested by Westmoreland) and that a more flexible bargaining position be adopted while actively seeking a political settlement.[dxcvii]

The next day McNamara asked the Chairman of the Joint Chiefs, the Director of the CIA, the Secretary of the Navy and the Secretary of the Air force to comment on his recommendation to the president.[dxcviii]

That same day (May 20) the Joint Chiefs sent McNamara two memorandums taking strong exception to his recommendations with a request that the memos be forwarded to the president.[dxcix]

On June 1, CIA Director Richard Helms responded to McNamara's memorandum saying:

> In general, we do not believe that any of the programs presented in your memorandum are capable of reducing the flow of military and other essential goods sufficiently to affect the war in the South or to decrease Hanoi's determination to persist in the war.[dc]

Two days later the Secretary of the Air Force, Harold Brown, responded to Secretary McNamara's memorandum saying that he was in favor of intensifying the bombing of North Vietnam's roads, bridges, rails and other lines of communication.[dci]

As Washington was debating how to best proceed with this war, the Marines in Vietnam were engaged in heavy fighting on the ground in the Que Son Valley.[dcii]

One of those Marines was Steve Kelsey, one of the more popular "Air Force Kids" I got to know and like at Wright Patterson A.F.B. when I returned home during college breaks in the mid "60s." Steve was a "Princeton Man"; very handsome, very smart, very athletic, very nice, and *all* the girls liked him very much.

After graduating from Princeton, in June 1965, Kelsey entered the Marine Corp's Officer Candidate School at Quantico, Virginia; this was followed by Infantry Basic School. Kelsey finished both programs at the top of his class.[dciii] His first duty assignment was Defense Language School in Monterrey, California, where he was sent to learn Vietnamese, and where he finished first in his class.[dciv]

After Reconnaissance Training at the Naval Amphibious School, Kelsey shipped out to Vietnam in late April 1967 and, upon arriving, was sent to the An Hoa Marine Combat Base in the Que Son Valley. There he was assigned to F (Foxtrot) Company 2nd Battalion, 5th Marine Regiment as platoon commander of the 2nd platoon.[dcv]

In a May 23 letter to his wife, Kelsey described how proud he was of his platoon, which had just returned from an operation more quickly:

> ...and more successfully than I thought we would. The Company [he said] climbed for two days over a mountain range down into the back end of a little valley on the edge of our TAOR (Tactical Area of Responsibility). When we got to the valley floor...I finally found out why we are here. We could observe [the enemy] running around in uniform with helmets on. We found out later, they had a stronghold on the valley, schooled the local people and taxed them and billeted their people with them. When it was over we had 16 VC kills...

> The valley was lush with food everywhere---water, tons of rice, bananas, pineapple, water buffalo, etc. but the people have been quite impoverished by the VC levees. In fact, they are operating quite a little Garden of Eden. Before they could react to our presence we began sweeping with my platoon on the point. We swept the whole afternoon for many miles and through many villages...[dcvi]

Lieutenant Colonel David B. Brown[*] USMC (Ret), and his daughter Tiffany Brown Holmes, described this operation saying that:

---

[*] Lt. Col. Brown was Commanding Officer of Fox Company 2/5 from July 1968 to January 1969, and a Silver Star recipient.

Fox's hard-charging-war-machine reputation became well established within the battalion. From 11 May to 20 May during smaller-sized search and destroy operations Fox ripped up Antenna Valley, netting twenty enemy killed, three POWs captured, and thirty-eight detainees collected, without sustaining any causalities. While Fox was slugging it out in An Hoa and the Antenna Valley, Operation Union, later known as Union I, took place thirty miles southeast of An Hoa from 28 April through 12 May.[dcvii]

Union I was a battle for control of the agriculturally rich Que Son Basin, where some 60,000 Vietnamese had lived under communist control for twenty years. Shortly after Union I was completed, two separate reconnaissance patrols spotted three to four thousand more NVA soldiers in the Que Son Valley.[dcviii]

It was then decided that a second operation (Union II), to be spearheaded by the 1st Division's 5th and 7th Marine Regiments, would be conducted to clear the valley. It was further decided the 1st and 3d battalions would take the lead in the 5th Regiment's sweep, and that the 2nd battalion's most aggressive company, Fox Company, would be attached to the first battalion for extra firepower.[dcix]

On June 3, Fox Company, which had been designated a "forward company" in this sweep, was taking small arms fire when NVA communication (com) wire was spotted near an open rice paddy that Fox had to cross. Since Fox's C.O., Captain Jim Graham, thought the com wire indicated a nearby enemy presence, he asked to have the paddy "prepped" from the air or by artillery before he crossed it. This request, however, was denied by the commander of the battalion to which Fox was attached and Fox was ordered to move out.[dcx]

Pursuant to orders, Fox moved out and when it reached the middle of the paddy:

> In the heat of the tropical summer afternoon the NVA initiated their attack with unrelenting bursts of machine gun fire from the tree line that stood directly in front of the 1st Platoon. Another machine gun fired from an area with a small pagoda on it located in front of [Kelsey's] 2nd Platoon. Within a millisecond, fifty to one hundred automatic and semi-automatic arms were unleashed upon [the Marines] from the bounding hedgerows in front. A machine [gun] and two automatic weapons on Hill B fired on them from behind. B-40 rockets roared four feet above the paddies impacting on the far side. Another .51 caliber machine gun located on Hill A, opened up twenty seconds later. Mercilessly it fired into the backs of the 2nd Platoon. A torrent of 82mm mortars rained onto the rice field and the trapped Marines. …
>
> Through the wall of lead, men of the 2nd Platoon instinctively launched their final assault attempting to gain superiority. …[dcxi]

Silver Star recipient, Staff Sergeant Louis "Rick" Barnes, said half of the 2nd platoon was killed in the first few minutes after the enemy began firing and, he added:

> With Lt. Kelsey's radioman shot and my good friend Lance Corporal Westphal dying in my arms the decision was made to assault the tree line.…
>
> Lt. Kelsey myself and Cpls. Golbrect and O'Brien assaulted the machine gun bunker directly in front of us. Lt. Kelsey's steadfast courage inspired more Marines from the second

platoon to follow his lead. It was without fear of his own safety that he upheld his honor and devotion to duty inspiring all who witnessed his actions on that afternoon of June 2nd 1967.

After silencing the first machine gun and many NVA in front of us, Lt. Kelsey and myself formed a small fighting force of some 20 Marines under the Command of [Medal of Honor winner][dcxii] Captain Graham.

Another machine gun was now laying heavy fire into the remaining Marines from a tree line on the other side of a short open rice paddy.

Lt. Kelsey turned to me and stated he wanted two men. He went on to state he was going to flank the second machine gun in front of us. It was leading this second assault on a machine gun position that Lt. Kelsey was cut down by heavy enemy fire and sustained mortal wounds.[dcxiii]

The next morning the Regiment Commander, who had asked for, and received, the second battalion's most aggressive company,[dcxiv] flew in and said to those in Fox who had survived, and had not yet been evacuated:

Marines, I put Fox into the center of the breach and your company was the lynchpin in defeating an enemy regiment. I had always heard of your fighting ability…your braveness. Today you have exceeded your reputation. You men exemplify the heroic character of the 5th Marine Regiment and the United States Marine Corps. With you I mourn your losses. We can never bring them back. They were brave Marines who did not die in vain. (Then, saluting in each direction he said) Men of

Foxtrot, I salute you and your magnificent fighting company.[dcxv]

Steve's high school friend and roommate at St. Paul's, (Sen.) John Kerry, said he was crushed when he heard about Kelsey's death and that when he died the world lost someone who was destined for great success and leadership.[dcxvi]

There is a story behind every name on "The Wall"; this was part of Steve Kelsey's story. More can be found in *My Brother Stevie: A Marine's Untold Story*, a moving book by his sister Marianne Kelsey Orestis who, in spite of Steve's valor, was unsuccessful in her attempt to have the Marine Corps recognize his heroism posthumously.

In order to offset the fierce fighting on the ground the Joint Chiefs, over the objection of Secretary McNamara, called for intensified bombing of North Vietnam. To address this difference of opinion it was announced on June 28, 1967, that the Senate Subcommittee on Military Preparedness would be holding hearings that summer.

Two days later in Vietnam the Armed Forces Council of South Vietnam selected Chief of State, Nguyen Van Thieu (instead of Premier, Nguyen Cao Ky) to run for president on its ticket in the upcoming presidential election. Ky was selected to run as vice president, which he tearfully agreed to do.[dcxvii]

On August 9, 1967, the previously announced Senate Subcommittee Hearings on Preparedness started in executive session.[dcxviii] According to the Pentagon Papers the hearings had been called because:

Earlier this year many statements appeared in the press which were calculated to belittle the effectiveness of the air campaign over North Vietnam. Many of these statements alleged, or at least implied, that all military targets of significance had been destroyed, that the air campaign had been conducted as effectively as possible, and that continuation of the air campaign was pointless and useless---possibly even prolonging the war itself. At the same time reports were being circulated that serious consideration was being given in high places to a cessation of the air campaign over North Vietnam, or a substantial curtailment of it. Many of these reports were attributed to unnamed high Government officials.

In view of the importance of the air campaign, on June 28, 1967, the subcommittee announced it would conduct an extensive inquiry into the conduct and effectiveness of the bombing campaign over North Vietnam.[dcxix]

Admiral U.S. Grant Sharp, Commander in Chief of the Pacific was called as the subcommittee's first witness to give the military objectives in bombing North Vietnam. He was followed by a number of other senior military officers including each Service Chief and the commander and former deputy commander of the 7th Air Force in Saigon.[dcxx]

Secretary McNamara was called on August 25 as the last subcommittee witness and asked to rebut the contention that civilian restrictions were hindering military progress in the war.[dcxxi] The argument he made was said to have been "one of his masterful performances" but it failed to persuade,[dcxxii] and he would be out as Secretary of Defense in three months.

After completing the inquiry, the Senate subcommittee issued a report on August 31, 1967, which concluded that the military had not been able to achieve its objectives due to overly restrictive civilian controls.[dcxxiii]

On September 3, the Thieu/Ky ticket was elected to serve a four-year term as president and vice president of South Vietnam. They received 35% of the vote; an unknown lawyer who wanted to negotiate with the NLF, received 17% of the vote, and the remaining 48% of the vote was split among 8 other candidates.[dcxxiv]

On September 24 the Americans for Democratic Action charged that the United States was "in league with a corrupt and illegal government [in South Vietnam] supported by a minority of the people." [dcxxv] It is true that the Thieu/Ky ticket did not receive more than 50% of the vote, but it is also true that the ticket pretty substantially defeated its opposition in this 10-man election.

In an attempt to show his reasonableness and jump start negotiations, President Johnson took his peace efforts public during a speech in San Antonio, Texas on September 29 where he basically repeated the offer that had been delivered privately to Hanoi in August.[dcxxvi] In this speech the president said:

> "Why not negotiate now"? So many ask me. The answer is we and our South Vietnamese allies are wholly prepared to negotiate tonight.

> I am ready to talk with Ho Chi Minh and other chiefs of staff tomorrow. I am ready to have Secretary of Rusk meet with their Foreign Minister tomorrow.

> I am willing to send a trusted representative of America to any spot on this earth to talk in public or private with a spokesman of Hanoi.

> As we have told Hanoi time and time and time again, the heart of the matter is this: The United States is willing to stop all aerial and naval bombardment of North Vietnam when this will

lead promptly to productive discussions. We assume that while discussions proceed, North Vietnam would not take advantage of this bombing cessation or limitation.[dcxxvii]

Instead of responding favorably to this request for peace negotiations North Vietnam started putting the first elements of its 1968 "Tet offensive" in place in early October when General Giap (the Commanding General at Dien Bien Phu) began positioning troops outside a Garrison near Khe Sanh.[dcxxviii]

On October 11, Speaker of the House John W. McCormick (D) criticized those he thought were hindering the administration's attempts to bring the war to a conclusion saying that, "If I was one of those [who dissented and heartened the enemy] my conscience would disturb me the rest of my life."[dcxxix]

At a press conference the next day Secretary Rusk warned that if Hanoi refused to even discuss the president's peace offer in San Antonio it:

> would reflect a view in Hanoi that they [could] gamble upon the character of the American people and of our allies in the Pacific [to prevail].[dcxxx]

On October 21, in spite of the appeals for solidarity by Speaker McCormick and Secretary Rusk, approximately 100,000 Americans gathered to protest the war on the national mall in Washington D.C., and later that day 35,000 of those gathered on the Mall continued across the Potomac River to the Pentagon with a goal of shutting it down.[dcxxxi]

A little over a week later Secretary McNamara sent an eyes-only memorandum to the president telling him that the public's support for the war would decline even further over the next year if the administration continued to follow its present course of action. In this memorandum he said that if the present course of action was pursued: additional ground forces, in the form of draftees or reservists, would be needed; 11,000 to 15,000 more Americans would be killed in the coming year, and another 30,000 to 45,000 would be wounded and need hospitalization.[dcxxxii] To avoid this catastrophe McNamara recommended that the U.S unilaterally stop bombing the North before year's end in order to jump start negotiations. He also recommended transferring more responsibility for the war to South Vietnam and reviewing ground operations in the South with a view toward reducing causalities.[dcxxxiii]

After receiving this memorandum the president, on November 2, held a secret meeting with members of an advisory group he had assembled, known as the Wise Men.[*] At this meeting he asked how he could best unite the divided country and, in response, he was told that the best path to unity would be to show the press there was a "light at the end of the tunnel." That is, according to the "Wise Men," the American people needed to be given more optimistic reports.[dcxxxiv]

And, the three-week battle of Dakto from November 3 to November 22 immediately provided the opportunity for optimistic reports. This battle took place in the central highlands around Hills 823, 830, 875, and 882 (hills in Vietnam were designated by their height in meters) and was one of the fiercest of the war. During the Dakto battle the

---

[*] The Wise Men included, Dean Acheson, former Secretary of State; General Omar Bradley, former General of the Army; W. Averell Harriman, former Ambassador-at-Large; Henry Cabot Lodge, former Ambassador to Vietnam; George Ball, former Under Secretary of State; Arthur Dean, attorney and Korean War negotiator under Eisenhower; General Matthew B. Ridgeway, former Commander of the United Nation Forces in Korea; General Maxwell Taylor, former Chairman of the Joint Chiefs of Staff and former Ambassador to Vietnam; Cyrus Vance, former Deputy Defense Secretary; McGeorge Bundy, former National Security Advisor; Douglas Dillion, former Treasury Secretary, Justice Arthur Goldberg, and Justice Abe Fortas.

Americans suffered approximately 280 casualties while inflicting an estimated 1,400 casualties on the NVA's First Division, rendering three of the four regiments in the Division inoperative.[dcxxxv]

Therefore, in a November 17, 1967, press conference the president was able to report that:

> We are making progress [in Vietnam]. We are pleased with the results we are getting. We are inflicting greater losses than we are taking... The fact that the population under free control has constantly risen...is a very encouraging sign... overall we are making progress.[dcxxxvi]

And, as part of a public relations campaign, General Westmoreland was brought back to the States on November 22 to give an optimistic report on the war, and he complied by reporting that the battle around Dakto was, "the beginning of a great defeat for the enemy."[dcxxxvii]

Westmoreland, however, might not have been so upbeat if an enemy document captured earlier that year had been translated at the time.[dcxxxviii] The captured document, not translated until 1968, read:

> The central headquarters has ordered the entire army [of North Vietnam] and people of South Vietnam to implement general offensive and general uprising in order to achieve a decisive victory...use very strong military attacks in coordination with uprisings of the local population to take over towns and cities. Troops should flood the lowlands. They should move toward liberating the capital city, Saigon, take power and try to rally enemy brigades...to our side.[dcxxxix]

At the end of November, in what probably was also intended to be an optimistic report, President Johnson announced that McNamara would be leaving his job as Secretary of Defense and joining the World Bank as its new president.[dcxl] McNamara later said he did not know if he quit or if he was fired.[dcxli] He was fired.

McNamara was replaced by Washington attorney Clark Clifford, a "Dove" who temporarily put on "Hawk's" clothing to get the job.[dcxlii] While Johnson was to become deeply disappointed in Clifford's true views, these views should not have come as a surprise since Clifford had vigorously opposed a major commitment of U.S. ground forces in Vietnam as early as 1965.[dcxliii]

On December 20, General Westmoreland, by then aware of the enemy's "countrywide win the war effort," so informed his superiors.[dcxliv]

At the end of December there were 485,000 Americans in Vietnam. During that year 9,300 were killed in action, and 12,700 were wounded. During the same period 12,700 South Vietnamese were killed in action and 29,400 were wounded.[dcxlv]

On January 20, 1968, a disgruntled NVA lieutenant surrendered to Marines at the Khe Sanh garrison, and offered highly classified information indicating Hanoi was planning a campaign to take Khe Sanh and the surrounding area.[dcxlvi] According to the lieutenant, this campaign would be the most intense of the war and its purpose was to gain bargaining power for the North during any future peace negotiations. The defector further advised that General Giap was personally in charge and that he planned to begin the battle that very day by attacking an outpost on nearby Hill 861.[dcxlvii]

In the pre-dawn hours of January 21, the NVA began its prolonged battle for Khe Sanh by shelling the outpost on Hill 861 with rockets and mortars, and this barrage was followed by a 250-soldier ground assault that was repelled.[dcxlviii] The next day General Westmoreland predicted Hanoi was preparing for more than just an attack on Khe Sahn noting that, "All of [the enemy's] military campaigns are associated with a political objective or a psychological objective, and if he [could] win a spectacular victory, he would be portrayed in the eyes of the world and the South Vietnamese people as a strong force."[dcxlix]

One week after the battle for Khe Sanh was initiated, the Tet truce of 1968 began, but was soon to be broken by communist attacks.[dcl] On January 30, 1968, General Wheeler, informed a concerned Senate that 40,000 enemy troops had surrounded the garrison at Khe Sanh, which was defended by only 6,000 Marines. Wheeler, however, said the Marines were prepared to defend the garrison because approximately 34,000 allied troops were located in the surrounding terrain which resulted in a matching troop level of about 40,000. Furthermore, he said, the U.S. had superior air power.[dcli]

The same day (January 30) the Senate unanimously confirmed Clark Clifford as the new Secretary of Defense.[dclii]

The next day the Lunar New Year (Tet) truce was broken when approximately 80,000 NVA soldiers and VC guerrillas simultaneously attacked virtually every town and city in the south hoping that South Vietnam would collapse amid a "general uprising."[dcliii] On the same day the president told his cabinet, in an emergency meeting, that:

> …We can dodge it (the Tet offensive) by being weak-kneed if we want to. I said in San Antonio that we have gone as far as we could—farther, I might add than the military wanted. We made it clear how much we want to talk, and not bomb, just so long as there is some prompt and productive response. But if you sneak in at night and hit us (during a truce) we cannot stop bombing. Now we have their answer with this new offensive.

It should satisfy every dove who loves peace as much as any mother does.[dcliv]

Walter Cronkite, reporting on this offensive, said on the evening news that:

> ...The biggest Communist offensive of the Vietnam War has begun. In an unprecedented display of military strength, the Vietcong have attacked eight major South Vietnamese cities, scores of towns and villages, and five American airfields, and early Wednesday, Vietnam time, the Communists struck at the heart of Saigon, and seized part of the new American embassy...[dclv]

After making this report Cronkite packed his bag and left for Vietnam to cover the war in person.

In spite of the gloomy reporting about the attacks in Saigon, the South Vietnamese Army and police reacted quickly and by noon the next day rallied to crush the communist commandos in Saigon.[dclvi] When the NVA tried to follow the commandos into Saigon they, too, were repelled after three days of ferocious street fighting.[dclvii] Within days, the VC commandos and NVA soldiers attacking the remaining cities and towns in South Vietnam were overwhelmed by allied troops and either killed or captured,[dclviii] except at Khe Sanh and in Hue the "ancient capital of Vietnam and cultural center of the country."[dclix]

In Hue and around the garrison at Khe Sanh, the battle raged on, and the North expressed an intention to launch a second wave of attacks designed "to destroy the Government of Vietnam and its armed forces."[dclx]

On February 27, Cronkite, back in the United States after a month in Vietnam, began his television address saying:

Tonight, back in more familiar surroundings in New York, we'd like to sum up our findings in Vietnam, an analysis that must be speculative, personal, and subjective. Who won and who lost in the great Tet offensive against the cities? I'm not sure. The Vietcong did not win by a knockout, but neither did we. The referees of history may make it a draw. Another standoff may be coming in the big battles expected south of the Demilitarized Zone. Khesanh could well fall, with a terrible loss in American lives, prestige and morale, and this is a tragedy of our stubbornness there. ...[dclxi]

And he concluded saying that the only rational way out for the United States was:

to negotiate, not as victors, but as an honorable people who lived up to their pledge to defend democracy, and did the best they could.[dclxii]

According to a Gallup poll at the time Cronkite was "the most trusted man in America,"[dclxiii] and after this telecast Johnson reportedly told an aide that if he had lost Cronkite, he had lost the average citizen.[dclxiv] So much for uniting the country with good news from the press.

While a later poll would show that Johnson lost many "average citizens" after Tet, American fighting forces on the ground in Vietnam won decisively. According to The Pentagon Papers, the Vietcong at the outset of Tet:

... blatantly announced their aim as the overthrow of the Saigon regime. But the Allied forces fought well and the main thrust of the attacks on Saigon, Danang, [Khe Sanh] and elsewhere were blunted with the enemy suffering enormous causalities. Only in Hue did the communists succeed in capturing the city temporarily. There the fighting continued as the most costly part of the war for nearly a month before the Viet Cong were finally rooted out of their strongholds.[dclxv]

On March 2, Radio Hanoi thanked Senators Mike Mansfield, Sherman Cooper, Robert Kennedy and Eugene McCarthy for attempting to suspend the bombing of North Vietnam.[dclxvi]

Two days later Secretary Clifford's "A to Z Reassessment" group (consisting of Clifford, former Secretary McNamara, Deputy Secretary of Defense Paul Nitze, CIA Director Richard Helms, General Maxwell Taylor, Assistant Secretary of State for Far Eastern Affairs William Bundy, and Paul Warnke, head of the politico-military-policy-office in the Pentagon)[dclxvii] completed its study of the Joint Chiefs' request to increase the authorized troop level in Vietnam by 200,000 soldiers and to call up the reserves.

After much debate within the group, and among sub-Cabinet civilian officials, a recommendation was made to immediately:

> deploy to Vietnam an estimated total of 22,000 additional personnel (approximately 60% of which would be combat). [And, immediately] … deploy three tactical fighter squadrons… [about 1,000 men]. This would be over and above the four battalions [about 3,700 men] already planned for deployment in April which in themselves would bring us slightly above the 525,000 authorized level.[dclxviii]

It was then decided to take the balance of the request under advisement. The next day Wheeler told Westmoreland that his request for 206,000 additional troops was all but dead in view of the "Reassessment" group's March 4 recommendations.[dclxix]

President Ky said on March 10 that Hanoi's Tet offensive had made it necessary to mobilize in South Vietnam.[dclxx] The same day, Frank McGee of NBC News reported that the U.S. was losing the war.[dclxxi]

Lt. General Robert E. Cushman USMC, held a March 11 news conference in which he said "the battle for surrounded Khe Sanh is a 'titanic firepower struggle' which he is convinced we, the allies, can win."[dclxxii]

The March 17 sweep of My Lai, led by Captain Ernest Medina, was described far differently in the Army Daily Summary[dclxxiii] than it was in subsequent court-martial charging papers. The relevant part of the Army Daily Summary described the sweep saying:

> The infantry company led by Captain Ernest Medina…engaged and killed 14 Vietcong while moving toward the village. They also captured three M-1 rifles and detained 10 suspects. One of the suspects told an interpreter that 35 Vietcong had moved into the village two hours earlier.
> [dclxxiv]

President Johnson announced on March 22 that General Westmoreland was going to be the next Army Chief of staff and would be leaving Vietnam in mid-1968.[dclxxv]

Even though U.S. and ARVN forces had soundly defeated the enemy during the Tet Offensive, support for the war in America, according to a March 25 Harris poll fell from 74% before Tet to 54% afterward. Furthermore, according to this this poll, 60% of those questioned thought the Tet Offensive represented a defeat of America's objectives in Vietnam.[dclxxvi] Six days later, President Johnson announced he would not seek reelection. [dclxxvii]

At the beginning of April, Don Sider of *Time* magazine and Col. David E. Lownds, the commanding officer at Khe Sanh, walked the base camp perimeter in the sunset and, according to Sider:

> Lownds stood very tall, looking out for the first time the master of all he could see. It had to be a supreme moment, [Sider] thought. He had survived and won. [Sider] asked [Lownds] what he was thinking, expecting a properly heroic victory statement—something out of Douglas MacArthur, or maybe John Wayne.

> [Instead, Lownds said softly] I've just been wishing that I could meet the man who was running their side. I'd like to compare notes with him."[dclxxviii]

The official number of enemy casualties at Khe Sanh was 1,602, but this number, like all body counts in Vietnam, was an estimate and Lownds put the 77-day count at two North Vietnamese Divisions,[dclxxix] or ten to fifteen thousand men. The U.S. lost 476 men[dclxxx] and its allies lost approximately 800.[dclxxxi]

Overall Tet ended with the South Vietnamese people fighting hard along with their ARVN troops, instead of joining the NVA as Hanoi had thought would happen. During this offensive U.S. and ARVN forces lost 1,100 and 2,300 men respectively, while the NVA and VC lost 40,000 men with the VC taking the bulk of the losses.[dclxxxii]

Even though the U.S. decisively won the Tet offensive on the battlefield and even though Johnson was "deeply opposed to abandoning a policy in which he had invested so much, particularly in view of the improved situation in South Vietnam,"[dclxxxiii]" he reluctantly did so because of "an 'abominable' fiscal situation, panic and demoralization in America, near universal opposition in the press, and his own 'overwhelming' disapproval in the polls."[dclxxxiv] To add to the country's problems Martin Luther King was assassinated on April 4.

President Johnson announced on April 10 that General Creighton W. Abrams would replace the departing Westmoreland.[dclxxxv]

Less than two weeks later Secretary Clifford said the South Vietnamese had acquired the capability to begin to ensure their own security [and would be taking] over more of the fighting."[dclxxxvi]

At the end of April, the American embassy announced that during the Tet Offensive the NVA and VC had executed more than 1,000 civilians in Hue,[dclxxxvii] and it was observed that the "enemy's …cruelty to those he sought to 'liberate" radically changed the outlook of South Vietnam's populace."[dclxxxviii]

On May 4, President Johnson announced that formal peace talks would begin in Paris around May 10.[dclxxxix] One week later, the negotiations between the United States and North Vietnam began at a time when the hopes of North Vietnam's leaders were boosted by the growth of America's antiwar movement which the leaders in the North reportedly followed on the radio every day.[dcxc]

Personal visits from Jane Fonda, former Attorney General Ramsey Clark, and others[dcxci] further boosted North Vietnam's confidence. Ms. Fonda, in particular: (1) made radio broadcasts from North Vietnam in which she told U.S. servicemen they were war criminals and advised them not to follow orders (2) posed on an anti-aircraft gun pretending to shoot down American planes,[dcxcii] and (3) held a press conference, in a red Vietnamese dress where she announced that she was ashamed of America's actions in the war and that she would struggle along with North Vietnam.[dcxciii]

Hanoi stated on May 22 that negotiations would remain deadlocked until the U.S. unconditionally stopped its bombing of North Vietnam. The U.S., in response, said that any bombing halt must be accompanied by mutual troop withdrawals from the DMZ; this was rejected by Hanoi.[dcxciv]

Less than three weeks later, General Westmoreland publicly said, at his change of command ceremony, that communist infiltration into South Vietnam would continue, and victory could not be achieved so long as Washington prohibited the U.S. military from cutting off the Ho Chi Minh Trail with ground attacks in Laos.[dcxcv]

Westmoreland's successor, General Creighton Abrams, almost immediately changed tactics. It was said that under Abrams "Instead of thrashing about in the deep jungle, seeking to bring the enemy to battle at times and places of his own choosing [on search and destroy missions] allied forces now set up positions sited to protect populated areas from invading forces."[dcxcvi] That is to say, "(t)he appropriate measure of merit... Abrams thought [was] not 'body count' but 'population security'—security from coercion and terrorism for the people of South Vietnam's villages and hamlets."[dcxcvii]

President Thieu signed a new mobilization bill on June 19 which provided that men between the ages of 18 and 43 were eligible for induction into the armed forces.[dcxcviii]

Two weeks later, Congress passed a $6 billion supplemental spending bill for Vietnam and, while substantial, this actually represented the beginning of financial constraints on Vietnam spending.[dcxcix]

Less than three weeks into August, President Johnson revealed that he had offered to halt the bombing of North Vietnam many times but Hanoi would not reciprocate and, therefore, he said, he would not stop bombing because it would put U.S. troops in danger. The president went on to attack his critics saying, "there are some among us who appear to be searching for a formula which would get us out of Vietnam and Asia on any terms, leaving the people of South Vietnam and Laos and Thailand ... to an uncertain fate."[dcc] The same day sixty-one percent of those questioned in a Harris poll sided with the president and opposed a halt in the bombing of North Vietnam even after being reminded that the Paris peace talks would not progress until the bombing ceased.[dcci]

On August 26, the Democratic National Convention opened in Chicago with dissent among the politicians inside[dccii] and 10,000 anti-war activists protesting outside.

During the second week of September the president said that according to General Abrams, "the military capacity of the enemy to hurt our forces would greatly increase" should the U.S. stop bombing the northern panhandle without reciprocal de-escalation.[dcciii]

Secretary General U Thant, opened his September 26th annual report to the UN General Assembly by stating that the war in Vietnam was a nationalist struggle that should be resolved by the Vietnamese people. He then repeated his request for a bombing halt and called on the parties to the Paris Peace talks to find a way to reunify North and South Vietnam and neutralize the Indochina peninsula.[dcciv]

October was a month of protests and concessions. Two hundred active duty soldiers, 100 reservists, and 700 veterans organized and led 7,000 anti-war protesters on an October 11th march through the streets of San Francisco.[dccv] Eleven days after that protest, (October 22) President Thieu announced that he had agreed to a bombing halt. [dccvi] However, this did not stop some 50,000 people from protesting the war in London on October 29th.[dccvii]

Two days later, (October 31) President Johnson, in a nationally televised speech, said that North Vietnam had agreed to let South Vietnam join the peace negotiations and the United States had agreed to give the NLF a role in the negotiations but would "not recognize [them] in any form." [dccviii] In addition, in spite of his vows to continue bombing North Vietnam two months earlier, the president announced that he had changed his mind and would stop the bombing in an attempt to facilitate peace negotiations. [dccix] In return, North Vietnam seemingly agreed it would not attack South Vietnamese cities, move large quantities of troops or supplies into the South, or fire on unarmed U.S. reconnaissance aircraft over the North. [dccx]

President Thieu told his General Assembly on November 2 that South Vietnam was going to boycott the Paris Peace talks because of the NLF's participation. And, after Johnson's announcement, Vice President Ky added that America's decision to stop bombing North Vietnam meant that "we can trust the Americans no longer—they are just a band of crooks." [dccxi] Four days later, Richard M. Nixon defeated Vice President Hubert Humphrey in the presidential election. [dccxii]

On November 12, Secretary Clifford told Saigon that if they did not come to Paris soon the U.S. would begin the peace negotiations without them. [dccxiii] Meanwhile, air reconnaissance revealed that since the bombing halt had begun the movement of NVA troops and supplies had quadrupled and all the bombed-out bridges between the 17th and 19th Parallels had been repaired. [dccxiv]

On December 31, 1968, there were 536,000 Americans in Vietnam; during that year 14,500 were killed in action and 46,700 were wounded. During the same period 27,900 South Vietnamese were killed in action and 70,600 were wounded. [dccxv]

A December Gallup Poll showed that most Americans wanted the South Vietnamese to take over the fighting, and to take the lead in peace negotiations.[dccxvi]

SUMMARY

In April 1967, General Westmoreland, with the backing of National Security Advisor Rostow, requested authority to insert U.S. troops into Laos at the 17th parallel to stop the flow of soldiers and material down the Ho Chi Minh Trail into South Vietnam. President Johnson, at the behest of Secretary McNamara and Secretary Rusk, however, denied this request. This was too bad because according to Bui Tin, the NVA Colonel who accepted South Vietnam's surrender in 1975, Hanoi would not have won the war had Westmoreland's plan been implemented.[dccxvii] In short, Westmoreland's plan might well have provided the "light at the end of the tunnel" called for by the "Wise Men."

Even though there was no "light at the end of the tunnel" General Westmoreland was summoned back to the States in November 1967 to optimistically report on the status of the war, a report that he could give because of the recent U.S. success at Dakto. Unfortunately, however, this optimism would ring hollow to many Americans a few months later when Hanoi threw an 80,000-man attack against every major city and town in South Vietnam.

Optimism in the U.S. was further dampened when the legendary General Giap led a 40,000-man attack against a strategically located U.S. garrison 18 miles south of the DMZ. This siege at Khe Sahn held the nation's attention for 77 days, with Walter Cronkite opining halfway through the battle that the U.S. could "well lose." However, the 6,000 Marines in the garrison outlasted Giap who, after two and a half months of fighting, took the remainder of his men and left the "titanic firepower struggle."

The rest of the year consisted of other "titanic firepower struggles" throughout Vietnam during which time U.S. and South Vietnamese forces lost 14,000 and 27,000 men respectively while the enemy lost over 160,000 men in wave after wave of Kamikaze-type attacks. These massive losses caused North Vietnamese leaders to engage (unbeknownst to the rest of the world) in "debates—and recriminations—over the strategy that (was) proving to be so costly in manpower."[dccxviii]

North Vietnam, had confidently begun Tet with the assumption there would be a general uprising by the people in South Vietnam against their "puppet government"; however, "(t)here were no popular uprisings, and the government troops, instead of deserting, fought back aggressively."[dccxix] Hanoi's biggest loss during Tet was not on the battlefield. Its biggest loss came when the South Vietnamese people failed to revolt against their government as expected and, instead, fought hard in defense of their country.

But, even with this success, most of the American public viewed Tet as a serious military defeat at the hands of the communists. South Vietnam's Ambassador to the United States said it was a "time when U.S. public opinion and misconception snatched defeat from the jaws of potential victory."[dccxx]

Much of this "misconception," it is safe to say, was shaped by press coverage like the commentary in the *Washington Post* two days into Tet, where it was said that:

> The war in Vietnam [was] unwinnable and the longer it goes on the more the Americans, already badly overexposed, will be subjected to losses and humiliations, even in places of maximum security. ...[dccxxi]

In this regard, Professor George C. Herring,[*] said that during Tet:

> The media continued to depict [its] events in highly unfavorable and sometimes distorted terms. Early reports of a smashing enemy victory went largely uncorrected. The fact that the United States had hurled back the attacks and quickly stabilized their position was lost in the image of chaos and defeat. For those television and newspaper commentators who had long opposed the conflict, Tet provided compelling evidence of its folly.[dccxxii]

Peter Braestrup, Saigon bureau chief for the *Washington Post* during Tet, later wrote that:

> Rarely has contemporary crisis-journalism turned out, in retrospect, to have veered so widely from reality. Essentially the dominant themes of the words and film from Vietnam (rebroadcast in commentary, editorials and much political rhetoric at home) added to a portrait of defeat for the allies. Historians, on the contrary, have concluded that the Tet offensive resulted in a severe military-political setback for Hanoi in the South. To have portrayed such a setback for one side as a defeat for the other—in a major crisis abroad—cannot be counted as a triumph for American journalism.[dccxxiii]

In spite of what the press had to say, 1968 was actually a good year militarily for the United States because: (1) it had repelled Hanoi's best shot during Tet, and (2) it had deemphasized search and destroy

---

[*] Herring is the author of *America's Longest War* which was first published in 1977 and is the "standard work in the field [that has] enjoyed extensive classroom use."

missions and reemphasized protection of the villages and hamlets in the countryside.

Even though the military had a good year on the battlefield, the press did not report it as such; therefore, "with no light at the end of the tunnel" a majority of the American public had come to believe the decision to go to war had been a mistake. As a result, President Johnson fired: Secretary McNamara, General Westmoreland, and himself.

While the military had a good year on the battlefield in 1968 it would have been a better year had the plan to interdict the Ho Chi Minh trail, proffered by General Westmoreland in 1967, been adopted. And, Westmoreland publicly vented his frustration with the president's decision during his change of command ceremony in June 1968 when he said that victory could not be achieved so long as the military was prohibited from conducting ground attacks in Laos to prevent communist infiltration into South Vietnam.[dccxxiv]

Photographs January 1967 to November 1968

On January 3, 1967, elements of the 25th Infantry Division engage in a search and destroy mission during Operation Ala Mona 25 miles NW of Saigon. (From the VA 029723 Robert Lafoon Photograph Collection, courtesy of the Vietnam Center and Sam Johnson Vietnam Archive, Texas Tech University.)

On January 17, 1967, a tank from the 4th Calvary 25th Infantry Division engages in a blocking action in the Iron Triangle along the Saigon River during Operation Cedar Falls. (From the VA029784 Robert Lafoon Photograph Collection, courtesy of the Vietnam Center and Sam Johnson Vietnam Archive, Texas Tech University.)

Areas near TayNinh and An Loc being sprayed with defoliation agents in January 1967. (National Archives)

In January 1967, a machine gunner in the 25th Infantry Division fires his M-60 machine gun into an area in the Iron Triangle (near Saigon) where a VC sniper was spotted. (From the VA029696 Robert Lafoon Photograph Collection, courtesy of the Vietnam Center and Sam Johnson Vietnam Archive, Texas Tech University.)

On April 24, 1967, a member of the 1st Cavalry Division Reconnaissance Squadron is lowered into a tunnel during a search and destroy mission west of Duc Pho in Quan Ngai Province. (National Archives)

Marines of the 3/4 (3rd Battalion, 4th Marine Regiment) board a helicopter carrier in Okinawa as they prepare to depart for Dong Ha, Vietnam in May 1967. (From the VA031501 David DeChant Photograph Collection, courtesy of the Vietnam Center and Sam Johnson Vietnam Archive, Texas Tech University.)

On June 7, 1967, members of the 25th Infantry Division take a break, before entering a village during a search and destroy mission in Tinh Nghia province 17 km southwest of Cu Chi and east of the Oriental River. (National Archives)

In July 1967, a Marine "stands" watch on Hill 950 as Mass is conducted below. (National Archives)

On August 28, 1967, Ninth Infantry Division soldiers ford the "Killer Swamp" in the Mekong Delta during Operation Coronado. (National Archives)

On September 4, 1967, a Medevac helicopter being guided in to pick up Fourth Infantry Division soldiers wounded during a Search and Destroy Mission in the central highlands about 300 miles northeast of Saigon. (National Archives)

Marines crossing rice paddies under heavy machine gun fire in June 1967, about twenty-five miles south of Da Nang. (National Archives)

General William C. Westmoreland. Commanding General Military Assistance Command, Vietnam, on September 21, 1967. (National Archives)

A CH-47 Chinook recovering a disabled 9th Infantry Division UH-1C (Huey) gunship in the Mekong Delta on October 19, 1967. (From the VA029646 Robert Lafoon Photograph Collection, courtesy of the Vietnam Center and Sam Johnson Vietnam Archive, Texas Tech University.)

One of the hundred thousand protestors on the National Mall on October 21, 1967, extends some "flower-power" to the MPs overseeing the event. (National Archives)

On October 21, 1967, thirty-five thousand protestors, of the hundred thousand on the Mall earlier in the day, marched on to the pentagon where they were restrained by Military Police. (National Archives)

On October 26, 1967, a unit in the 4th Infantry Division checks out cave for enemy activity. (National Archives)

A tunnel rat in the 25th Infantry Division clearing a tunnel during a search and destroy mission in the Iron Triangle north of Saigon on November 27, 1967. (National Archives)

On November 23, 1967, members of the 173rd Airborne Brigade temporarily pinned down by mortar fire during their assault on Hill 87. (National Archives)

In November 1967, members of Navy Seal Team One move down the Bassac River on a Seal team Assault Boat (STAB). (National Archives)

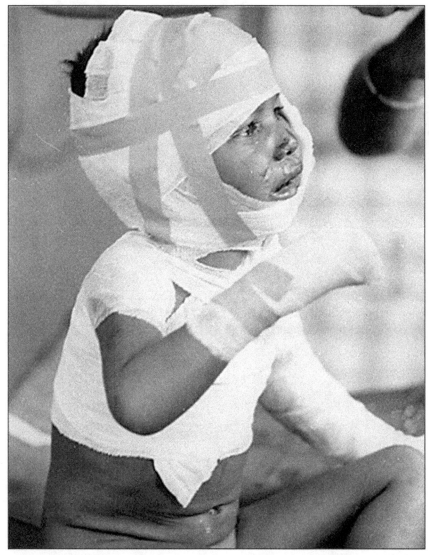

On December 6, 1967, the VC attacked Dak Son (75 miles northeast of Saigon) leaving 252 dead and many others wounded and homeless; this three-year old child is one of the wounded and homeless. (National Archives)

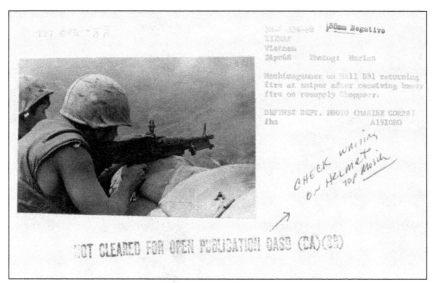

On April 2, 1968 a Marine on Hill 881 attempting to eliminate a sniper shooting at resupply helicopters. (National Archives)

Marine machine gunners call for more ammunition during a battle south of the DMZ in 1968. (National Archives)

In January 1968, members of the 25th Infantry Division relax during Operation Yellowstone. (National Archives)

To the delight of an onlooker a protestor burns his draft card during an anti-draft rally in New York City on January 14, 1968. (National Archives)

The Tet Offensive begins on January 30, 1968, with a rocket attack on the U.S. Air Base in Da Nang. (National Archives)

Wounded and tired South Vietnamese on January 30, 1968 after an early morning Tet attack on their village near Da Nang Air Base. (National Archives)

On February 6, 1968, a wounded Marine from the Fifth Marine Regiment is being attended to by a Medic during the battle for Hue. (National Archives)

Attack on Saigon during Tet 1968. (National Archives)

President Johnson and Secretary of Defense McNamara listen to Tet updates during a Cabinet meeting on February 7, 1968. (National Archives)

Walter Cronkite interviews the Marine Corps commander overseeing the defense of Hue during Tet offensive on February 20, 1968. (National Archives)

On February 29, 1968, Twenty-Fifth Infantry Division soldiers wait for an airlift outside of Saigon, during Operation Tra Hung Doa. (From the VA029958 Bryan Grigsby Photograph Collection, courtesy of the Vietnam Center and Sam Johnson Vietnam Archive, Texas Tech University.)

This "short-timer," down to his last month, is a First Cavalry Division (Airmobile) Sky Trooper fighting in Operation Pershing. (National Archives)

Hue city officials identify the remains of some 2,800 civilians rounded up and executed by NVA and VC forces during the 1968 Tet Offensive. (National Archives)

During Operation Worth in March 1968, Marines of the 1st Battalion 7th Regiment sit by their foxhole under a sign that reads, "Home is where you dig." (National Archives)

A draft resistance march on March 4, 1968, at Yale University. (National Archives)

On March 17, 1968, a gun crew of Battery B, 1st Battalion, 83rd Artillery, engages in a fire mission in support of Operation Jeb Stuart in North Central Vietnam. (From the VA002929 Bryan Grigsby Photograph Collection, courtesy of the Vietnam Center and Sam Johnson Vietnam Archive, Texas Tech University.)

A group of refugees being transported to a safer area near Saigon after a VC attack on their village in March 1968. (National Archives)

Marines protect their ears as an M-48 tank fires its 90mm gun during an April 1968 road sweep southwest of Phu Bai. (National Archives)

On April 5, 1968, a Ninth Infantry Division soldier rests his 45-pound 90mm recoilless rifle on a rock in front of a burning VC village in the Mekong Delta. (National Archives)

On May 7, 1968, a twelve-year old in an ARVN Airborne unit displays his M-79 grenade launcher after a day long battle outside of Saigon. (National Archives)

On July 21, 1968, President Johnson listens to a tape sent to him from Vietnam by his son-in-law, Marine Corps Captain Charles Robb. (National Archives)

On October 17, 1968, an Air Force door gunner firing his mini-gun during a rescue mission. (National Archives)

```
EEA659                              Received: Washington CommCen
OO WTE10                           9:08 PM EST Saturday 02 NOV 1968
DE WTE 4183
                                   Received: LBJ Ranch CommCen
FROM WALT ROSTOW                   8:34 PM CST Saturday 02 NOV 1968
 TO   THE PRESIDENT
CITE CAP82650          SECRET

S E C R E T

THE NEW MEXICO REFERENCE MAY INDICATE AGNEW IS ACTING.
TWO REPORTS FOLLOW.

REPORT ONE:

     ON NOVEMBER TWO INSTANT, A CONFIDENTIAL SOURCE, WHO HAS
FURNISHED RELIABLE INFORMATION IN THE PAST, REPORTED THAT
MRS. ANNA CHENNAULT CONTACTED VIETNAMESE AMBASSADOR, BUI DIEM,
AND ADVISED HIM THAT SHE HAD RECEIVED A MESSAGE FROM HER BOSS
(NOT FURTHER IDENTIFIED), WHICH HER BOSS WANTED HER TO GIVE
PERSONALLY TO THE AMBASSADOR. SHE SAID THE MESSAGE WAS THAT
THE AMBASSADOR IS TO "HOLD ON, WE ARE GONNA WIN" AND THAT HER
BOSS ALSO SAID " HOLD ON, HE UNDERSTANDS ALL OF IT". SHE
REPEATED THAT THIS IS THE ONLY MESSAGE "HE SAID PLEASE TELL
YOUR BOSS TO HOLD ON." SHE ADVISED THAT HER BOSS HAD JUST
CALLED FROM NEW MEXICO.

REPORT TWO

     THE NOVEMBER ONE, LAST, EDITION OF THE "WASHINGTON POST,"
A DAILY NEWSPAPER IN THE WASHINGTON, D.C. AREA, CARRIED AN
ARTICLE CONCERNING MRS. ANNA CHENNAULT. THE ARTICLE INDICATED
THAT MRS. CHENNAULT INTENDED TO PROCEED TO NEW YORK CITY
WHERE SHE WOULD AWAIT THE ELECTION RESULTS ON NOVEMBER FIVE,
NEXT, WITH PRESIDENTIAL NOMINEE RICHARD M. NIXON.

     ON NOVEMBER TWO, INSTANT, AT SEVEN TEN A.M., MRS.
CHENNAULT'S CAR WAS OBSERVED IN THE PARKING GARAGE AT
TWO FIVE ONE ZERO VIRGINIA AVENUE, N.W.

     AT ONE FORTY FIVE P.M., SHE DEPARTED HER RESIDENCE AND
ENTERED THE AUTOMOBILE. IT WAS BEING DRIVEN BY HER CHAUFFEUR
AND PROCEEDED TO THE BALTIMORE-WASHINGTON PARKWAY WHERE IT WAS
LAST OBSERVED HEADING NORTH AT TWO FIFTEEN P.M.

     ARRANGEMENTS HAVE BEEN MADE WITH THE NEW YORK OFFICE OF
THE FBI FOR THEM TO OBSERVE THE CAR EN ROUTE AND TO
UNDERTAKE DISCREET SURVEILLANCE WITH REFERENCE TO HER
ACTIVITIES WHILE IN NEW YORK.

                                   DECLASSIFIED
                                   E.O. 13526, Sec.
                                   By ___ NARA, Date 12-19-00
DTG: 030208Z NOV 1968      SECRET
```

NSC report to President Johnson relating the activities of a Nixon presidential campaign staffer who was under surveillance by the FBI because Johnson thought Nixon was attempting to sabotage his peace talks with North Vietnam. (National Archives)

CHAPTER SEVEN
January 1969-February 1973

When Richard Milhouse Nixon was sworn in as president of the United States on January 20, 1969, he promised that "after a period of confrontation [we would soon be] entering an era of negotiation" in Vietnam.[dccxxv]

To achieve his goal Nixon planned: to have South Vietnamese troops take over the fighting (Vietnamization); to gradually increase the bombing of North Vietnam until a serious Hanoi came to the negotiating table; to end the draft, and to normalize relations with Beijing.

As a step toward normalizing relations with Beijing, Nixon hoped to visit China by the end of his second term. When Nixon's National Security Advisor, Henry Kissinger, heard about this goal his comment was, "Fat chance."[dccxxvi] However, an ongoing border dispute between China and Russia gave Nixon a small opening.[dccxxvii]

On January 28, 1969, the NLF delegation in Paris made it clear to Nixon that there would be no discussions about POWs until (1) all allied troops were withdrawn from South Vietnam, and (2) a political settlement was reached between the government in Saigon and the NLF without interference from the United States.[dccxxviii]

During a February 6 news conference President Nixon confirmed that he wanted to withdraw troops from Vietnam but, he said, before doing so he wanted to see progress in the peace talks.[dccxxix]

Vice President Ky announced on February 10 that South Vietnam would negotiate a settlement of its political problems with the VC after North Vietnam and the United States withdrew from his country.[dccxxx]

North Vietnam began its 1969 "Tet Offensive" on February 23 and, even though it suffered an estimated 100,000 casualties, Hanoi again considered the offensive to be a success because "it boosted the anti-war movement in the U.S. ..." [dccxxxi]

As soon as this offensive began General Abrams and Ambassador Bunker recommended that the U.S. immediately bomb the North in retaliation.[dccxxxii] Nixon, however, refused because he thought it would produce "a violent outburst of domestic protest" which, in turn, would destroy his "efforts to bring the country together in support of (his) plan for peace." [dccxxxiii]

In retrospect, Nixon later said, "if we had [retaliated] then...I think we would have ended the war in 1969 rather than in 1973" and, he added, this, "was my biggest mistake as President." [dccxxxiv] While this may have been a big mistake, his biggest mistake was yet to come.

On March 18, B-52's, began covert bombing attacks on communist camps in Cambodia based on secret orders from Nixon,[dccxxxv] who said the operation was "the first turning point in his administration's conduct of the Vietnam War."[dccxxxvi]

According to a March 22 Gallup Poll, 32% of those questioned: favored greatly escalating the Vietnam War; 26% favored pulling out; 19% favored continuing the same policies, and 21% did not voice an opinion.[dccxxxvii] Two weeks later another Gallup Poll revealed that 60% of those expressing an opinion, approved of the way Nixon was handling the war.[dccxxxviii]

On April 16, Cambodia reestablished diplomatic relations with the U.S. after a four-year break.[dccxxxix] The next day Hanoi again rejected the proposal of mutual withdrawals from South Vietnam and continued to demand an immediate unilateral withdrawal of U.S. troops.[dccxl] At the end of April the U.S. reached its peak of 543,400 troops in Vietnam.[dccxli]

The NLF presented a 10-point peace plan at the Paris peace talks on May 8. The plan, among other things, called for: an unconditional withdrawal of U.S. and allied troops from South Vietnam; the establishment of a coalition government between the NLF and the Saigon government; South Vietnam to be able to settle its own affairs without foreign interference, free elections in South Vietnam, and an eventual unification of North and South Vietnam.[dccxlii]

On May 9, the *New York Times* published a front-page article accurately describing the covert B-52 raids in Cambodia. Within hours, Henry Kissinger told FBI Director J. Edgar Hoover to determine who leaked the information. Thereafter, over the next two years, Kissinger's assistant, General Alexander Haig, directed the FBI to wiretap the telephones of specifically identified reporters and National Security Council staff members.[dccxliii]

The NVA began advancing from Laos toward Hue through the A Shau Valley on May 10, and they were intercepted by elements of the 101st Airborne Division during Operation Apache Snow. After ten days of furious fighting the 101st took Hill 937 ("Hamburger Hill") at a cost of 56 lives and 56 wounded while the NVA lost 597 men and had 420 wounded.[dccxliv]

President Nixon responded to the NLF's 10-point plan making a counter-offer on national television on May 14. His proposal was that U.S., allied and NVA troops mutually withdraw from South Vietnam over a 12-month period and that NVA troops also withdraw from Laos and Cambodia during this period. In addition, he proposed internationally supervised elections in South Vietnam. This proposal differed from the October 1966 Manila proposal where the U.S, said it would withdraw from South Vietnam six months after the NVA left.[dccxlv]

During a White House meeting on the same day Singapore Prime Minister, Lee Kunan Yee, warned President Nixon, not to hastily withdraw from South Vietnam.[dccxlvi]

A week after the 101st took Hamburger Hill, Senator Edward Kennedy (D) condemned the military's recent actions particularly the "senseless and irresponsible" fight to take Hamburger Hill calling it battle madness.[dccxlvii] General Abram's responded saying, "I think it's better to fight the 29th in the A Shau," than in Hue where so many civilian causalities have already been incurred.[dccxlviii] On May 28, the U.S. left Hamburger Hill.[dccxlix]

President Thieu concluded a four-day trip to South Korea on May 30 vowing that he would "never" accept a coalition government with the NLF, but he also said that communists could participate in elections if they were, "willing to lay down their weapons, abandon the communist ideology and abandon atrocities..."[dccl]

On June 8, the U.S. re-opened operations in the Ashua valley which included another fight for Hamburger Hill.[dccli] The next day President Thieu, President Nixon and General Abrams met on Midway Island and (over the silent objection of Thieu and Abrams) Nixon announced that 25,000 U.S. troops would be withdrawn and replaced by 25,000 South Vietnamese troops during the next two months.[dcclii]

The NLF announced on June 10 in Paris that it was forming a Provincial Revolutionary Government (PRG) in South Vietnam,[dccliii] and the following day the PRG said it would be responsible for the internal and foreign policy of South Vietnam and the NLF would continue to be "the organizer and leader of the resistance."[dccliv]

By June 15, the PRG was recognized by Bulgaria, Cambodia, China, Cuba, Czechoslovakia, East Germany, Hungary, Mongolia, North Korea, North Vietnam, Poland, Romania, Syria, the Soviet Union, and Yugoslavia.[dcclv] By comparison, in 1969 South Vietnam was recognized by approximately 60 nations.[dcclvi]

On June 17, around 1,000 NVA troops took control of Hamburger Hill.[dcclvii] Slightly more than two weeks later U.S. troops started withdrawing from Vietnam when a battalion in the 9th Infantry Division was sent home.[dcclviii]

In mid-July, Ho Chi Minh said there could be no free elections in South Vietnam so long as the U.S. remained there and so long as the present South Vietnamese government remained in power.[dcclix]

In a Cold War boost for the U.S., Neil Armstrong became the first man to walk on the moon on July 20.[dcclx]

Five days after Armstrong's walk Nixon announced on Guam that in the future the U.S. would defend non-communist countries in Asia against nuclear attack, but added that these countries would have to defend themselves in conventional wars. This came to be known as the Nixon Doctrine.[dcclxi]

At the end of July, President Nixon told India's Prime Minister, Indira Gandhi, that President Thieu was one of the top five leaders in the world, thereby, demonstrating his solidarity with Vietnam's president.[dcclxii]

In August 1969, President Nixon began making overtures to China through the president of Pakistan.[dcclxiii] Also in August, Henry Kissinger began secret meetings with the North Vietnamese by telling them that a mutual withdrawal of troops would end the war while adding that a refusal to accept this proposal would result in grave consequences. The North, in response, said that the NLF's 10-point program was the only proposal it would accept.[dcclxiv]

On August 26, 1969, Ed Collins and I landed at Tan Son Nuit AFB in the middle of the night and, in the process of deplaning, we filed past the guys boarding who made it clear we were the FNGs (F---ing New Guys) and they were the "short timers."

They were "So short [they said] that they could sleep in a match box" or, "So short they could leave the room without opening the door" or, "So short they could play handball against the curb." Or, were so "short" for a hundred other stupid reasons.

But, as everyone in Vietnam knew, you could never be too "short." Ask Jim Heiman who, while waiting in our office for a ride to the airstrip on his last day, was hit in the face by shards of flying glass from a fluorescent light bulb that had been jarred loose from its overhead fixture.

We occasionally had falling fluorescent bulbs in our office due to vibrations from heavy outgoing artillery above us on Hon Cong Mountain, where Division Artillery was located. In order to catch the falling bulbs, we put tape across the bottom of the fixtures but, in this case, the tape had rotted and did not do its job. While the flying glass hit Jim's face it missed his eyes, and he caught his flight out.

Jim, however, was lucky when compared to the two 9th Infantry Division soldiers who had been killed a month earlier when hit by incoming artillery while waiting in their Out-Processing Center for a flight home; he was also lucky when compared to the twenty-one others who were injured in the same attack.[dcclxv] You never could be too short.

On the morning of August 27, Collins and I reported to the MACV Staff Judge Advocate's office to get our duty stations but were preempted by Aubrey Daniel* (the Calley prosecutor) and his entourage.

After Daniel was taken care of, Collins, I believe, was told he would be based in the coastal city of Nha Trang. In any event, since he was a military judge, he would not be spending much time in one place as judges traveled all over their designated areas conducting court-martial proceedings.

I was assigned to the Fourth Infantry Division which had an area of operations in the central highlands near the junction of Laos and Cambodia this area, as one writer accurately described it, consisted of "uncountable rugged mountain peaks covered by a thick tangle of triple canopy jungle... [that] not only served as an end to...the infamous Ho Chi Minh Trail...it also allowed the NVA to stage massive forces in a secluded nearly impregnable region."[dcclxvi]

Control of the central highlands was strategically important because it prevented the NVA from moving eastward to the coast, and cutting Vietnam in half.[dcclxvii]

After a C-130 ride the next day, I found myself about sixteen kilometers south of Pleiku at Camp Enari, the 4th Infantry Division base camp. When I checked into the replacement depot I was (are you kidding me) billeted across the hall from John Cavetto, a Sigma Phi

---

* Daniel was two years ahead of me in law school but our paths never crossed.

Epsilon pledge brother at the University of Richmond. Cavetto had transferred after his first year and I had not seen him in six years; when we met again, he was a Captain in the Artillery.

Before reporting to my JAG unit, I (like everyone else) went through "in-country processing" that began with field training, and ended with presentations on the protocols of war under the Geneva Conventions.

On August 30, 1969, Ho Chi Minh sent a letter to President Nixon rejecting his July 15 peace proposal and urged, instead, that the NLF's 10-point plan be accepted. In short, Ho said, "the United States must cease its war of aggression" withdraw from Vietnam and give the people there the right of self-determination.[dcclxviii]

On August 31, I got my permanent "hooch mate," Tom Chenault, a Captain in the Chemical Corps, who gave me many tips most of which I took to heart. But even though he told me not to bother putting a mosquito net over my cot I put one up anyway, not only because of the mosquitos, but also because it provided protection from the many rats running around on the rafters.

Tom should have followed my lead on this one because, even though he had been lucky for eight months, not long after I got there one of those rafter rats took a misstep in the middle of the night and landed squarely on his stomach. We spent the next couple of hours locating and assembling Tom's mosquito net.

A week or so later Tom started to think I was bad luck when the "people sniffer" helicopter* he volunteered on was brought down by

---

* "People sniffers" were helicopters with detector equipment that, at some risk, flew at low levels trying to locate the enemy.

sniper fire. But, when he and the rest of the crew were rescued just before they were captured (or shot) he began to think otherwise.

A few days later I had a bit of luck myself when a helicopter I was on was forced to land (at Camp Holloway) because a heavy fog had rolled in out of nowhere on a bright sunny day. When I returned to the helicopter after the fog lifted my pilot said he would not be going on because his preflight check had revealed that a massive crack had somehow developed in one of his overhead rotor blades. Correctly sensing irritation on my part, he added, that if the fog had not forced him to land the blade most certainly would have broken off long before we reached our destination (Camp Radcliff) and we would not be standing anywhere right now. I said thank you fog, and found another ride going my way.

On September 3, 1969, Ho Chi Minh died at the age of 79.[dcclxix]

Two days later, Lieutenant William Calley was charged with killing 109 My Lai villagers.[dcclxx]

On the other side of the "Calley coin" were soldiers in Vietnam like Sergeant James Barta who was willing to risk court-martial for refusing an order to plant land mines outside the wire of his fire support base. He was willing to risk court-martial, he said, because the perimeter was already very well secured and because the mines would literally be overkill in view of the village children who played there every day.

Whether Sergeant Barta was right or wrong remains to be seen. The point is he was willing to risk a lot for those village kids. Apparently this matter was handled in some way satisfactory to Barta, because I never heard from him again.

On September 6, 1969, Hanoi announced that Ho Chi Minh would be jointly succeeded by Le Duan, the first Secretary of North Vietnam's Communist Party, Truong Chin, Chairman of the National Assembly, General Vo Nguyen Giap, Defense Minister, and Premier, Pham Van Dong.[dcclxxi]

Three days later Ho Chi Minh was buried with 250,000 people in attendance including Soviet Premier Aleksei Kosygin, Chinese Vice-Premier Li Hsiennien, and Cambodia's Prince Sihanouk.[dcclxxii] The following day Prince Sihanouk expressed his support for North Vietnam, and asked the United States to leave South Vietnam.[dcclxxiii]

In mid-September President Nixon temporarily took the wind out of the sails of the protest movement by cancelling the 32,000-man November draft call and the 18,000-man December draft call.[dcclxxiv] But, the movement was soon reinvigorated by the trial of the "Chicago Seven" which began on September 23 and continued for five months.[dcclxxv]

During the first week of October President Nixon met with Premier Phouma of Laos in the White House and assured him the U.S. would insist on the withdrawal of North Vietnamese troops from Laos and Cambodia as part of any settlement of the Vietnam War.[dcclxxvi]

In a speech on November 3, President Nixon asked the country's "Silent Majority" to support his search for peace through Vietnamization.[dcclxxvii] The next day seventy-seven percent of those questioned in a Gallup Poll expressed their support for Nixon's plan and only 6% opposed it.[dcclxxviii]

In spite of this apparent support, 9,000 federal troops had to be assembled in Washington, D.C. on November 12 to help 1,200 National Guardsmen and 3,700 policemen serve as security for an upcoming anti-war rally.^{dcclxxix} The following day the New Mobilization Committee's "March against Death," headed by 46,000 relatives of servicemen killed in Vietnam, began at Arlington National Cemetery.^{dcclxxx} By November 15, the "March against Death" had grown to over 250,000 people who marched down Pennsylvania Avenue and gathered on the Mall near the Washington Monument. From there around 6,000 of the more radical demonstrators, led by members of the Youth International Party (Yippies), broke away and marched to the Justice Department throwing bottles and burning U.S. flags in support of the "Chicago Seven." At the Justice Department, the protestors were repelled by tear gas and approximately one hundred were arrested.^{dcclxxxi}

In mid-December 1969, Congress slowed down the war effort when it prohibited the introduction of U.S. troops into Laos and Thailand with DOD funds.^{dcclxxxii} But, Nixon secretly began to make headway on his own with low level talks between U.S. and Chinese officials that were scheduled to begin at the end of the year.^{dcclxxxiii}

At the end of 1969, the U.S. troop level in Vietnam was down to 475,000, from a peak of 543,000 in June 1969, and during the year South Vietnam's forces went from 850,000 to over a million, while communist forces in South Vietnam went from 290,000 to 240,000.^{dcclxxxiv} During 1969, nine thousand Americans were killed in action, and 33,000 were wounded. During the same period 21,800 South Vietnamese were killed in action and 65,000 were wounded.^{dcclxxxv}

My hooch mate's Date of Estimated Return from Overseas (DEROS) was in January 1970 and I was sorry to see him leave. He was a fun guy who had scrounged a TV from somewhere and when 10:00 P.M. rolled around we would often be watching a tape of the Johnny Carson show out of Saigon. But I quit watching when he left because I was not very good at adjusting the "rabbit ears" to pick up the signal from Saigon, and because watching the Carson show alone was not that much fun.

On January 30, 1970, Nixon said he would continue to drawdown the combat troop level in Vietnam regardless of the progress in Paris, but added that increased fighting by North Vietnam during these withdrawals would be handled "more strongly than…in the past."[dcclxxxvi]

A February 14, Gallup Poll reflected that 55% of those questioned opposed an immediate withdrawal from Vietnam and that 35% (up 14% from the last poll) favored immediate withdrawal.[dcclxxxvii]

On February 21, Henry Kissinger continued his secret meetings with North Vietnam, but no progress was made then or in follow up meetings on March 16 and April 4 of that year.[dcclxxxviii]

At the end of February I completed six months in the Fourth Division which made me eligible for transfer to a place that had things like, air conditioners, hot and cold running water, flush toilets, indoor showers, and sinks.

One of our latrines

However, at the time, I was representing a defendant charged with murder, robbery, and a number of other offenses and could not leave until after the trial.

On March 10, 1970, Captain Ernest Medina and four others were charged with having committed a number of crimes at My Lai in 1968. The crimes charged ranged from premeditated murder to rape and maiming. Captain Medina was Lt. Calley's C.O. as well as the C.O. of others charged with committing crimes at Mylai.[dcclxxxix]

On March 11, approximately 20,000 Cambodians attacked the North Vietnamese embassy as well as the VC (Provisional Revolutionary Government) embassy protesting the presence of their military forces in Cambodia.[dccxc] A week later pro-West Lt. General Lon Nol took control of Cambodia from Prince Sihanouk in a bloodless coup.[dccxci] Three days later Sihanouk agreed to become the leader of the Cambodian communists at a secret meeting with North Vietnam's Prime Minister Pham Van Dong, and Chinese Premier Zhou Enlai in Peking.[dccxcii]

In April 1970, as part of Nixon's Vietnamization program, the 4th Division's 3rd Brigade was sent home and deactivated. The remainder of the Division was to be moved from Camp Enari outside of Pleiku to Camp Radcliff outside of An Khe on the other side of the Mang Yang pass.

I had flown over the Mang Yang Pass a number of times, but this move meant we would be traveling through the pass on Highway 19 where convoys were often ambushed.[dccxciii] As we departed, I was generally aware of the problem the French had encountered fifteen years earlier as they travelled along Highway 19 in the opposite direction, to Pleiku,[dccxciv] but I was unaware of the specifics of that trip which were detailed in Bernard Fall's book *Street Without Joy*.

According to Colin Powell, *Street Without Joy* was read by young officers during their early combat training,[dccxcv] many of whom carried "dog-eared" copies with them as they shipped out to Vietnam.[dccxcvi] However, I had not received combat training or read *Street Without Joy*.

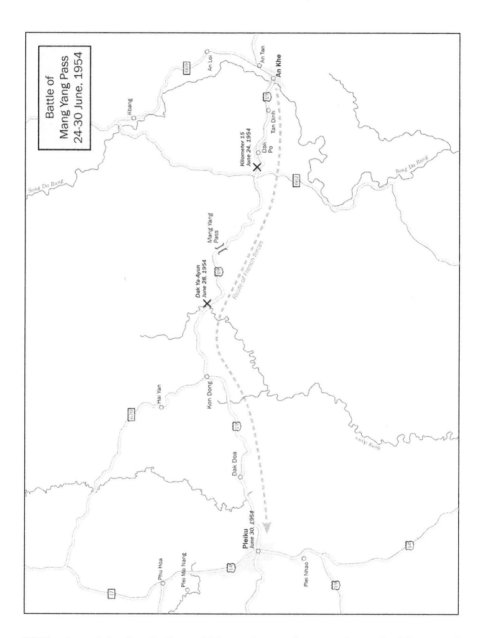

If I had read the book, I would have learned more about the history of the street (Highway 19) where the French were massacred in the last big battle of the French/Indochinese war. I would have learned that the massacred unit, known as *Groupement Mobile* 100, or G.M. 100 was ordered to evacuate An Khe on 23 June 1954[dccxcvii] and move to Pleiku and that, as ordered, it left the next morning at 0300 hours.[dccxcviii] I would have also learned that when the unit approached Kilometer 15 on Hwy 19 at about 1400 hours on 24 June the Commanding Officer of the 1st company of the 43rd Infantry sensed a problem and volunteered to take his company into the "high grass" to reconnoiter the area.[dccxcix]

It was there at Kilometer 15, according to Fall, that:

> Two Communist machine guns opened up at a range of about 30 yards, catching [the company] broadside…. It was about 1420 on [the CO's] watch, and he and his men knew they were going to die right there, in the tall grass in the narrow highland valley….[dccc]

*****

In the Headquarters Company the ambush looked quite different [but also at 1420]… As if swallowed up by an earthquake, the whole headquarters convoy now disappeared in clouds of dust and shattered metal as salvo upon salvo of well-aimed artillery and mortar fire slammed into it. The armored platoon was simply knocked out of the fight before it could search out the guns which were destroying it. Within four minutes, the three half-tracks and one M-8 were afire and exploding. The last M-8, though also immobilized registered on a machine-gun nest which, from a nearby hilltop, was raking the stopped vehicles with its fire, and covered it with canister shells. At 1425, the Group's Radio truck collapsed in flames, thus depriving the doomed task force of its central control…

*****

At 1500 a mighty roar, reverberating from the surrounding mountains, shook the whole column while huge flames shot skyward and pieces began to rain down on the battlefield: the engineers' ammunition trucks had begun to explode under the impact of the Viet-Minh shells.

*****

At 1900 the remnants of Mobil Group 100 gathered for the final battle as an organized unit: the breakout from Kilometer 15, from the steel trap which had been chewing them to pieces for the past six hours....[dccci]

After five days of fighting the remnants of G.M. 100 reached Pleiku on 29 June 1954.[dcccii]

When we started down Highway 19 in the opposite direction to An Khe in April 1970, I had only vaguely heard about "Kilometer 15" but I did know I was travelling through a valley surrounded by mountains and high grass; therefore, riding shotgun, I stayed alert until we reached Camp Radcliff.

The First Calvary Division (Airmobile) was the first occupant of Camp Radcliff; when the "Cav" left the 173rd Airborne Brigade moved in and when they left we moved in. The good news about this move was that I got another fun hooch mate, and our new hooch did not have rats on the rafters. The bad news was we did have snakes in the high grass outside the hooch.

But more good news about Camp Radcliff was that it had a hospital where I could get a broken thumb (basketball injury) evaluated. And, when I got to the hospital (are you kidding me) there sat Richard

Reynolds who I had represented in that robbery case back at Fort Sam Houston. We shook hands and laughed like long lost friends. In response to my question, he said he had been released from jail shortly after the trial and after several months of training sent to Vietnam. We were only able to talk for a few minutes before he was called in but, as I recall, Reynolds was serving as a combat medic. He was a likable guy and hopefully he used his military training to become a first responder or maybe even a doctor, who knows.

On April 20, Cambodian Premier Lon Nol sent President Nixon a personal request for military aid following reports that communists had more than doubled their area of control in his country.[dccciii] Within a week of Lon Nol's request leaders of the communist movements in Indochina, (Prince Norodum Sihanouk, the deposed leader of Cambodia; Prince Souphonouvong, leader of the Pathet Lao in Laos; Nguyen Huu, President of the Provisional Revolutionary Government of South Vietnam, and Pham Van Dong, Prime Minister of North Vietnam) met in China and pledged to remove the United States and all other opposition forces from Indochina. Chinese Premier Zhou Enlai closed the meeting with his stamp of approval.[dccciv]

In response to Lon Nol's request, President Nixon formally authorized the use of U.S. troops to fight in Cambodia alongside the ARVN on April 28.[dcccv] Two days later Nixon announced this decision in a televised speech.[dcccvi] And, two days after this speech rioting students, protesting the expansion of the war into Cambodia, burned a ROTC building to the ground at Kent State University which, in turn, inspired protests on a number of different campuses.[dcccvii] To stop the riots at Kent State the Mayor of Kent, Ohio called in National Guardsmen on May 2 and when the riots continued the Guardsmen fired into a group of students killing four and wounding eleven. After this incident students at 100 colleges and universities around the country pledged to strike.[dcccviii]

Virtually simultaneously with the Kent State shooting, elements of the 4th Infantry Division and 22nd ARVN Division combined to launch a joint operation into the Fish Hook area of Cambodia about 50 miles west of Pleiku City. Six hundred and eighty-five enemy troops were killed and 118 were detained,[dcccix] while the Americans lost 12 and had 48 wounded. [dcccx]

On May 1 and 2, 1970, Nixon sent 128 planes to bomb two different provinces in North Vietnam; thereby breaking the bombing pause instituted in 1968 by President Johnson.[dcccxi]

California's Governor, Ronald Reagan shut down all 28 campuses of the University of California system on May 6 due to campus unrest created by the Kent State shooting. In addition, the entire 18 campus Penn State University System joined more than 100 colleges and universities throughout the nation in shutting its doors while students on more than 300 other campuses boycotted classes.[dcccxii]

Two days after the major campus closures, President Nixon justified the movement of U.S. troops into Cambodia, saying it would give the South Vietnamese 6 to 8 more months of training time, and he also took this occasion to promise the withdrawal of 150,000 more U.S. troops from Vietnam by spring.[dcccxiii] The same day protesting students disrupted approximately 400 colleges around the nation and closed 200 completely.[dcccxiv] Another rally the next day brought seventy-five to one-hundred thousand people to the White House to protest the war.[dcccxv]

In addition to the unrest this incursion caused, it also scuttled Nixon's plan to work with China as the Chinese broke off communications with the State Department.[dcccxvi]

In the midst of this incursion the murder case I had been working on finally went to trial at a small installation in the central highlands (the name of which I cannot recall); however, I do remember that on the first day of trial we received incoming and the judge "sua sponte" declared a recess so we could head for the bunkers. When the trial ended, I only had four months left in-country so I decided to remain in the 4th because I liked the people and time went by faster at the Division level.

After this trial I went on R&R where I experienced the scariest moment of my "Vietnam year" on the then deserted Hawaiian island of Kauai. It was there I foolishly jumped off a long pier with the intention of riding the waves back to shore. Unfortunately, I had jumped into an ocean with a strong undertow and after 10 to 15 minutes of hard swimming found myself going sideways and backwards. Completely exhausted, I started treading water in order to rest---only to find I had drifted over a sand bar and was swimming in about 4 feet of water. I walked most of the way in from there; Merry Christmas in May.

But not everyone had a merry R&R. I cannot forget a Sergeant who got home a few days early for R&R, only to find his wife in bed with a neighbor. And, instead of getting a tearful apology, his wife told him she was going to be filing for an immediate divorce. A divorce he did not want because he was sure he could change her mind when he returned.

When the Sergeant got back to Vietnam, he stopped by JAG to see if his wife could get a divorce while he was away, and when told the short answer was no, he seemed relieved as he headed out to spend the next six months in the jungle as the First Sergeant in an infantry company. War takes its toll in many ways.

On May 27, South Vietnam and Cambodia agreed to restore diplomatic relations after 17 years of hostilities.[dcccxvii]

President Nixon, in a nationally televised speech on June 3, told the nation that the allied invasion of Cambodia had been the "most successful operation of the long and difficult war," and added that 17,000 of the 31,000 U.S. troops sent to Cambodia had been returned to Vietnam.[dcccxviii] Five days later, during a speech in Hanoi, deposed Prince Sihanouk said that Cambodia would stand with the Vietnamese Communists in their effort to defeat U.S. "imperialism."[dcccxix]

Senator Robert Dole* (R) proposed repealing the Southeast Asia (Gulf of Tonkin) Resolution on June 24 in an amendment to the Foreign Military Sales Act; this proposal passed the Senate (81 to 10),[dcccxx] but did not pass in the House.

By the end of June, the last of the U.S. combat troops in Cambodia returned to South Vietnam.[dcccxxi]

I started my official "short" countdown on August 1 and it went smoothly with two exceptions. The first was a "hot landing" that had to be made on a firebase because a sniper had shot down the resupply helicopter before us; the second was the night sappers, got inside the wire and blew up several nearby hooches.[dcccxxii]

---

* Senator Dole was a World War II hero, the Republican vice presidential nominee in 1976, and its presidential nominee in 1996.

August 26, 1970, was my DEROS date and my countdown ended with no more incidents. It was good to touch the green green grass of home until a custom's official, going through my duffle bag, found "narcotics" in my shaving kit. When I explained that this "contraband" was unused medication for wisdom teeth I had pulled just before I left the official consulted with his boss, and they decided to confiscate the pills and allow me to pass. My year in Vietnam was over, and when I exited customs into the San Francisco airport I was greeted by neither cheers nor jeers.

Before going to my next duty station in Virginia I went back to visit my family in San Antonio where I was met by my wife and 6-month-old daughter. Back at Ft. Sam my wife and I were invited over to Tim and Karen's (our road trip partners) for dinner and to look at our road trip pictures. But, after dinner I was still on Vietnam time so we had to get a raincheck on the pictures. Unfortunately, we never got to use that raincheck because a month or so later Karen ran off with her dance teacher to end, what seemed to be, the perfect marriage.

Vice President Agnew, during a speech on August 27 in Saigon, attended by President Thieu and Vice President Ky, praised the South Vietnamese people for enduring "so much in freedom's cause" and promised that there would "be no lessening of U.S. support."[dcccxxiii]

At the end of August ninety-three percent of the South Vietnamese people were safely under government control; about 185,000 people were under VC control, and approximately 1 million people lived in areas controlled by neither.[dcccxxiv]

On September 1, the U.S. Senate, by a vote of 55 to 39, rejected a McGovern/Hatfield proposal to have all troops out of Vietnam by December 31, 1971, and by a vote of 71 to 22 it also rejected a proposal to prohibit the use of future draftees in Vietnam.[dcccxxv]

In a televised speech on October 7, President Nixon proposed: a "ceasefire in place" throughout Indochina; a release of POWs, and an Indochina peace conference to negotiate an end of the fighting. At this peace conference the president said the U.S. would be willing to negotiate a timetable for the withdrawal of U.S. troops and accept a political solution agreeable to the South Vietnamese people. Nixon, however, rejected the idea of ousting President Thieu.[dcccxxvi]

Later in October Nixon renewed his attempt to establish diplomatic relations with the Chinese by personally asking Pakistan's president to carry an entreaty to China on his behalf.[dcccxxvii]

Speaking at West Point on November 16 Vice President Ky said that the communists would overrun Cambodia if South Vietnamese forces were withdrawn, and added that his government was concerned that the U.S. would yield to the "pressure of the antiwar groups" and leave too quickly.[dcccxxviii]

Less than a week later Radio Hanoi reported "wave after wave" of U.S. bombers striking targets ranging from Haiphong to Hoabinh southeast of Hanoi.[dcccxxix]

On December 8, a note from Chinese Premier Zou Enlai was delivered to the White House by Pakistan's Ambassador to the United States, it read:

> In order to discuss the subject of the vacation of Chinese territories called Taiwan, a special envoy of President Nixon's will be most welcome in Peking.[dcccxxx]

Kissinger responded to China on plain white paper, through a Romanian backchannel, saying that an:

American envoy would be willing to come and talk 'on a broad range of issues' facing the two countries… With respect to the U.S. Military presence on Taiwan… the policy of the United States government is to reduce its military presence in the region of East Asia and the pacific as the tensions diminish.[dcccxxxi]

Two days later Lt. Calley's attorney began his defense by contending, in his opening statement, that Calley was not guilty of the charges against him because he was following the lawful orders of his company commander, Captain Ernest Medina, who told him they were finally going to meet the enemy in Mylai, (during Tet) and ordered him to kill "every living thing" in the village. He further argued that the evidence would show Calley carried out this order under the watchful eyes of the task force commander Lt. Col. Frank Barker on the ground and the Americal Division commander, General Samuel W. Coster, in the air.[dcccxxxii]

By the end of December there were 334,000 Americans in Vietnam. During that year 4,221 were killed in action, and 15,211 were wounded. During the same period 23,346 South Vietnamese were killed in action and 71,582 were wounded.[dcccxxxiii]

In January 1971, Congress prohibited the use of ground forces in Laos and Cambodia, but not the use of air power,[dcccxxxiv] and it also repealed the Southeast Asia (Gulf of Tonkin) Resolution.[dcccxxxv] After the Gulf of Tonkin Resolution was repealed Nixon "primarily drew on the constitutional authority of the president as commander-in-chief to protect the lives of U.S. military forces in justifying [his] actions and policies in prosecuting the war."[dcccxxxvi]

Cambodia's Premier Lon Nol suffered a stroke on February 8, and in April he turned his duties over to Deputy Premier, Stirik Matak.[dcccxxxvii]

W. Averell Harriman, former head of the U.S, delegation to the Paris peace talks, and one of Johnson's Wise Men, led an antiwar teach-in on February 22 at Yale University.[dcccxxxviii]

Operation Phoenix began on March 1. This operation, run by the South Vietnamese and endorsed by the United States: (1) increased the People's Self Defense Force from 500,000 to 1,000,000 rural civilians, (2) created a large "people's intelligence network" to gather covert information about communist activity, and (3) eventually jailed or killed approximately 14,000 individuals thought to be VC agents.[dcccxxxix]

Between March 5 and 8, Chinese Premier Zhou Enlai visited North Vietnam during which time he and North Vietnamese Premier, Pham Van Don, issued a joint communiqué in which China gave its all-out support to North Vietnam in its struggle against the United States.[dcccxl]

At the end of March, Lieutenant Calley was found guilty of murdering at least 22 civilians and was sentenced to life in prison at Fort Leavenworth. After Calley's conviction and sentencing the public began to vocally complain that he was being made the scapegoat.[dcccxli]

In response to the public outcry, President Nixon had Calley removed from the Ft. Benning stockade on April 3 and placed in house arrest.[dcccxlii] Thereafter, Calley's sentence was reduced to 20 years by the Third Army Commander, Lt. Gen. Albert O. Connor, and further reduced to 10 years by the Secretary of the Army. In 1974, Calley, still under house arrest, was paroled by President Nixon after having served one-third of his 10-year sentence.[dcccxliii] Of the fourteen men charged in the My Lai incident Calley was the only one convicted.[dcccxliv]

Through the first three months of 1971 the scuttled communications between China and the United States stumbled along, but slowly. However, things changed in April when a nineteen-year-old American ping-pong player at the World Table Tennis Championships in Japan hitched a ride with the Chinese to an event Japan was sponsoring for the players. To show his appreciation, the American gave the Chinese team captain a T shirt and China, thinking this "thank you" was a signal from Washington, invited the U.S. Ping-Pong team to Beijing the following week.[dcccxlv] During a reception for the Americans in Beijing, Premier Zhou Enlai told them they had opened a new chapter in relations between the United States and China.[dcccxlvi]

Zhou Enlai followed up on these remarks to the ping-pong team by sending a message to Washington on April 21 through a Pakistani backchannel. In this message he reaffirmed China's "willingness to receive publicly in Peking a special envoy of the president of the United States (for instance Mr. Kissinger) or the U.S. Secretary of State or even the president of the United States himself for a direct meeting."[dcccxlvii]

By May 1971, the United States, as a result of this "Ping-Pong diplomacy," was corresponding directly with China. On May 9, Henry Kissinger informed Premier Zhou Enlai, in response to his April 21 invitation, that he would be the one coming to Peking.[dcccxlviii] On June 2, Zhou Enlai sent a reply approving Kissinger's trip to China and added that Chairman Mao had expressed the "pleasure" of meeting with President Nixon soon thereafter. In Kissinger's opinion this was "the most important" communication since World War II.[dcccxlix] Nixon, when advised of this invitation, said, "Let us drink to generations to come who may have a better chance to live in peace because of what we have done."[dcccl]

On June 13, the *New York Times* began publishing the leaked "Pentagon Papers" that had been compiled by the DOD at the request of Secretary McNamara. These papers contained classified information about the internal decision making process that led to U.S. involvement in Vietnam and about civilian and military decisions made during the war, up until Secretary McNamara's departure.[dcccli] In rapid-fire judicial proceedings, first in a federal district court and subsequently in the Supreme Court it was held that the government had failed to meet its heavy burden of prior restraint and, therefore, the courts' refused to enjoin publication of these papers.

As these papers were being published in early July 1971, my good friend Bill Thomas, a high school, college and law school classmate, and also a Vietnam Veteran, called to tell me he had just heard our high school classmate and friend Jim Morrison, of the Doors, had been found dead in Paris under mysterious circumstances. In response, I told Bill I thought he had faked his death so he could disappear and do some serious writing.

The circumstances surrounding Morrison's death are, to say the least, suspicious, but I am no longer confident he faked his death and, even if he did, I am confident he is no longer alive. Bill, on the other hand, continues to believe there is strong circumstantial evidence indicating Morrison did not die in Pairs as reported and further believes he and his son may even have encountered him in Flagstaff, Arizona, in the early 1990s.[dccclii]

Kissinger secretly met with Zhou Enlai in Beijing on July 9 and out of this meeting came an invitation for President Nixon to visit the Peoples Republic of China early in 1972.[dcccliii] President Nixon, in a stunning announcement on July 15, 1971, issued simultaneously in Washington, Peking and worldwide, said he planned to visit China before May 1972 where he hoped to "seek normalization of relations between the two countries and to exchange views on questions of concern to both sides."[dccccliv] "In a single stroke," it was said, "the president had confounded all of his enemies: the Soviets, the North Vietnamese, the press and the liberal Democrats."[dccclv]

In August 1971, South Vietnam's presidential candidates General Duong Van (Big) Minh and Vice President Ky withdrew from the race contending the election was rigged.[dccclvi] In the ensuing one-man presidential election, 87% of the nation's eligible voters showed up at the polls, in spite of communist attacks to discourage turnout, and 94% of those voting cast their votes for Thieu. Upon being reelected Thieu freed over 2,300 VC POW's.[dccclvii]

On September 30, the U.S. Senate for the second time approved a Mike Mansfield sponsored amendment to the military procurement bill calling for the withdrawal of U.S. troops from Southeast Asia within six months.[dccclviii]

By mid-October, Cambodia's Premier Lon Nol suspended his National Assembly and said he would govern by executive decree because the "sterile game of democracy" was hampering his war-torn country in its fight against communism.[dccclix]

October also found Kissinger in China where he began drafting the communique Nixon and Mao would sign at the February 1972 summit.[dccclx] Shortly after Kissinger's October visit to China, Zhou Enlai went to Hanoi and started pressuring North Vietnam to accept a compromise settlement that would let the Thieu government remain in place while passing along other American peace proposals, thus tacitly endorsing them.[dccclxi]

On December 9, the 138th session of the Paris peace talks adjourned and, for the first time, no future meetings were scheduled. This adjournment continued into 1972 when the Hanoi and VC delegates became angry and refused to negotiate after the U.S. suggested that they get together and develop a "more comprehensive" approach.[dccclxii]

By the end of December, there were 156,800 Americans in Vietnam. In that year 1,381 were killed in action and 4,767 were wounded; during the same time period 22,738 South Vietnamese were killed in action and 60,939 were wounded.[dccclxiii]

The Paris peace talks reconvened on January 6, 1972, at which time the Communist delegations said American POWs would not be returned until the United States: (1) withdrew its forces from South Vietnam, (2) withdrew its support for Thieu, and (3) stopped its Vietnamization program.[dccclxiv]

On January 25, President Nixon responded to domestic criticism that he had not made his best effort to end the war saying that between August 4, 1969, and August 16, 1971, his National Security Advisor, Henry Kissinger, had held 12 secret meetings with Le Duc Tho, a member of North Vietnam's politburo and/ or Xuan Thuy, Hanoi's chief delegate to the Paris peace talks, but Hanoi had discontinued these talks. This, Nixon said, was followed on October 11, 1971, with a secret offer to: (1) enter into a cease fire agreement that would be accompanied with the release of all POWs, (2) simultaneously withdraw all U.S. and communist troops from South Vietnam, Cambodia and Laos, and (3) to hold a presidential election in South Vietnam overseen by a number of different factions, where President Thieu would resign a month before the election.[dccclxv]

The next day Henry Kissinger expanded on Nixon's statement saying Hanoi insisted that, as a part of any settlement, the U.S. would have to end all future assistance to South Vietnam and would have to remove everything it had ever given to them. These requirements were deal breakers, he said, because they would have insured the fall of the Saigon government.[dccclxvi]

North Vietnamese officials released a communiqué at the end of January expressing their displeasure with President Nixon and Henry Kissinger for disclosing the substance of secret talks.[dccclxvii]

President Nixon and Mao Zedong met in Beijing on February 21 and discussed their mutual interest of "resisting the spread of Soviet influence."[dccclxviii] At the time, Nixon said his visit would be "the week that changed the world,"[dccclxix] and it was. More particularly, it immediately changed the dynamics of the Vietnam War. Walter Isaacson, the author of *Kissinger*, perhaps best described how things changed afterward, noting that:

> With the suddenness of the breaking of ice on a lake, the opening to China made the Vietnam War an anachronism. For Beijing and Washington, and Moscow as well, the clash in the Southeast Asian jungle—both as an ideological struggle and as a strategic one—abruptly seemed a nettlesome historical holdover. Now that they considered the Soviets rather than the Americans to be their prime antagonists, the Chinese would no longer be as thrilled by the prospect of a triumph by North Vietnam, which was [now] aligned with Moscow. Likewise, now that it found itself being played off against Beijing, Moscow found itself more interested in détente than prolonging American agony in Vietnam. And in the U.S., the need to stop the spread of the Chinese Communist menace—which is one way the war had been justified—no longer seemed quite as pressing.[dccclxx]

On March 16, 1972, VC and NVA troops attacked 41 South Vietnamese targets (mostly local militia units) over a period of 24 hours.[dccclxxi] A week after these attacks W. J. Porter, as directed by President Nixon, announced an end to the Paris Peace talks until there could be a "serious discussion" of the agenda at hand, and until the communists ended their offensive in South Vietnam. In response, North Vietnam and the NLF said they would not resume the talks until the U.S. stopped the bombing of North and South Vietnam, but they then withdrew that demand.[dccclxxii]

On March 30, one hundred and fifty thousand NVA and thousands of VC troops, supported by heavy rocket and artillery fire, mounted the heaviest attacks against Khe Sanh and the northern part of South Vietnam since 1968.[dccclxxiii]

Two days later twelve to fifteen thousand NVA troops, supported by artillery and Sea to Air Missiles (SAMs), drove the ARVN's 3rd Division out of the DMZ. The NVA's objective was to take Quantri City, the capital of Quantri Province, and then move on to Hue and Danang.[dccclxxiv] Hanoi's plan during this offensive was to: "(1) impress the communist world and its own people with its determination, (2) capitalize on U.S. anti-war sentiment and possibly hurt President Nixon's chances for reelection, (3) prove Vietnamization was a failure, (4) damage South Vietnamese forces and the Thieu regime's stability, (5) gain as much territory as possible, and to (6) accelerate negotiations on their own terms."[dccclxxv]

President Nixon, discouraged by the progress of peace negotiations with Hanoi, asked his Joint Chiefs on April 5 for new options that would force serious negotiations. This was a question the JCS had wanted to hear for a long time.[dccclxxvi]

In early April, the NVA expanded its offensive by committing all but one of its combat divisions as it moved into the central highlands from Laos and Cambodia.[dccclxxvii]

By April 23, the North Vietnamese offensive had driven 250,000 civilians from their homes and, while slowing on two fronts, continued in the central highlands.[dccclxxviii]

In spite of this offensive, President Nixon announced a few days later that 20,000 more troops would be withdrawn in May and June; at the same time, however, the U.S. Navy doubled the number of its combat ships off the coast of Vietnam.[dccclxxix]

President Nixon finally responded to the NVA offensive on May 8 when he announced that he had ordered the immediate mining of all major North Vietnamese ports to prevent the flow of goods into North Vietnam, and he warned foreign ships in those ports that the mines would be activated in three days. He further announced that all rail lines into North Vietnam from China would be bombed to further stem the flow of war material into North Vietnam. And, he added, these actions would continue until "(1) all U.S. POW's were returned, and (2) an internationally supervised cease-fire began."[dccclxxx]

That same day the mining operation commenced,[dccclxxxi] and continued into 1973 when over 11,000 mines were deposited into North Vietnam's ports and waterways.[dccclxxxii] By May 9, the U.S. bombing of North Vietnam reached 1967-1968 levels when bombing had been at its highest.[dccclxxxiii]

On May 10, China, the Soviet Union, and their eastern allies denounced President Nixon's decision to mine North Vietnam's ports.[dccclxxxiv] But, said Vietnam War critic Roger Morris, Peking and

Moscow's cautious indifference to the U.S. counter-offensive was more effective than the counter-offensive itself.[dccclxxxv]

According to Walter Isaacson:

America's mining of Vietnam's harbors was a major provocative move, one that in a different environment could have provoked a military showdown with Moscow, especially since some of its ships were in Haiphong harbor and were hit by bombs. As it was, there would be only a few muted protests in St. Vladimir's Hall.[dccclxxxvi]

Only 13 days after the mining began President Nixon, in another first, met with General Secretary Brezhnev in Moscow [dccclxxxvii] where "détente" (the relaxation of tensions between western and communist nations) began to take shape.[dccclxxxviii]

Hanoi launched a 120,000-troop Easter Offensive against South Vietnam on May 30, but this offensive was repelled by ARVN troops and American air power.[dccclxxxix] During this offensive an estimated 100,000 North Vietnamese were killed while an estimated 30,000 South Vietnamese died in action and another 78,000 were wounded.[dcccxc]

On June 9, President Nixon began to step up airpower in Vietnam by tripling the number of USAF fighter-bombers in Southeast Asia; tripling the number of aircraft carriers (from 2 to 6) with two more in route, and quadrupling the number of B-52s.[dcccxci]

On December 14, President Nixon told the North Vietnamese they would feel the consequences if they did not begin to negotiate "seriously." When, in Nixon's opinion, they did not start negotiating seriously, Hanoi did begin to suffer the consequences during a "Christmas bombing" known as "Linebacker II."[dcccxcii] After twelve days, Hanoi said it would continue peace negotiations once bombing above the 20th Parallel was stopped.[dcccxciii]

In response, Nixon ordered a halt to the "Christmas bombing" during which time Hanoi and Haiphong were reduced to rubble by more bombs than had been dropped in the three preceding years.[dcccxciv]

On January 8, 1973, serious negotiations between Washington and Hanoi began, and on January 23, 1973, Nixon announced that an agreement to end the war had been reached and that a cease fire would go into effect at 0800 hours on January 28, 1973.[dcccxcv]

On January 27, Washington announced the termination of the draft[dcccxcvi] and, the same day, Lt. Colonel William B. Noble was killed by an artillery shell at 2100 hours making him the last U.S. serviceman killed in Vietnam before the peace treaty went into effect.[dcccxcvii]

On February 12, 1973, Hanoi released 20 U.S. POWs and between February 12 and February 27 one hundred and twenty-two more POWs were released. However, the release program temporarily came to a halt on February 27 when Hanoi accused the U.S. of encouraging South Vietnam to violate the cease-fire agreement.[dcccxcviii]

SUMMARY

When Richard Nixon became president of the United States in January 1969, he promised to bring all the troops (and POWs) in Vietnam home and turn the ground war over to the South Vietnamese. He also privately expressed hope of ending the Vietnam War as well as the Cold War by taking advantage of a rift between China and Russia.

However, Nixon, like Johnson, refused to abandon the people of South Vietnam and President Thieu. Therefore, the fighting continued with North Vietnam mounting a second Tet offensive in February 1969. As in "Tet 68" Hanoi once again suffered heavy causalities, losing over 100,000 men but, once again, it believed the offensive was a success because of the adverse impact it had on the American public.

Hanoi was correct about this adverse impact as evidenced by the 400,000 war protestors who gathered shortly after Tet 69 for a three-day rally outside of Woodstock, New York and by the 250,000 more who marched down Washington D.C.'s Pennsylvania Avenue in November.

Opponents of the war were further galvanized on April 30, 1970, when Nixon announced that he had sent combat troops into Cambodia. This incursion was viewed as illegal in Congress and in colleges where students at Kent State University were killed when the National Guard was called in to control the rioting.

By May 8, 1970, two hundred colleges and universities were shut down and classes were disrupted by students on 400 of the campuses remaining open. In Washington D.C., seventy-five to one hundred thousand people gathered at the White House to protest the war.

Meanwhile, back in the jungle a young "Buck" Sergeant who had heard the 4th Infantry Division might be ordered into Cambodia went to his JAG office looking for someone to represent him if he refused to go. He was a very young infantryman (20-21) who had "earned his stripes" in the bush, and who had no problem finishing his tour in the bush, but did not want to participate in, what he thought, was an illegal war in Cambodia.

This young sergeant ended up in my office and I told him I would be happy to represent him but added that, off the top of my head, I thought an order to fight in Cambodia would probably be a lawful order. Units of the Fourth Division were subsequently ordered into Cambodia; however, I do not know if this sergeant received orders to go, as I never saw him again.

If I had seen him again as a defendant his case would have been difficult to win because the Gulf of Tonkin Resolution (which was in effect until January 1971) gave the president the authority to:

> take all necessary steps, *including the use of armed force to assist any* member or *protocol state* of the Southeast Asia Collective Defense Treaty *requesting assistance in defense of its freedom.* (Emphasis mine)

Since the president of Cambodia (a protocol state of the Southeast Asia Collective Defense Treaty) requested U.S. assistance on April 20, 1970, Nixon had the legal authority to commit U.S. troops to Cambodia, which he did on April 28, 1970.

Legal, or not, the Cambodian incursion was not popular at home or in Hanoi which, as a result, increased its fighting in the South. In turn, Nixon viewed this increased fighting in the South as a violation of

Johnson's 1968 bombing halt and went on the offensive with strategic bombing of the North.

As part of this bombing increase the Air Force tripled the number of its fighter-bombers in Southeast Asia, more than tripled the number of aircraft carriers; quadrupled the number of its B-52's, and, by May 9, reached 1967-1968 bombing levels, when the bombing of North Vietnam was at its height.

Even though the North was increasing its fighting in the South and even though negotiations in Paris remained at a stalemate, Nixon continued to reduce the number of troops in Vietnam. By December 31, 1970, U.S. troop strength was down to 334,000, and by April 26, 1971, it was down to 281,000; the lowest level since July 1966. And, by December 31, 1971, there were only 157,000 U.S. troops in Vietnam.

For those who remained, however, the fighting was far from over. On January 21, 1972, for example, very angry soldiers on Firebase Melanie took extreme exception to the administration's assertion that those left in South Vietnam were only there in a "defensive" posture and were not in combat.[dcccxcix]

In January 1972, the stalled Paris peace talks reconvened, but the Communist delegation again said that one of its preconditions to an agreement was the removal of President Thieu who had been reelected in August 1970. Abandoning the Thieu government and the people of South Vietnam, however, remained a deal breaker for Nixon; therefore, no meaningful negotiations took place at the reconvened Paris peace talks.

On February 16, 1972, negotiations were still stalled in Paris, and at home only 52% of those questioned in a Gallup Poll approved of the way the war was being handled. But Nixon's popularity began to rise after he visited the Peoples Republic of China on February 21. On this first-ever trip to Communist China Nixon began the process of normalizing relations and establishing diplomatic ties between the two countries. A few months later Nixon's popularity rose even further when, with another first, he met General Secretary Brezhnev in Moscow and they launched dente.

While Nixon was getting along better with China and Russia in 1972 not even his troop reductions had brought better results from North Vietnam; therefore, he ordered the mining of all major North Vietnamese ports on May 8. This action was denounced by China, the Soviet Union, and their eastern allies; however, they offered no military resistance.

The heavy air attacks Nixon ordered on May 8 were widened on May 23 to include bridges, pipelines, power plants, troops, troop training facilities, and rail lines.

Throughout this period the U.S. continued to reduce its troop level which by June 30, 1972, was down to 47,000, but as the U.S. reduced its troop levels, its pressure through airpower increased.

At the end of June, Nixon, in an attempt to reduce tension among the younger generation, announced that in the future no draftee would go to Vietnam unless he volunteered to do so.

As October began Nixon's eyes were on the upcoming presidential election in November and he very much wanted to announce that a peace agreement had been reached before this election. He, therefore, stepped-up the bombing to make Hanoi more inclined to deal and, in fact, over the next three weeks a draft cease-fire agreement was hammered out. However, in the haste to come up with this peace agreement President Thieu had been excluded from the process, and when he was finally shown the draft he rejected it outright calling it a "surrender of the South Vietnamese people to the Communists" because it did not recognize South Vietnam as a sovereign state. To address Thieu's (valid) concerns negotiations began again and were ongoing when Nixon defeated "peace-candidate" George McGovern on November 7, 1972, with 97% of the electoral vote.

While Nixon may have won the election, Kissinger was getting nowhere with Hanoi and the deadlocked negotiations completely ended on December 14. When negotiations broke down Nixon, with his new found mandate, told Hanoi that if they did not start to negotiate "seriously" they would suffer the consequences. When, in Nixon's opinion, Hanoi refused to begin serious negotiations he ordered the so-called "Christmas bombing" of the densely populated area between Hanoi and Haiphong. This bombing probably would have brought retaliation by China and/or Russia if Nixon had not first paved the way by establishing "diplomatic relations" with the two countries but, as it was, there were only some muted protests.

With no intervention by China or Russia Hanoi began to negotiate in earnest and during these negotiations a draft agreement that provided for a sovereign North and South Vietnam was finally reached. Even so, Nixon knew that no matter what agreement was hammered out Thieu would still be concerned about the safety of his country; therefore, Nixon sent him two secret letters of assurance to induce him to sign any future peace agreement. In the first letter, dated November 14, 1972, Nixon absolutely assured Thieu that if Hanoi refused to abide by the terms of an agreement he would "take swift and retaliatory action."[cm] In a second letter, dated January 5, 1973, Nixon promised Thieu that the U.S. would "respond with full force should the settlement be violated by North Vietnam."[cmi]

On January 27, 1973, a peace agreement, the centerpiece of which provided for a sovereign North and South Vietnam that would eventually be unified by "peaceful means," was finally signed. But a major negative to the agreement, from President Theiu's point of view, was that it left approximately 150,000 NVA soldiers in South Vietnam.[cmii]

In spite of this negative, Thieu had been convinced to sign because of the two letters of assurance from Nixon.[cmiii] And, it did seem like Nixon would be able to fulfill his promises since he had just been reelected with 97% of the electoral vote and had just brought the war to an end by applying maximum pressure on the North. The United States, after all, had similarly promised to enforce the Korean cease-fire and, by 1973, peace in Korea had been on-going for two decades.[cmiv]

President Nixon took office in January 1969 promising to end the war and, while it took him four years, he did so in 1973. Unfortunately, 20,000 more Americans had to die.

When Nixon became president, he inherited an imperfect situation and four years later he reached an imperfect solution that had: U.S. troops out of Vietnam; POW's on their way home; a sovereign South Vietnam in control of over 75% of its territory and 93% of its population, and more than a million men in its armed forces.

Nixon, however, "had no illusions that the North Vietnamese would willingly abide by the cease-fire. But he did expect to compel compliance by threatening and, if necessary, resuming—the bombing that had caused Hanoi to accept the cease fire in the first place. As Kissinger recalled, the hope was "'that Nixon's renown for ruthlessness would deter gross violations.'"[cmv]

PHOTOGRAPHS 1969 to 1973

A wounded comrade being carried through troubled waters in 1969. (National Archives)

A member of the 3rd Battalion 9th Marines wounded during Operation Dewy Canyon in the A Shau Valley on February 20, 1969. (National Archives)

NORTHERN _____ *District of* ILLINOIS _____

_____ EASTERN _____ *Division*

THE UNITED STATES OF AMERICA

vs.

DAVID T. DELLINGER, et al.

INDICTMENT

IOLATION; Title 18, United States
Sections 371, 231(a)(1)

On March 20, 1969, a grand jury returned an Indictment against the Chicago Eight (eventually Seven). All defendants were charged with conspiring to incite a riot; six were charged with crossing state lines with the intent to incite a riot, and two were charged with instructing others in the construction and use of an incendiary device. (National Archives)

On March 26, 1969, a tired Fourth Infantry Division Captain and his men on patrol in the Central Highland's Chu Pa Mountains. (From the VA002321 Douglas Pike Photograph Collection, courtesy of the Vietnam Center and Sam Johnson Vietnam Archive, Texas Tech University.)

On March 26, 1969, in the early morning fog, elements of the Fourth Infantry Division lay down covering fire in the dense Central Highland jungle. (From the VA002328 Douglas Pike Photograph Collection, courtesy of the Vietnam Center and Sam Johnson Vietnam Archive, Texas Tech University.)

In April 1969, assault helicopters prepare to take Fourth Infantry Division Special Forces to designated locations in the central highlands during Operation Wayne Grey. (National Archives)

On October 16, 1969, a Medevac helicopter on its way to pick up an injured member of the 101st Airborne Division. (National Archives)

On October 17, 1969, members of the 101st Airborne Division discuss tactics outside a Montagnard village in the central highlands. (National Archives)

The author on the Nha Trang airstrip in 1969.

On May 4, 1970, the Mayor of Kent, Ohio called in 1,300 National Guardsmen to help control Kent State University students who had been rioting for several days in protest of the U.S. incursion into Cambodia. This confrontation tragically resulted in 4 dead students (two of whom were not protesting) and the wounding of nine others one of whom was paralyzed for life. (National Archives)

Reaction on Kent State campus as the National Guard fired 67 shots into a crowd killing four and wounding nine in 13 seconds. America was outraged but not only at the National Guard; according to a Gallup Poll taken at the time, 58 percent of those interviewed blamed the students for the violence. Sharing this opinion was a passerby, paralyzed during the incident who, after coming out of an induced coma, sent an open letter to the protestors which he began by saying, "Dear communist hippie radical, I hope by the time you read this, you are dead." (National Archives)

Old Shoes, 5/23/1970. (National Archives)

MIG hit on left wing by the 20mm canon of an F-105 in an undated photograph. (National Achieves)

On January 15, 1970, members of the 101st Airborne Division (Airmobile) play baseball with children of the Ap Uu Thoung hamlet, near Hue, as part of the 101st Division's pacification operation. (National Archives)

On March 21, 1970, a member of the First Air Calvary Division catches some rays while enjoying a Pepsi and reading the Stars and Stripes. (National Archives)

A Navy Patrol Craft Fast (PCF)-38 patrolling the Cai Ngay canal in April 1970. (National Achieves)

On May 14, 1970, a Montagnard girl in the central highlands watches a
convoy move toward Djerang to help support the Cambodian incursion.
(National Archives)

An ARVN soldier in Phanh-Ban, 17 miles east of Danang, after half the village was destroyed on the night of June 10, 1970. (National Archives)

On August 21, 1970, members of the 25th Infantry Division cross a stream during a Search and Clear Operation near Fire Support Base Kien in Tay Ninh Province. (National Archives)

Members of the 1st ARVN Division move along a trail on October 8, 1970, during an assault operation near Firebase O'Reilly. (National Archives)

On January 19,1971, a squad leader in the 11th Light Brigade coordinates an attempt to take out a sniper on Hill 56 (seventy miles southeast of Chu Lai). (National Archives)

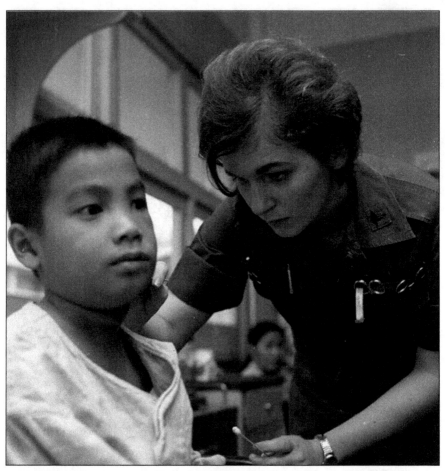

On July 12, 1971, an Army nurse treats a Vietnamese boy in the Pediatrics Ward of the 3rd Field Hospital, slightly Northwest of Saigon. (National Archives)

B-52 landing in Thailand at U-Tapo AFB, in October 1972. (National Archives)

On December 5, 1972, B-52s leave Guam as part of the Linebacker missions over North Vietnam. (National Archives)

On January 23, 1973, President Nixon holds a press conference at the White House to announce that an agreement to end the war had just about been reached. (National Archives)

In February 1973, POWs react to "wheels up" as their plane leaves Hanoi. (National Archives)

On February 12, 1973, a group of women await the return of their loved ones at Camp Pendleton in California. (National Archives)

CHAPTER EIGHT
February 1973-April 1975

In a secret letter dated February 1, 1973, President Nixon informed Hanoi that the United States would give North Vietnam billions of dollars in reconstruction, and other, aid. But, if for no other reason, this promise was later considered null and void because Vietnam had not kept the terms of the peace agreement; therefore, Congress passed a series of resolutions prohibiting any such payments.[cmvi]

On February 17, Mao Zedong told Henry Kissinger that, "We were enemies in the past, but now we are friends."[cmvii] At the same time, Mao proposed establishing a "'strategic line' which extended from Europe, Turkey, Iran [and] Pakistan, to Japan, China and the United States...opposing the Soviet Union irrespective of ideological position."[cmviii]

Only four days later the Laotian government, led by Souvanna Phouma, reached a cease-fire agreement with the Communist led Pathet Lao after 20 years of fighting.[cmix]

By March 1973, conditions in South Vietnam were greatly improved; therefore, as a countermeasure, Hanoi began preparing for an all-out offensive in the South. This, in turn, caused Nixon to threaten intervention in the event the North violated the cease-fire agreement.[cmx]

In May 1973, Washington established a United States Liaison Office in Beijing and Beijing established a Chinese Liaison Office in Washington as a step toward building formal diplomatic relations.[cmxi]

On June 4, 1973, Congress passed the Case-Church amendment blocking presidential spending on U.S. military activities in Indochina after August 15.[cmxii]

In a little-noticed incident a year earlier (in June 1972) five men were arrested and charged with breaking into the Democratic National Headquarters at the Watergate Hotel in Washington D.C.[cmxiii] A year later, on June 27, 1973, John Dean (then Legal Counsel to the president) appeared before Congress and testified that Nixon was deeply involved in trying to cover up this break-in.[cmxiv]

On August 3, President Nixon sent a letter to Congress expressing his grave personal reservations about the potentially dangerous consequences of the Case-Church legislation that cut off funding for U.S. military activities in Indochina. (Document 1)

At midnight on August 14, the bombing of Cambodia ended as required by the Case-Church amendment.[cmxv]

Candidates from President Thieu's party swept the August 26th national elections in South Vietnam.[cmxvi]

On Yom Kipper 1973, (October 5) Syria and Egypt, backed by the Soviet Union, attacked Israel, but Israel's counter attack, in what is known as the Yom Kipper war, almost destroyed the Egyptian forces. At this point, Moscow threatened to intervene but when Nixon countered, by putting the U.S. military on worldwide alert, the Soviets backed off and agreed to a ceasefire.[cmxvii]

On October 10, Vice President Spiro Agnew pleaded guilty to criminal tax violations and resigned; he was replaced by Congressman Gerald R. Ford, Jr, (R).

Six days after Agnew's resignation, Henry Kissinger and Le Duc Tho were awarded the Nobel Peace Prize for negotiating the Paris Peace Accords. Kissinger accepted his award while Le Duc Tho refused to accept his until he felt there was truly peace in Vietnam.[cmxviii]

On October 24, U.S. Intelligence reported that Hanoi had infiltrated 70,000 men into South Vietnam since the cease-fire.[cmxix] And, during the same month, North Vietnam attempted to get military aid from Moscow and Peking but was turned down by both.[cmxx]

At the end of December of that year (1973) the estimated size of the South Vietnamese armed force was 1,110,000.[cmxxi]

In spite of the cease-fire, 237 Americans were killed in action in 1973 and 24 were wounded. During the same year 27,901 South Vietnamese were killed in action and 131,936 were wounded.[cmxxii]

On January 4, 1974, President Thieu asserted that the war had restarted and he responded to North Vietnam's attacks by ordering counterattacks to retake lost territory. This fighting ended any outward attempt to adhere to the 1973 Paris Peace Accords.[cmxxiii]

At the end of March, South Vietnam's Information Minister said that North Vietnam was planning an offensive designed to conquer South Vietnam.[cmxxiv]

Laotian Premier Souvanna Phouma, (a U.S. Ally) formed a coalition government on April 5 with the communist Pathet Lao forces headed by Prince Souphanouvong.[cmxxv]

In early May, the House Judiciary Committee initiated impeachment hearings against President Nixon to determine his role in the Watergate break-in, and the House voted to impeach him on July 30, 1974.[cmxxvi] Nixon resigned the presidency on August 9th to avoid a trial in the Senate. Before starting down the red carpet to board his awaiting helicopter, Nixon turned to Ford, who had assumed the presidency, and said, "Goodbye, Mr. President;" to which Ford replied, "Goodbye, Mr. President."[cmxxvii]

Within a month Ford pardoned former President Nixon.[cmxxviii] In addition, a week after pardoning Nixon, Ford offered amnesty to those who evaded the draft during the Vietnam War.[cmxxix]

In November 1974, a year after China and Russia turned down North Vietnam's request for help, they (China and Russia) informed Kissinger that, in their opinion, South Vietnam was doomed and, therefore, they were considering ways to expand their influence in the area---China in Cambodia and Russia in Vietnam.[cmxxx]

South Vietnamese intelligence reported on December 3 that it had obtained North Vietnamese documents indicating the NVA planned to sharply increase its fighting in the South during the upcoming months.[cmxxxi]

In 1974, two hundred and seven U.S. servicemen were killed in action. During the same year, according to U.S. records, 31,000 South Vietnamese were killed in action and 155,000 were wounded. South Vietnam, however, reported that 80,000 South Vietnamese were killed in 1974 (more than in any other year of the war).[cmxxxii]

On January 1, 1975, the communist Khmer Rouge in Cambodia began their assault on Phnom Penh.[cmxxxiii]

As February 1975 drew to a close, a bipartisan congressional delegation sent by President Ford arrived in Vietnam to assess the situation on the ground and, upon return, all but one recommended increasing military and humanitarian aid to Vietnam. Even so, a week later the Democratic caucus in both the House and Senate voted to oppose further aid to Vietnam and Cambodia.[cmxxxiv]

On March 24, Hanoi set the end of April 1975 as its timetable for capturing Saigon.[cmxxxv]

Three days later President Ford sent General Weyland, the Army Chief of Staff and former MACV commander, on a weeklong mission to Vietnam to evaluate the situation and, upon arrival, Weyland assured Thieu that Ford steadfastly supported South Vietnam.[cmxxxvi] When he returned from this mission Weyland informed Congress that South Vietnam could not survive without additional aid from the United States and when reporters asked if South Vietnam could survive even if given additional aid, Weyland said there was "a chance."[cmxxxvii]

In March 1975, due to pressure from the antiwar movement in the United States and the failure of the Cambodian government to deter the Khmer Rouge, the United States terminated its assistance to Cambodia.[cmxxxviii]

On April 9, ARVN forces resolutely defended the city of Xuan Loc (outside of Saigon) against the swarming North Vietnamese Army and South Vietnamese General Le Minh Dao said, "I don't care how many divisions the other side sends against me...I will knock them down!"[cmxxxix] The next day, President Ford, impressed by the ARVN stand at Xuan Loc, appeared before a joint session of Congress and personally requested assistance for the beleaguered people of Indochina.[cmxl]

On April 16, 1975, approximately eight months after Congress forced the U.S. to stop bombing in Cambodia, its capital (Phnom Penh) fell to the Khmer Rouge regime.[cmxli]

Within two weeks of the fall of Phnom Penh North Vietnamese tanks knocked down the gates of the presidential palace and acting President Duong Van (Big) Minh surrendered the Republic of Vietnam (South Vietnam) to NVA Colonel Bui Tin of the Democratic Republic of Vietnam (North Vietnam) ending the war (for the second time) between North and South Vietnam.[cmxlii]

SUMMARY

When North and South Vietnam entered into a cease-fire agreement in January 1973 life in the South actually began to improve causing a discouraged Hanoi to start making plans to try and take over South Vietnam by force. While making those plans, however, North Vietnam did recognize that if it exercised this option Nixon might start bombing again.

But U.S. intervention never came (as promised) because the U.S. Congress banned further military spending in Indochina after August 15, 1973, without Congressional approval (which also never came). This ban was enacted in spite of Nixon's August 3, 1973, letter to Congress explaining the potential consequences of the legislation.

South Vietnam's goal, on the other hand, was to unite Vietnam through "peaceful means" as provided for in the 1973 Paris Peace Accords. To this end, Saigon persistently attempted to get Hanoi to set an election timetable; however, all such attempts were rebuffed while Hanoi continued to weigh its military options.

As Hanoi's intention became more apparent South Vietnam's Information Minister warned on March 30, 1974, that North Vietnam was planning a takeover of the South. Even so, on April 4 the U.S. House of Representatives rejected Nixon's request to increase military aid to South Vietnam.

This rejection, however, should not have come as a surprise since Nixon's role in the Watergate cover-up was becoming more apparent. Moreover, his fortunes worsened when the House Judiciary Committee opened impeachment hearings against him in May 1974, and worsened even further on July 30, 1974, when the House voted to impeach him.

A week later, on August 5, with Nixon now basically a lame duck, Congress reduced military aid to South Vietnam to $1 billion from $2.8 billion the year before.[cmxliii]

Nixon resigned the presidency on August 9 in order to avoid a trial in the Senate, and immediately after his resignation the House proposed reducing military aid to South Vietnam to $700 million instead of the $1 billion it had just appropriated.[cmxliv] Upon learning of this further reduction, the Ambassador in Saigon sent the Secretary of State a "Secret" cable in which he strenuously argued against Congressional approval of this lower amount. As part of his argument, he pointed out that Hanoi was discouraged and disappointed because the people of South Vietnam had not wanted to become communists when the war ended. In addition, he said Hanoi was discouraged and disappointed by serious economic problems and was trying to decide whether to use its limited resources to help alleviate these problems or to put the resources into its military and attack South Vietnam.

According to this August 1974 cable, recent intelligence showed that if Hanoi should come to conclude the U.S. was:

> disengaging politically and economically from the South they would suspend serious economic planning and hold their resources in reserve to use militarily against South Vietnam at some opportune moment [possibly] as early as the Spring of 1975 when the South Vietnamese Government equipment and material shortages could be most severe if there is no additional assistance. Hanoi's long and short-term intentions thus hinge critically on its current estimates of the extent and durability of U.S. commitments to the South Vietnamese.

> We believe that a reduction in Military Assistance to the RVN by over 50 percent of the Administration's request will tip the

balance in Hanoi irrevocably in favor of the military option.[cmxlv] (Document 2)

This plea fell on deaf ears and two days after Nixon's resignation, Congress further reduced U.S. military aid to South Vietnam to $700 million.[cmxlvi]

By September 1974, with the United States now clearly disengaging, the NVA had pushed to within 15 miles of Hue and on December 3 South Vietnam's intelligence came into possession of documents showing that Hanoi planned to sharply increase its fighting in the spring.

U.S. military aid to Saigon was down to $583 million by 1975 which was "half the level judged necessary even in the absence of a major North Vietnamese offensive."[cmxlvii] Accordingly, in early 1975 the Chairmen of South Vietnam's Joint General Staff issued a directive to his troops telling them that "From this moment on we must conserve and economize on the use of each individual bullet, each drop of gasoline."[cmxlviii]

On January 6, 1975, Phuoc Long Province, about 60 miles north of Saigon, fell with no intervention by the United States (as threatened publicly and promised privately by Nixon) leaving President Thieu to ask, "How can the free world abandon us?"[cmxlix] This was more than a fair question since sixty to one hundred thousand South Vietnamese had been killed in action while defending their country in 1973 and 1974.

Well aware of South Vietnam's sacrifice, President Ford, on January 28, asked Congress for an additional $500,000 to help this beleaguered country, but his plea fell on deaf ears. Therefore, on February 26, he sent a bipartisan congressional delegation to evaluate the situation on the ground. Upon their return all but one member recommended increasing military and humanitarian aid to the embattled nation, yet Congress refused to act.

This, again, was not a proud moment in American history considering that, in January 1973, South Vietnam signed a peace agreement that left 150,000 NVA soldiers in its midst, after being induced to do so by a U.S. promise to intervene if North Vietnam broke the cease-fire agreement. Not only did the United States fail to intervene, it also deprived Saigon of the funding necessary to defend itself.

The decision to abandon South Vietnam to communism in 1975 was not a proud moment, but it should not have come as a surprise as it was eerily similar to its decision to abandon China, an ally throughout World War II, to communism in 1949.

PHOTOGRAPHS & DOCUMENTS FROM 1974 TO 1975

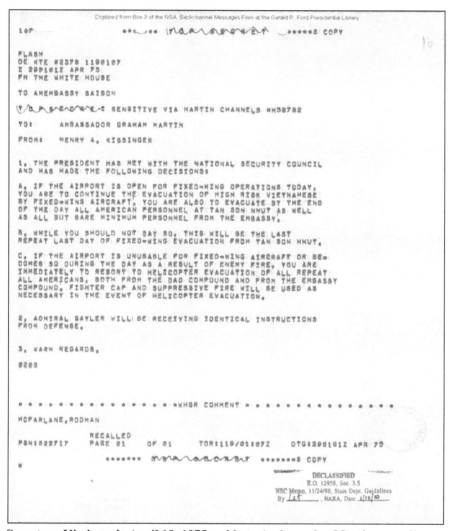

Secretary Kissinger's April 19, 1975, cable to Ambassador Martin regarding the evacuation of Saigon. (National Archives)

JOHNNY CASH

September 10, 1974

President Gerald Ford
The White House
Washington, District of Columbia

Dear Mr. President:

June and I support you and your decisions concerning pardons and amnesty.

We are much pleased to see that you are praying for guidance and wisdom, for that is our daily prayer for you. Remember that you can't do the will of God without getting a lot of people against you. Always take strength in knowing that God is with you, and when He is with you, men will not stand against you long.

God bless you and your family. If we can ever do anything for you, let us know.

Sincerely,

Johnny Cash

JC/lg

A September 10, 1974, letter Johnny Cash sent to President Ford commending him on the pardon of Nixon and the granting of amnesty to Vietnam War resisters. (National Archives)

```
Robert + Unchinged
6 May 1975

O 191801Z APR 75
FM THE WHITE HOUSE
TO AMEMBASSY SAIGON
ZEN
T-O-P-S-E-C-R-E-T SENSITIVE EXCLUSIVELY EYES ONLY
DELIVER AT OPENING OF BUSINESS VIA MARTIN CHANNELS WH50728

APRIL 19, 1975

TO:     GRAHAM MARTIN

FROM:   SECRETARY KISSINGER

    1. THANKS FOR YOUR 0715.

    2. MY ASS ISN'T COVERED. I CAN ASSURE YOU I WILL BE
HANGING SEVERAL YARDS HIGHER THAN YOU WHEN THIS IS ALL OVER.

    3. NOW THAT WE ARE AGREED THAT THE NUMBER OF AMERICANS
WILL BE REDUCED BY TUESDAY TO A SIZE WHICH CAN BE EVACUATED
BY A SINGLE HELICOPTER LIFT, THE EXACT NUMBERS ARE COMPLETELY
UP TO YOU. THAT HAVING BEEN DECIDED, I WILL STOP BUGGING
YOU ON NUMBERS, EXCEPT TO SAY THAT YOU SHOULD ENSURE THAT THE
EMBASSY REMAINS ABLE TO FUNCTION EFFECTIVELY.

    4. YOU SHOULD GO AHEAD WITH YOUR DISCUSSION WITH THIEU.
IN YOUR SOUNDINGS RELATIVE TO HIS POSSIBLE RESIGNATION,
HOWEVER, THE MATTER OF TIMING IS ALSO OF GREAT SIGNIFICANCE.
IN ANY EVENT ANY RESIGNATION SHOULD NOT TAKE PLACE PRECIPITATELY
BUT SHOULD BE TIMED FOR MAXIMUM LEVERAGE IN THE POLITICAL
SITUATION. YOU SHOULD KNOW, ALTHOUGH YOU SHOULD NOT INTIMATE
THIS TO THIEU, THAT WE THIS MORNING HAVE MADE AN APPROACH TO
THE SOVIET UNION. WE SHOULD NOT BE SANGUINE ABOUT ANY RESULTS
BUT, IF THERE ARE ANY, THEY COULD EASILY INVOLVE THIEU AS ONE
OF THE BARGAINING POINTS.

    5. YOU SHOULD ALSO KNOW THAT THE FRENCH HAVE APPROACHED US
WITH THE IDEA OF RECONVENING THE PARIS CONFERENCE. WE
TOLD THEM WE WERE OPPOSED AND FELT IT WOULD BE COUNTERPRO-
DUCTIVE.

    WARM REGARDS.
```

GERALD R. FORD LIBRARY

DECLASSIFIED
E.O. 12356, Sec. 3.4
MR 93-39, #53; NSC ltr 2/14/94
By Ut, NARA Date 11/10/94

(196)

Secretary Kissinger's April 19, 1975, cable to Ambassador Martin assuring him that between the two his (Kissinger's) rear end would be the most exposed when everything was over. (National Archives)

President Ford, on April 28, 1975, ordering the evacuation of the last Americans from Vietnam. (National Archives)

```
252              *******          S E C R E T        *****   S COPY
                                                                              4/29/75
FLASH
ESA673TR2659
DE RUKOIR #0000 1191220
Z 291215Z
FM AMEMBASSY SAIGON

TO SECSTATE WASHDC 0000

S E C R E T SAIGON 00000

    PLAN TO CLOSE MISSION SAIGON APPROXIMATELY 0430
SAIGON TIME, DEPENDENT ON PERFORMANCE OF MILITARY EVACUATION
CHANNELS.
    DUE TO NECESSITY TO DESTROY COMMO GEAR, THIS IS THE LAST
SAIGON MESSAGE TO SECSTATE.
S E C R E T
BT
```

```
. . . . . . . . . . . . . . *WHSR COMMENT . . . . . . . . . . . . . . . . . .

HAK, SCOWCROFT, LL

            RECALLED
PSN:023695  PAGE: 01    OF 01    TOR:119/19:32Z   DTG:291215Z APR 75

            *******         S E C R E T       *******S COPY
0
        DECLASSIFIED
Authority  NLF MR 80-19 Doc #1
By      RAR   NLF Date 11/4/80
```

Last telegram sent from the American Embassy in Saigon. Within 18 hours of its April 29, 1975, transmission, 1,000 American civilians and 7,000 South Vietnamese were evacuated. Saigon fell to the NVA on April 30, 1975. (National Archives)

A Marine rescues a refugee baby during Operation Eagle Pull when Cambodia was evacuated in 1975. (National Archives)

A South Vietnamese helicopter pilot and his family arrive on the USS Enterprise in the 1975 evacuation of Saigon during Operation Frequent Wind. (National Archives)

A South Vietnamese refugee mourns the loss of her fallen country in May 1975. This poignant photograph appeared on the cover of the November/December edition of the 2018 Vietnam Veterans of America Magazine. (From the VA002722 Bryan Grigsby Photograph Collection, courtesy of the Vietnam Center and Sam Johnson Vietnam Archive, Texas Tech University.)

CHAPTER NINE
December 1975-2001

When the Vietnam War ended in April 1975 the fighting was over yet the Cold War continued and so did frosty relations between the United States and Vietnam. One thing that added to these frosty relations was the "unaccounted for POW issue," and this problem grew over the years. In December 1975, U.S. officials concluded that "no Americans [were] still being held in Indochina" and that "a total accounting …is not now, and never will be possible."[cml]

The problem started to grow in 1978, when it was determined that there were 224 unaccounted for U.S. POWs in Vietnam. The problem grew further in 1980, when the number of unaccounted for POWs increased to 2,500 after U.S. officials decided to include those identified as "killed in action/body not recovered" in the "unaccounted for POW" count.[cmli] Thereafter, "unaccounted for POWs" became a major issue in post-war relations with Vietnam.

After taking control of South Vietnam in 1975, North Vietnam set aside the NLF in July 1976 and unified North and South Vietnam as the Socialist Republic of Vietnam (SRV). This marked the beginning of dark and violent times in Vietnam, Cambodia and Laos.[cmlii] Because of Vietnam's "ferocious and barbarous aggression Cambodia broke off diplomatic relations with the SRV on December 31, 1977. In January 1978, Vietnam wiped out half of Cambodia's army and took control of 400 square miles of Cambodian territory along the Vietnam-Cambodia border.[cmliii]

Meanwhile back in the states, President Jimmy Carter pardoned some 10,000 Vietnam-era draft evaders in January 1977, and he also began the process of upgrading the discharge certificates of approximately 100,000 Vietnam-era deserters.[cmliv]

While the Vietnam War had ended in 1975 the Cold War had not, and in July 1977, the Soviet Union sent a number of SS-20 missiles to satellite countries in Eastern Europe and those countries, in turn, set the sites of those missiles on major Western European targets.[cmlv]

On July 3, 1978, China terminated all economic assistance to Vietnam because seventy to ninety thousand ethnic Chinese had been forced to flee the country just to survive.[cmlvi] Moreover, the following month, China recalled its delegation from Hanoi after accusing Vietnam of occupying its border territory.[cmlvii]

The United States began formal diplomatic relations with China on January 1, 1979.[cmlviii]

In January 1979, Vietnam installed a puppet government in Cambodia after taking military control of the country. The next month China, in retaliation for Vietnam's invasion of Cambodia and to punish Hanoi for mistreating the ethnic Chinese in Vietnam, sent more than 200,000 troops up to 40 miles inside Vietnam along their 480-mile common border.[cmlix]

The United States (now the mediator) criticized Vietnam for invading Cambodia and called on China to withdraw its troops from Vietnam while the Soviet Union advised China it needed to stop before it was too late. Vietnam, in the meantime, asked the United Nations "to force the aggressive Chinese troops to withdraw from Vietnam."[cmlx]

In early March 1979, China announced its withdrawal from Vietnam and later said it had lost 20,000 troops during the fighting and that Vietnam had lost 50,000.[cmlxi]

Although Vietnam was no longer daily front-page news, the international Cold War power struggle continued. On the positive side, President Carter and General Secretary Brezhnev signed the 2nd Strategic Arms Limitation Treaty (SALT II) in mid-June 1979.[cmlxii] On the negative side, the Soviet's SS-20 missiles remained aimed at Western Europe, which prompted NATO, in response, to say that it planned to obtain long-range U.S. Pershing II and cruise missiles and aim them at Soviet cities.[cmlxiii] And, most disturbing, Soviet Special Forces ousted the government in Afghanistan on December 27, 1979, and replaced it with a puppet government controlled by Moscow.[cmlxiv]

The usually nonaggressive President Carter responded forcefully to this invasion saying, in his January 23, 1980, State of the Union address, that:

> ... during the last three and a half decades, the relationship between our country, the United States of America, and the Soviet Union is the most critical factor in determining whether the world will live at peace or be engulfed in global conflict...

> But [with the invasion of Afghanistan] the Soviet Union has taken a radical and an aggressive new step. It's using its great military power against a relatively defenseless nation. The implications of the Soviet invasion of Afghanistan could pose the most serious threat to the peace since the Second World War...

> The Soviet Union is going to have to answer some basic questions: Will it help promote a more stable international environment in which its own legitimate, peaceful concerns can be pursued? Or will it continue to expand its military power far beyond its genuine security needs, and use that power for colonial conquest? The Soviet Union must realize that its

decision to use military force in Afghanistan will be costly to every political and economic relationship it values.

****

This situation demands careful thought, steady nerves, and resolute action, not only for this year but for many years to come. It demands collective efforts to meet this new threat to security in the Persian Gulf and in Southwest Asia…

****

Meeting this challenge will take national will, diplomatic and political wisdom, economic sacrifice, and, of course, military capability. We must call on the best that is in us to preserve the security of this crucial region.

Let our position be absolutely clear: An attempt by any outside force to gain control of the Persian Gulf region will be regarded as an assault on the vital interests of the United States of America, and such an assault will be repelled by any means necessary, including military force.[cmlxv]

On March 9, 1980, China pledged to back the Cambodian guerrillas fighting the Vietnamese supported government in Cambodia.[cmlxvi] And, on the same day, negotiations between Vietnam and China again broke down because Vietnam refused to discuss its invasion of Cambodia.[cmlxvii]

Also in March 1980, UNICEF announced, "That the prospect of famine [in Cambodia] ha[d] significantly increased" because of a second harvest failure and because of logistical problems.[cmlxviii] And, in October of that year, the UN General Assembly approved a resolution calling on Vietnam to withdraw its troops from Cambodia.[cmlxix]

Ronald Reagan was sworn in as president of the United States on January 20, 1981, and with his election came a "renewed push [by the U.S.] to win the Cold War."[cmlxx] When asked at his first press conference, on January 29, 1981, whether he thought the Cold War would continue or if he thought détente might be possible, the president said:

> Well, so far detente's been a one-way street that the Soviet Union has used to pursue its own aims. I don't have to think of an answer as to what I think their intentions are; they have repeated it. I know of no leader of the Soviet Union since the revolution, and including the present leadership, that has not more than once repeated that their goal must be the promotion of world revolution and a one-world Socialist or Communist state, whichever word you want to use.
>
> Now, as long as they do that and as long as they, at the same time, have openly and publicly declared that the only morality they recognize is what will further their cause, meaning they reserve unto themselves the right to commit any crime, to lie, to cheat, in order to attain that [end] and that [this] is moral, not immoral, and we operate on a different set of standards, I think when you do business with them, even at a detente, you keep that in mind.[cmlxxi]

While addressing the British Parliament on June 8 of that year, President Reagan took on the topic of Soviet totalitarianism in the twentieth century saying:

> We're approaching the end of a bloody century plagued by a terrible political invention—totalitarianism. Optimism comes less easily today, not because democracy is less vigorous, but because democracy's enemies have refined their instruments of

repression. Yet optimism is in order, because day by day democracy is proving itself to be a not-at-all-fragile flower. From Stettin on the Baltic to Varna on the Black Sea, the regimes planted by totalitarianism have had more than 30 years to establish their legitimacy. But none—not one regime—has yet been able to risk free elections. Regimes planted by bayonets do not take root.

He then gave his views on the Cold War and the Soviet economy saying:

...the gifts of science and technology have made life much easier for us, they have also made it more dangerous. There are threats now to our freedom, indeed to our very existence, that other generations could never even have imagined.

There is first the threat of global war. No President, no Congress, no Prime Minister, no Parliament can spend a day entirely free of this threat. And I don't have to tell you that in today's world the existence of nuclear weapons could mean, if not the extinction of mankind, then surely the end of civilization as we know it. That's why negotiations on intermediate-range nuclear forces now underway in Europe and the START talks—Strategic Arms Reduction Talks— which will begin later this month, are not just critical to American or Western policy; they are critical to mankind.

*****

Sir Winston Churchill refused to accept the inevitability of war or even that it was imminent. He said, "I do not believe that Soviet Russia desires war. What they desire [are] the fruits of war and the indefinite expansion of their power and doctrines.

But what we have to consider here today while time remains is the permanent prevention of war and the establishment of conditions of freedom and democracy as rapidly as possible in all countries.

Well, this is precisely our mission today: to preserve freedom as well as peace. It may not be easy to see; but I believe we live now at a turning point…

In conclusion, he stated:

I have discussed on other occasions… the elements of Western policies toward the Soviet Union to safeguard our interests and protect the peace. What I am describing now is *a plan* and a hope for the long term—the march of freedom and democracy *which will leave Marxism-Leninism on the ash-heap of history* as it has left other tyrannies which stifle the freedom and muzzle the self-expression of the people. And that's why we must continue our efforts to strengthen NATO even as we move forward with our Zero-Option initiative in the negotiations on intermediate-range forces and our proposal for a one-third reduction in strategic ballistic missile warheads. (Emphasis mine)

Our military strength is a prerequisite to peace, but let it be clear we maintain this strength in the hope it will never be used, for the ultimate determinant in the struggle that's now going on in the world will not be bombs and rockets, but a test of wills and ideas, a trial of spiritual resolve, the values we hold, the beliefs we cherish, the ideals to which we are dedicated…[cmlxxii]

On November 10, 1982, Léonard Brezhnev died and Yuri Andropov became the next general secretary of the Communist Party and Chief of State.[cmlxxiii]

In a speech on March 8, 1983, Reagan said that he would not agree to a nuclear freeze with the Soviets but that he would agree to a cut in weapons and, explaining his reasoning, he said:

> During my first press conference as President, in answer to a direct question, I pointed out that, as good Marxist-Leninists, the Soviet leaders have openly and publicly declared that the only morality they recognize is that which will further their cause, which is world revolution ...

> Well, I think the refusal of many influential people to accept this elementary fact of Soviet doctrine illustrates an historical reluctance to see totalitarian powers for what they are. We saw this phenomenon in the 1930s. We see it too often today.

> This doesn't mean we should isolate ourselves and refuse to seek an understanding with them. I intend to do everything I can to persuade them of our peaceful intent, to remind them that it was the West that refused to use its nuclear monopoly in the forties and fifties for territorial gain and which now proposes a 50-percent cut in strategic ballistic missiles and the elimination of an entire class of land-based, intermediate-range nuclear missiles. At the same time, however, they must be made to understand we will never compromise our principles and standards. We will never give away our freedom. We will never abandon our belief in God. And we will never stop searching for a genuine peace. But we can assure none of these things America stands for through the so-called nuclear freeze solutions proposed by some.

The truth is that a freeze now would be a very dangerous fraud, for that is merely the illusion of peace. The reality is that we must find peace through strength.

I would agree to a freeze if only we could freeze the Soviets' global desires. A freeze at current levels of weapons would remove any incentive for the Soviets to negotiate seriously in Geneva and virtually end our chances to achieve the major arms reductions which we have proposed. Instead, they would achieve their objectives through the freeze …

… let us be aware that while they preach the supremacy of the state, declare its omnipotence over individual man, and predict its eventual domination of all peoples on the Earth, they are the focus of evil in the modern world.

…because [the Soviets] … do not "raise their voices," because they sometimes speak in soothing tones of brotherhood and peace, because, like other dictators before them, they're always making "their final territorial demand," some would have us accept them at their word and accommodate ourselves to their aggressive impulses. But if history teaches anything, it teaches that simple-minded appeasement or wishful thinking about our adversaries is folly. It means the betrayal of our past, the squandering of our freedom.

So, I urge you [not]… to ignore the facts of history and the aggressive impulses of an evil empire, to simply call the arms race a giant misunderstanding and thereby remove yourself from the struggle between right and wrong and good and evil…

I believe we shall rise to the challenge. I believe that communism is another sad, bizarre chapter in human history whose last pages even now are being written...[cmlxxiv]

President Reagan, in his "Star Wars" (Strategic Defense Initiative) speech on March 23, 1983, spoke about the need for a national anti-ballistic missile system which he justified because of the Soviet's massive arms buildup saying that:

> ...During the past decade and a half, the Soviets have built up a massive arsenal of new strategic nuclear weapons—weapons that can strike directly at the United States.

> [On the other hand, he said] (t)he United States introduced its last new intercontinental ballistic missile, the Minute Man III, in 1969, and we're now dismantling our even older Titan missiles. But what has the Soviet Union done in these intervening years? Well, since 1969 the Soviet Union has built five new classes of ICBM's, and upgraded these eight times. As a result, their missiles are much more powerful and accurate than they were several years ago, and they continue to develop more, while ours are increasingly obsolete....

> There was a time [he said] when we were able to offset superior Soviet numbers with higher quality, but today they are building weapons as sophisticated and modern as our own.

> As the Soviets have increased their military power, they've been emboldened to extend that power. They're spreading their military influence in ways that can directly challenge our vital interests and those of our allies.

What if free people could live secure in the knowledge that their security did not rest upon the threat of instant U.S. retaliation to deter a Soviet attack, [what if] we could intercept and destroy strategic ballistic missiles before they reached our own soil or that of our allies?[cmlxxv]

Not only did the rhetoric between the super powers indicate the Cold War was heating up, so did events around the world. The United States overthrew a communist regime in Grenada in October 1983 and replaced it with a democratic government.[cmlxxvi] NATO began deployment of U.S. cruise and Pershing II missiles aimed at Soviet cities in November 1983.[cmlxxvii] And, in July 1984, the Association of Southeast Nations condemned Vietnam's "illegal occupation" of Cambodia.[cmlxxviii]

On March 11, 1985, Mikhail Gorbachev succeeded Konstantin Chernenko (who had briefly succeeded Andropov) and became the general secretary of the Communist party, and Chief of State.[cmlxxix] With Gorbachev the head of state, tensions between the Soviet Union and the United States began to ease.

Tensions between the United States and Vietnam also began to ease in July 1986 when Le Duan, the co-architect of the war between Hanoi and Washington died clearing "the way for the ascension of a younger more reconciliatory generation of leaders to power."[cmlxxx] By December 19, 1986, all of Vietnam's wartime leaders had resigned from its politburo after which Nguyen Van Linh, was elected General Secretary of Vietnam's Communist Party. Shortly thereafter, he brought a series of economic reforms to Vietnam known as Doi Moi "the socialist world's version of the New Deal, introducing free-market reforms to save the communist state."[cmlxxxi]

Even though tensions between the U.S. and Vietnamese governments began to ease in 1986, relations between the two countries remained hampered because the American public was still fixated on the POW problem. Therefore, in January 1987, President Reagan made General John Vessey, Jr., formerly the Chairman of the Joint Chiefs of Staff, his personal emissary on POW/MIA affairs.[cmlxxxii]

In June 1987, President Reagan stood in front of Berlin's Brandenburg Gate and urged Gorbachev to ease Cold War tensions by tearing down the Berlin Wall saying:

> There is one sign the Soviets can make that would be unmistakable, that would advance dramatically the cause of freedom and peace. General Secretary Gorbachev, if you seek peace, if you seek prosperity for the Soviet Union and Eastern Europe, if you seek liberalization: Come here to this gate! Mr. Gorbachev, open this gate! Mr. Gorbachev, tear down this wall![cmlxxxiii]

To address the "POW/MIA problem" Reagan sent General Vessey to Hanoi in July 1987 to get a POW accounting and to discuss the emigration of Amerasians and the release and resettlement of reeducation camp detainees (i.e. political prisoners).[cmlxxxiv]

The Cold War really began to thaw on November 9, 1989, when the Berlin Wall came down.[cmlxxxv]

On January 20, 1989, George H.W. Bush was sworn in as president of the United States.

Finally, after 11 years of fighting, Vietnam finished the withdrawal of its troops from Cambodia on September 26, 1989. During the time of active hostilities some 23,000 Vietnamese soldiers were killed and 55,000 were wounded. [cmlxxxvi]

In 1989, the United States and Vietnam signed the Humanitarian Operation (HO) Agreement under which former reeducation camp detainees began arriving in the United States and the agreement ran until Hanoi released the last detainees in 1992. [cmlxxxvii]

In the summer of 1990, Iraq invaded Kuwait and threatened Saudi Arabia causing the United States, and other coalition forces, to invade Iraq on February 24, 1991. [cmlxxxviii] Announcing victory, after only one hundred hours of fighting, President H.W. Bush said that it was "a proud day for America." And, he added, "By God we've kicked the Vietnam syndrome once and for all." [cmlxxxix]

On July 1, 1991, the Warsaw pact formally disbanded. [cmxc]

In August 1991, the Senate established a Select Committee on POW/MIAs to "provide definitive answers to the many who believed Hanoi continued to hold live Americans in captivity and remained suspicious about a U.S. government cover-up." [cmxci]

Late December 1991, was a time of significant change. Gorbachev resigned on December 25th and the Soviet Union dissolved, officially ending the Cold War. [cmxcii] As a result of this collapse, the former Soviet Union was replaced on December 31 by fifteen independent states, one of which was Russia. [cmxciii]

On September 19, 1992, Vietnam disbanded its National Defense Council which had played such a prominent role during the war. [cmxciv]

The Senate Select Committee on POW/MIA Affairs issued a 1,233-page report on January 13, 1993; it concluded saying, "There is at this time, no compelling evidence that proves that any American remains alive in captivity in Southeast Asia."[cmxcv] Therefore, after "nearly twenty years and billions of dollars," members of congress:

> arrived at the same conclusions [U.S. officials] had in December 1975: 'No Americans are still being held as prisoners in Indochina' and 'a total accounting ... is not now and, never will be possible.'[cmxcvi]

However, even in the face of these findings, 67 percent of those responding to a public opinion poll taken in April 1993 believed Americans were "still being held in Southeast Asia."[cmxcvii] In this regard, historian H. Bruce Franklin opined, "the POW myth...has all the intensity of a religion" in the United States.[cmxcviii] Therefore, in spite of evidence to the contrary, politicians remained aware the public was still concerned about this issue.

On January 20, 1993, William Jefferson Clinton was sworn in as president of the United States.

In a speech on July 2, President Clinton again called for a full accounting of America's POW/MIA but he also took this opportunity to go along with forgiving Vietnam's $140 million debt to the International Monetary Fund; thereby, permitting the resumption of international lending to Vietnam which, by the fall of 1993, totaled almost $2 billion.[cmxcix]

On January 27, 1994, the Senate approved a non-binding bipartisan resolution urging President Clinton to lift the U.S. trade embargo on Vietnam.[m] A week later Clinton lifted the 19-year-old trade embargo on Vietnam.[mi] But, the House (ever mindful of public sentiment) passed a bill on October 5 which provided that Vietnam's accounting for MIAs must remain paramount to U.S. policy with Vietnam.[mii]

In April 1995, Hanoi said that approximately 282,000 ARVN troops and 882,000 NVA and VC Troops had been killed between 1954 and 1975 during the Vietnam War.[miii]

In 1995, Vietnam became a member of the Association of Southeast Asian Nations.[miv] Also, by 1995 over 1.4 million migrants had left Cambodia and Vietnam in the aftermath of the wars in those countries.[mv]

A CNN/USA *Today*/Gallup poll taken on July 11, 1995, revealed that 67 percent of the public backed normalizing relations with Vietnam and only 21 percent opposed it.[mvi]

Florida congressman Douglas "Pete" Peterson, who had spent six years as a POW, was confirmed on April 10, 1996, as the first U.S. ambassador to Vietnam and Le Van Bang was confirmed as Vietnam's first ambassador to the United States.[mvii]

On November 17, 2000, President Clinton began a three-day visit to Vietnam.[mviii] And, in December 2001, the United States granted Vietnam most favored nation (MFN) status.[mix]

SUMMARY

According to a recent account of the Vietnam War by the Smithsonian Institution, life in Vietnam after 1975 was unbearable because: "Whatever levels of cooperation under the fraternal banner of communism [that] might have existed during the [Vietnam War] quickly fell apart [after the war] as historical animosities prevailed. The following decades were a dark and violent time in Vietnam, Cambodia and Laos."[mx]

At the end of December 1977, this lack of cooperation in Indochina continued when Cambodia broke off diplomatic relations with Vietnam because of its "ferocious and barbarous aggression." In January 1978, Vietnam attacked Cambodia and took control of 400 square miles of its territory along the Vietnam-Cambodia border.

By July 1978, conditions in Indochina continued to erode when China terminated economic assistance to Vietnam because of the way the 1.5 million ethnic Chinese in Vietnam were being treated.

Almost exactly a year later the State Department estimated that 300,000 people had fled from Vietnam, Cambodia, and Laos during the prior year sending unwanted refugees into other Southeast Asian countries. At the same time Vietnam, in response to criticism, promised to stem the flow and the plight of its people at an international refugee conference in Geneva.[mxi]

On March 9, 1980, negotiations between Vietnam and China again broke down because Vietnam refused to discuss its invasion of Cambodia. On March 21, 1980, UNICEF announced, "That the prospect of famine [in Cambodia] ha(d) significantly increased," and, on October 22, the UN General Assembly approved a resolution calling on Vietnam to withdraw its troops from Cambodia.[mxii]

Dr. Gregory H. Stanton, who opposed U.S. involvement in the Vietnam War, changed his mind in 1980 when he, as Director of Genocide Watch, took a trip to Cambodia and:

> returned convinced that Americans should have used much different tactics in the Vietnam War, but that we were right to try to help the South Vietnamese defeat Communist takeovers. "I returned" [he said] "convinced that Congress's cutting off assistance to fight the Khmer Rouge and to enforce the Paris Accords doomed millions of Cambodians and Vietnamese to unspeakable deaths. I can never again believe that the fight against Communism in Southeast Asia was wrong ... I will never be able to forget the plaintive sorrow of the widow in Siem Reap who asked me, 'Why did you abandon us?'"[mxiii]

Robert F. Turner, Professor of Law at the University of Virginia, has explained that the people in Indochina were abandoned when:

> in May [1973] Congress enacted a new law that made it unlawful for the President to expend money in support of combat operations in the air, on the ground, or off the shores of North Vietnam, South Vietnam, Laos or Cambodia, after August 15 1973. In a very real sense Congress "threw in the towel" virtually snatching defeat from the jaws of victory. [North Vietnam's] Premier Phan Van Dong later remarked that the Americans would not come back "even if we offered them candy," and after Congress repeatedly cut assistance to the Saigon regime, Hanoi responded by sending virtually its entire army to complete the conquest of its southern neighbor.

> ... "I believe" [he said] "this was one of the most shameful episodes in American history. I was there at the end, and it took me years to fully recover emotionally from that experience.

After we withdrew, tens of thousands of South Vietnamese and more than a million Cambodians were executed. Tens of millions of others were consigned to a Stalinist tyranny and [in 1980] the Socialist Republic of Vietnam [was still] among the worlds 'dirty dozen' human rights violators."[mxiv]

When Vietnam's wartime leaders resigned from the Politburo in December 1986 the new leadership started instituting economic reforms and making military changes.

Clinton picked up on this signal when he became president and ended U.S. opposition to the settlement of Vietnam's $140 million debt to the International Monetary in July 1993; thereby, clearing the way for international lending to Vietnam.[mxv] And, Clinton continued to send positive signals on September 13, 1991, when he relaxed the United States trade embargo on Vietnam thereby allowing U.S. companies to bid on Vietnamese projects that use funds from international organizations.[mxvi]

Vietnam then took advantage of these opportunities and converted from a socialistic economy to a free-market economy and under capitalism it became a bustling country. In 2015, it hosted 8 million visitors, 400,000 of whom came from the United States. All of this caused USA Today to say that even though the communists won the war, the capitalists have taken over Ho Chi Minh City (Saigon) which is now a cosmopolitan city buzzing with entrepreneurial energy.[mxvii]

"The systematic changes that culminated with the dissolution of the Soviet Union in 1991 created an atmosphere of flexibility that reverberated widely in world geopolitics."[mxviii] Signaling "… that official and diplomatic relations between Washington and Hanoi might [soon] be different."[mxix]

PHOTOGRAPHS FROM 1982 to 2000

Dedication of the Vietnam Memorial "The Wall" on the National Mall in Washington D.C. on November 13, 1982. (National Archives)

On May 28, 1984, President Reagan laid a wreath at the tomb of the Unknown Soldier in honor of the Vietnam Era unknown. (From the VA031528 David DeChant Photograph Collection, courtesy of the Vietnam Center and Sam Johnson Vietnam Archive, Texas Tech University.)

On November 11, 1984 a statute honoring all those who served in Vietnam War was added to the Vietnam Memorial. (National Archives)

Another statute specifically honoring the eleven thousand women who served in Vietnam (eight of whom died)[mxx] was added to the Vietnam Memorial in 1993. (National Archives)

Vietnam's Prime Minister presented this bronze incense burner to President Clinton in July 1995 when the United States and Vietnam normalized relations. (National Archives)

CHAPTER TEN
Recap and Aftermath

"Having lived in Vietnam for six years, I have to a degree put down roots there and have come to care very deeply about what happens....Victory by the Communists would mean consigning thousands of Vietnamese, many of them of course my friends, to death, prison, or permanent exile...My heart goes out to the Vietnamese people—who have been sold out again and again, whose long history could be written in terms of betrayal and who, based on this long and bitter experience, can only expect that America too will sell them out. If America betrays the Vietnamese people by abandoning them, she betrays her own heritage."[mxxi]

Douglas Pike [*]
Saigon, August 1966

In August 1966, Douglas Pike, then a Foreign Service Officer with the State Department, expressed his concern that the United States might sell Vietnam out to communism. His concern was well founded.

When World War II came to an end in 1945, the Potsdam Declaration required Japan to surrender Indochina south of the 16th parallel to Great Britain and north of the 16th parallel to China. After Great Britain received southern Indochina it ceded the territory to France and shortly after China received northern Indochina it sold the territory to France.

France, thereafter, tried to reestablish the French Union made up of Laos, Cambodia and Vietnam, but soon found itself at war in northern Vietnam with stubborn communists led by Ho Chi Minh. When France

---

[*] One of the foremost scholars on the Vietnam War, now deceased, but formerly the director of the Indochina Archive at the University of California at Berkeley, Associate Director of Research at Texas Tech's Vietnam Center, and publisher of The Indochina Quarterly.

ran into trouble in this war it asked the United States for assistance but the U.S., not in favor of colonialism, was not inclined to help and turned its efforts to fighting communist expansion in other parts of the world.

However, everything changed in 1949 when, due to a lack of support from the United States, Nationalist China fell to Communist China which, in turn, resulted in the formation of the Sino/Soviet bloc. Matters worsened shortly thereafter when this bloc announced it would be backing North Vietnam in its conflict with France. After this announcement was made the U.S. rethought France's request for help, and between 1950 and 1954 provided it with more than $10 billion in aid.

Even so, France was unable to prevail in Indochina and departed in 1954 leaving North and South Vietnam to co-exist as, what even the Soviet Union agreed, were two separate states. However, in 1958, North Vietnam (still backed by the Sino/Soviet bloc) started sending guerillas into South Vietnam which was by then backed by the United States.

Fighting between the two countries continued until January 1973 when the conflict ended with a treaty that South Vietnam agreed to sign because President Nixon had promised the U.S. would intervene if North Vietnam violated its terms. However, when North Vietnam resumed hostilities Nixon, preoccupied with his own problems, reneged on his promise and left this responsibility to his successor, Gerald Ford.

On April 10, 1975, at 9 P.M., in a last-ditch effort to at least partially fulfil Nixon's promise, President Ford called for a joint session of Congress and delivered a moving plea on behalf of the people of Vietnam and Cambodia, a plea that was broadcast to the nation.

In a nutshell, this address outlined how America got involved in Indochina; its obligations, and what yet needed to be done. As he opened his address the president said, "I stand before you tonight after many agonizing hours in very solemn prayer for guidance by the Almighty;" continuing, he said:

A vast human tragedy has befallen our friends in Vietnam and Cambodia [which was also aligned with the United States]. Tonight, I shall not talk only of obligations arising from legal documents. Who can forget the enormous sacrifices of blood, dedication, and treasure that we made in Vietnam?

Under five Presidents and 12 Congresses, the United States was engaged in Indochina. Millions of Americans served, thousands died, and many more were wounded, imprisoned, or lost. Over $150 billion has been appropriated for that war by the Congress of the United States. And after years of effort, we negotiated, under the most difficult circumstances, a settlement which made it possible for us to remove our military forces and bring home with pride our American prisoners. This [1973] settlement, if its terms had been adhered to, would have permitted our South Vietnamese ally, with our material and moral support, to maintain its security and rebuild after two decades of war.

The chances for an enduring peace after the last American fighting man left Vietnam in 1973 rested on two publicly stated premises: first, that if necessary, the United States would help sustain the terms of the Paris accords it signed 2 years ago, and second, that the United States would provide adequate economic and military assistance to South Vietnam.

Let us refresh our memories for just a moment. The universal consensus in the United States at that time, late 1972, was that if we could end our own involvement and obtain the release of our prisoners, we would provide adequate material support to South Vietnam. The North Vietnamese, from the moment they signed the Paris accords, systematically violated the cease-fire and other provisions of that agreement. Flagrantly disregarding the ban on the infiltration of troops, the North Vietnamese illegally introduced over 350,000 men into the South. In direct violation of the agreement, they sent in the most modern equipment in massive amounts. Meanwhile, they continued to receive large quantities of supplies and arms from their friends.

In the face of this situation, the United States-torn as it was by the emotions of a decade of war-was unable to respond. We deprived ourselves by law of the ability to enforce the agreement, thus giving North Vietnam assurance that it could violate that agreement with impunity. Next, we reduced our economic and arms aid to South Vietnam. Finally, we signaled our increasing reluctance to give any support to that nation struggling for its survival.

Encouraged by these developments, the North Vietnamese, in recent months, began sending even their reserve divisions into South Vietnam. Some 20 divisions, virtually their entire army, are now in South Vietnam.

*****

The situation in South Vietnam and Cambodia has reached a critical phase requiring immediate and positive decisions by this Government. The options before us are few and the time is very short.

On the one hand, the United States could do nothing more; let the Government of South Vietnam save itself and what is left of its territory, if it can; let those South Vietnamese civilians who have worked with us for a decade or more save their lives and their families, if they can; in short, shut our eyes and wash our hands of the whole affair-if we can.

Or, on the other hand, I could ask the Congress for authority to enforce the Paris accords with our troops and our tanks and our aircraft and our artillery and carry the war to the enemy.

*****

I [instead] am asking the Congress to appropriate without delay $722 million for emergency military assistance and an initial sum of $250 million for economic and humanitarian aid for South Vietnam.

The situation in South Vietnam is changing very rapidly, and the need for emergency food, medicine, and refugee relief is growing by the hour. I will work with the Congress in the days ahead to develop humanitarian assistance to meet these very pressing needs.

Fundamental decency requires that we do everything in our power to ease the misery and the pain of the monumental human crisis which has befallen the people of Vietnam. Millions have fled in the face of the Communist onslaught and are now homeless and are now destitute. I hereby pledge in the name of the American people that the United States will make a maximum humanitarian effort to help care for and feed these hopeless victims.

And now I ask the Congress to clarify immediately its restrictions on the use of U.S. military forces in Southeast Asia for the limited purposes of protecting American lives by ensuring their evacuation, if this should be necessary. And I also ask prompt revision of the law to cover those Vietnamese to whom we have a very special obligation and whose lives may be endangered should the worst come to pass...

In Cambodia, the situation is [also] tragic. The United States and the Cambodian Government have each made major efforts, over a long period and through many channels, to end that conflict. But because of their military successes, steady external support, and their awareness of American legal restrictions, the Communist side has shown no interest in negotiation, compromise, or a political solution. And yet, for the past 3 months, the beleaguered people of Phnom Penh have fought on, hoping against hope that the United States would not desert them, but instead provide the arms and ammunition they so badly needed.

I have received a moving letter from the new acting President of Cambodia, Saukham Khoy, and let me quote it for you:

"Dear Mr. President," he wrote, "As the American Congress reconvenes to reconsider your urgent request for supplemental assistance for the Khmer Republic, I appeal to you to convey to the American legislators our plea not to deny these vital resources to us, if a nonmilitary solution is to emerge from this tragic 5-year-old conflict.

To find a peaceful end to the conflict we need time. I do not know how much time, but we all fully realize that the agony of the Khmer people cannot and must not go on much longer.

However, for the immediate future we need the rice to feed the hungry and the ammunition and the weapons to defend ourselves against those who want to impose their will by force [of arms]. A denial by the American people of the means for us to carry on will leave us no alternative but inevitably abandoning our search for a solution which will give our citizens some freedom of choice as to their future. For a number of years now the Cambodian people have placed their trust in America. I cannot believe that this confidence was misplaced and that suddenly America will deny us the means which might give us a chance to find an acceptable solution to our conflict."

This letter [Ford continued] speaks for itself. In January, I requested food and ammunition for the brave Cambodians, and I regret to say that as of this evening, it may be soon too late.

Members of the Congress, my fellow Americans, this moment of tragedy for Indochina is a time of trial for us. It is a time for national resolve.

We cannot…abandon our friends while our adversaries support and encourage theirs…

Let us put an end to self-inflicted wounds. Let us remember that our national unity is a most priceless asset. Let us deny our adversaries the satisfaction of using Vietnam to pit Americans against Americans. At this moment, the United States must present to the world a united front.

Above all, let's keep events in Southeast Asia in their proper perspective. The security and the progress of hundreds of millions of people everywhere depend importantly on us.

Let no potential adversary believe that our difficulties or our debates mean a slackening of our national will. We will stand by our friends, we will honor our commitments, and we will uphold our country's principles…[mxxii]

Two members of Congress[*] did not even wait for the president to finish his speech before they got up and left the chamber,[mxxiii] and there was no applause from those who remained; it was as if the United States, as a nation, had "shut [its] eyes and wash(ed) [its] hands of the whole affair."

Before washing its hands, however, maybe Congress should have thought back to when the United States might have been able to avoid this war. This opportunity presented itself in January 1957 when the Soviet Union proposed admitting North and South Vietnam into the United Nations as member states along with North and South Korea.

This was a major proposal which, according to the Pentagon Papers, "signaled that the USSR might [have been] prepared in the interests of 'peaceful coexistence,' to make a great power deal which would have lent permanency to the partition of Vietnam."

In short, the Vietnam War might have been avoided altogether if Russia's offer at the UN had been pursued, but it was not. Maybe the United States, by failing to pursue this offer, should have asked itself whether it might have owed the people of South Vietnam more before shutting its eyes and washing its hands of the whole affair. But, it did not.

Perhaps Congress should have also thought back to 1963 when the United States, at the direction of its president and its ambassador, over

---

[*] Congressmen Toby Moffett (D) and George Miller (D).

the strong objection of its military commander, had President Diem removed by coup because he was thought to be too autocratic.

This was a president who *Life Magazine* had called "The tough Miracle Man of Vietnam, [a leader] who has roused the country and routed the reds." This was a president who, according to Eisenhower, had "attained independence [for his country] in a situation so perilous that many thought it hopeless."

This was a man who had served faithfully, if not perfectly, over a nine-year span during which time less than a hundred and fifty Americans had died. This was a man who was murdered because he was liked by too many gullible people in the countryside. And, this was a man who, during the next two years, was followed by eight unsuccessful governments that led South Vietnam into total chaos.

Perhaps, after the United States had created this chaos, Congress might have wondered whether it owed the South Vietnamese people something more, before shutting its eyes and washing its hands of the whole affair. But, it did not.

Perhaps, before shutting its eyes and washing its hands, Congress should have thought about President Nixon's promise to intervene if North Vietnam violated the 1973 peace treaty. But it did not.

And perhaps, Congress should have thought about the many (sixty to one hundred thousand) South Vietnamese soldiers killed defending their country in the two years *after* the peace treaty was signed. But, it did not.

After Congress cut off funds to Cambodia and ignored the moving plea from its acting president, Cambodia fell to communism and the Khmer Rouge on April 16, 1975. In December 1975, the Khmer Rouge, headed by Pol Pot, instituted the "Killing Fields" where two to four million Cambodians would die over the next two years.[mxxiv]

When America reneged on its promise to help South Vietnam it fell to Hanoi, on April 30, 1975. This fall came when North Vietnamese tanks crashed through the presidential palace gates, and acting President "Big" Minh (the man who ordered the murder of President Diem in 1963) surrendered to North Vietnam's Colonel Bui Tin.

On April 30, 1975, President Ford asked Congress for $504 million to transport and care for the 120,000 South Vietnamese who had escaped South Vietnam; this request, however, was rejected by the U.S. House of Representatives on May 1, 1975.[mxxv]

By way of comparison, the United States offered a new life to 1.3 million people after World War II; opened its doors to 50,000 Hungarians when the Soviets crushed the Hungarian revolution in 1956, and welcomed over half a million Cubans who fled a communist dictatorship when Fidel Castro took control of Cuba in 1959.[mxxvi]

But, when help was requested for South Vietnamese refugees in 1975, (after 255,000 South Vietnamese soldiers had died in the fight against communism) the answer from Washington D.C. was no. As President Ford said: "Unbelievable!"[mxxvii]

After Congress refused to intervene, and the Vietnam War ended:

> Hanoi murdered up to 65,000 South Vietnamese who had cooperated with the United States;[mxxviii]

> Cambodia, our other ally, had two to four million people murdered in Pol Pot's "killing fields;"[mxxix]

Hundreds of thousands, (maybe more than a million) "Boat-people" died when over two million South Vietnamese fled communist tyranny in un-seaworthy boats;[mxxx]

Two and a half million South Vietnamese political prisoners were moved into "re-education" camps where rules were enforced with "Tiger Cages" and beatings, and where over a hundred and sixty thousand prisoners perished;[mxxxi]

Thousands of Montagnards were slaughtered while defending their religion and culture in the central highlands of Vietnam;[mxxxii]

Buddhism was placed under state control; its clergymen were arrested and imprisoned, and its property was confiscated;[mxxxiii]

Approximately one million South Vietnamese people were relocated by Hanoi into previously uninhabited mountainous areas where between thirty to a hundred thousand people perished,[mxxxiv] and

More than a million South Vietnamese people were relocated from the cities into the country to work on collective farms.[mxxxv]

Commenting on the mass exodus from Vietnam in 1980, Hoang Huu Quynh, a former member of the Vietnamese Communist Party, said, "More than any other people, the Vietnamese people hate exile, but today if Hanoi allowed the people to freely leave the country, even lampposts would apply for the right to leave. The Party has betrayed the people and the promises made to them…and as a patriot, I can no longer remain silent."[mxxxvi]

In the aftermath of America's withdrawal from Indochina, two to five million lives were lost,[mxxxvii] and over 1.4 billion people fled from Laos, Cambodia, and Vietnam.[mxxxviii] Those who remained lived in bitter tyranny.

Among the first to feel this tyranny were the Buddhists when, in August 1975, the communists created the Patriotic Buddhist Liaison Committee "to channel Buddhists…into organizations that would serve [Hanoi's] policies…"[mxxxix] In response, twelve monks and nuns immolated themselves in November 1975.[mxl]

In December 1977, Hanoi made life even more intolerable when it issued Resolution 297 requiring Buddhism, and other religions, to obtain prior government approval for services, investitures, appointment or transfer of clergy, religious meetings and religious training. In addition, every religion was required, under this resolution, to ensure that its followers carry out the policies of the state.[mxli]

During 1979, Joan Baez and 80 other activists (but not Jane Fonda) sent an open letter to Vietnam's leaders "speaking out against [their] brutal disregard of human rights" because of the "horror stories" they had:

> heard… from the people of Vietnam from workers and peasants, Catholic nuns and Buddhist priests, from the Boat people, the artists and professionals and those who fought alongside the NLF. The jails [the letter said] are overflowing with thousands upon thousands of detainees. People disappear and never return. People are shipped to re-education centers, fed a starvation diet of stale rice, forced to squat bound wrist to ankle, suffocated in connex boxes. People are used as human mine detectors, clearing live mine fields with their hands and feet. For many, life is hell and death is prayed for. [mxlii]

Continuing its repression of religion, all Buddhists in Vietnam were incorporated into the Vietnam Buddhist Church in November 1981 which, on the day it was established, "proclaimed itself a component of the People's Fatherland Front... [an] organization of the government's political party."[mxliii]

In 1983, the average per capita income in Vietnam was $150 a year[mxliv] when, according to the *New York Times Magazine*, its "leaders seemed overwhelmed by the problem of feeding 54 million people..."[mxlv] "Nothing [it was said] was more terrible than those ten years after the war," because of "the huge mistakes of the Stalinist economic policies, the economic policies of communism."[mxlvi]

So, it might be asked, with all the blood and treasure lost by the United States and South Vietnam and with the horrible consequences that predictably would befall those left behind, what caused the U.S. Congress to quit?

Kissinger and Nixon say the scales were finally tipped because of Watergate; meaning the consequences flowing from the June 1972 break-in of the Democratic National Headquarters at the Watergate Hotel by Republican operatives.

"Our domestic drama" Kissinger said "first paralyzed and then overwhelmed us."[mxlvii] And, he later added, "But for the collapse of executive authority as a result of Watergate I believe we would have succeeded [in saving South Vietnam]."[mxlviii]

Nixon was of the same opinion: "Had I survived" he said "I think that it would have been possible to have implemented the [peace] agreement. [And,] South Vietnam would still be a viable noncommunist enclave."[mxlix]

There is merit to this thinking. The Case-Church Amendment (that cut off funding for U.S. military activities in Indochina) was enacted on June 4, 1973, one month after the House Judiciary Committee had voted to initiate impeachment hearings against Nixon. Then, on August 11, 1974, two days after Nixon resigned to avoid conviction by the Senate, Congress reduced South Vietnam's aid to $700 million from $2.8 billion the year before, in spite of desperate pleas to the contrary by the U.S. Embassy in Saigon.

The ending in Vietnam was tragic for both America and for South Vietnam. Given this self-inflicted tragedy it is often asked if America did the right thing by going into Vietnam.

CHAPTER ELEVEN
Vietnam: Right? or Wrong?

"This is a world of chance, free will, and necessity---all interweavingly working together as one; chance by turn rules either and has the last featuring blow at events."

Herman Melville - - *Moby Dick*[ml]

American advisors first appeared in Vietnam in 1954, but it was not until June 26, 1965, that President Johnson formally committed troops to battle. And, two months later the Gallup organization began taking America's pulse on the war by asking the public if going into Vietnam was the right thing to do, or if it had been a mistake.

Gallup continued to conduct this poll over the next four years,[mli] and the results were:

	8/1965	1/1967	2/1968	1/1970	1/1971
Right thing to do	60%	52%	42%	32%	31%
It was a mistake	24%	32%	46%	57%	60%
No Opinion	9%	16%	12%	10%	9%

Beginning in 1985, twelve years after the U.S. left Vietnam, CBS asked the American public if the United States had done the right thing by going into Vietnam or if it should have stayed out, and then repeated this poll in four subsequent years.[mlii] The results were:

	2/1985	2/1992	5/1995	4/2000	1/2018
Did right thing	19%	18%	19%	24%	22%
Should have stayed out	73%	70%	72%	60%	51%
Don't know the answer	9%	12%	9%	16%	27%

So, in 1965, sixty percent of those polled thought that going into Vietnam was the right thing to do but, by 1971, sixty percent thought it had been a mistake to do so.

By 1985, seventy-three percent of those polled thought the United States should have stayed out of Vietnam while nine percent did not know the answer, but by 2018, fifty-one percent thought the United States should have stayed out while twenty-seven percent did not know the answer.

According to these polls, then, the American public was more uncertain of its answer in 2018 than it had been in 1985 indicating that Edward R. Morrow may well have been right when he said, "Anyone who isn't confused [about Vietnam] really doesn't understand the situation."[mliii]

To better understand the situation, it is helpful to know why Southeast Asia was so important to America in the first place, and that takes us back to 1941 when ninety percent of America's crude rubber and seventy-five percent of its tin came from that part of the world. In addition, Indochina controlled the "South [China] Sea area, including trade routes of supreme importance to the United States …"[mliv]

In fact, Indochina was so important to President Roosevelt in 1941 that he offered to negotiate a neutrality pact with the Japanese in an attempt to persuade Japan to leave the area. But Japan refused to negotiate and Roosevelt retaliated by freezing Japanese assets under U.S. control and by placing an embargo on oil going to Japan. These sanctions were levied knowing that there might be consequences, but Indochina was where Roosevelt drew the line on Japanese expansion.

Responding to the line drawn by Roosevelt, Japan attacked Pearl Harbor on December 7, 1941; thereby, ushering the United States into

World War II. When this war ended Indochina remained strategically important to the United States and, once again, it was where the United States drew the line in Asia. This time it was drawn as part of the Cold War fought in the aftermath of World War II.

While it has been said that the Cold War is "rapidly receding in the rear-view mirror of history..."[mlv] it was a very real war with very real consequences. And, America's,

> ...engagement in Indochina from the mid-1950's to 1975—*with the Vietnam War as the centerpiece*—was an integral part of the Cold War begun when the Kremlin leadership seized on the chaos and instability in the aftermath of World War II to press the global Marxist/Leninist agenda under the proclaimed leadership of the communist party of the USSR. Throughout East Asia, including Indochina, they were joined in that effort by Mao Zedong's China in 1949, albeit with some differences that were to emerge later.[mlvi] (Emphasis mine)

To be sure, "(b)oth the United States and the Soviet Union regarded the conflict...between North and South Vietnam... as a consequential engagement of the Cold War in a strategic region."[mlvii] It was, where North Vietnam "strongly backed by the Soviet Union and mainland China, sought to increase the number of those who lived behind the Bamboo Curtain."[mlviii]

Stalin set the stage for the Cold War in 1939 when he and Hitler, under the terms of a non-aggression agreement (the Molotov-Ribbentrop Pact) started carving out territory in Eastern Europe.[mlix] In addition, Stalin, at the same time, set his eyes on Asia when he sent a paid agent of the Communist International to Nationalist China in 1940 to help bring China back into the communist fold.

Even though Stalin's expansionist aspirations took a detour when he was attacked by Hitler in 1941, he was back on track by April 1945 when the Office of Strategic Services (OSS) warned President Roosevelt that:

> In the easily foreseeable future Russia may well outrank even the United States in military potential.

Even before World War II came to an end America's new adversary was quietly beginning to expand. This expansion began in February 1945, when Stalin was given control of Manchuria (in northern China) at the Yalta Conference and it continued in the waning days of World War II when he took control of northern Korea. Furthermore, Ho Chi Minh, the agent Stalin sent to China in 1940, had taken control of northern Vietnam with a band of guerillas armed with weapons given to him by the United States and China to fight the Japanese.

In addition to the Bamboo Curtain in Asia, "an iron curtain had descended across the [European] Continent (b)ehind [which lay] all the capitols of the ancient states of Central and Eastern Europe."

When Stalin's actions behind these "curtains" made it clear Russia was acting in opposition to the United States, George Kennan, Washington's Charge d' Affairs in Moscow, was asked to explain why. The reason, Kennan telegraphed back in February 1946, was because Russia was:

> …a political force committed fanatically to the belief that with US there can be no permanent *modus vivendi*, [they believe] it is desirable and necessary that the internal harmony of our society be disrupted, our traditional way of life be destroyed, the international authority of our state be broken, if Soviet power is to be secure…

Consequently in 1947, when Great Britain told President Truman it could no longer help finance Greece and Turkey in their fight against totalitarianism, Truman called for a joint session of Congress and told them it was imperative that the United States step in and fill the void because, without mentioning Russia by name, he said:

> One of the primary objectives of the foreign policy of the United States is the creation of conditions in which we and other nations will be able to work out a way of life free from coercion. This was a fundamental issue in the war with Germany and Japan. Our victory was won over countries which sought to impose their will, and their way of life, upon other nations…

> The peoples of a number of countries of the world have recently had totalitarian regimes forced upon them against their will. The Government of the United States has made frequent protests against coercion and intimidation, in violation of the Yalta agreement, in Poland, Romania, and Bulgaria. I must also state that in a number of other countries there have been similar developments…

> At the present moment in world history nearly every nation must choose between alternative ways of life. The choice is too often not a free one…

> I believe that it must be the policy of the United States to support free peoples who are resisting attempted subjugation by armed minorities or by outside pressures.

> I believe that we must assist free peoples to work out their own destinies in their own way…

Should we fail to aid Greece and Turkey in this fateful hour, the effect will be far reaching to the West as well as to the East. We must take immediate and resolute action.

I therefore ask the Congress to provide authority for assistance to Greece and Turkey in the amount of $400,000,000...

The seeds of totalitarian regimes are nurtured by misery and want. They spread and grow in the evil soil of poverty and strife. They reach their full growth when the hope of a people for a better life has died. We must keep that hope alive...

The free peoples of the world look to us for support in maintaining their freedoms. If we falter in our leadership, we may endanger the peace of the world—and we shall surely endanger the welfare of this Nation.

Great responsibilities have been placed upon us by the swift movement of events.[mlx]

Four hundred million dollars was subsequently appropriated and the first seed in the U.S. Cold War line of containment was officially planted.

After this speech a number of lines of containment were drawn. One of those lines was drawn in Southeast Asia by General Omar Bradley, Chairman of the Joint Chiefs of Staff who said in April 1950 that:

...a vital segment in the line of containment of Communism stretch(es) from Japan southward and around to the Indian Peninsula...

The security of...Japan, India, and Australia depend in a large measure on the denial of Southeast Asia to the Communists.

Unfortunately, this line was drawn after China was lost to communism in 1949 leading to the formation of the Sino/Soviet bloc. Thereafter, "…America's willingness to resist the Moscow-led Communist advances in Asia was put to the test in Korea"[mlxi] when a Sino/Soviet backed North Korea invaded South Korea. This time Truman, without hesitation, immediately extended help.

In addition to backing South Korea, the Truman administration made an initial $10 million appropriation to the French in 1950 to help them with their fight against the Vietminh and Ho Chi Minh who were backed by the Sino/Soviet bloc. When France left Indochina in 1954 President Eisenhower, President Kennedy, President Johnson and finally the Congress of the United States (by way of the 1964 Southeast Asia Resolution) stepped in to help defend South Vietnam.

Why the U.S. stepped in was explained by Secretary of State, Dean Rusk in 1965 when he was asked, "how …our honor [was] involved in Viet-Nam?" And, "how … our security [was] involved in those rice paddies and remote villages?" In response Rusk said there was:

> no need to parse these commitments in great detail. The fact is we know we have a commitment [the SEATO treaty]. The South Vietnamese know we have a commitment. The communist world knows we have a commitment. The rest of the world knows it.

*****

> [And if our allies] or more particularly, if our adversaries should discover that the American commitment is not worth anything. Then the world would face dangers of which we have not yet dreamed. And it is important for us to make good on that American commitment to South Viet-Nam.

The Vietnam War dragged on into the 1970s with no end in sight until Nixon shocked the world in 1971 when he announced a meeting between himself and Mao Zedong. This announcement was followed by a February 1972 summit in China where Mao and Nixon entered into the "Shanghai Communique" in which they agreed to resist "the spread of Soviet influence." In 1973, a year after this alliance was formed, the Vietnam War ended in a stalemate with two sovereign nations.

Unfortunately, two years later South Vietnam was invaded and conquered by North Vietnam while the United States stood by and watched. The fall of this U.S. ally resulted, as Secretary Rusk had predicted, in a:

> Worldwide Marxist-Leninist revolutionary wave and discernable bandwagoning [re-alliance] with the Soviet Union by frightened American allies and neutral countries...[mlxii]

But, as bad as this 1975 re-alliance was, it would have been much worse, from a Cold War perspective, if it had occurred in 1950 when China and Russia had just "linked to create a force that was impossible to defeat." It would have been worse if the United States had left Vietnam in 1963 right after it had engineered a coup that sent the South Vietnamese government into complete disarray. It would have been worse if the United States had left in 1966 when Mao declared that "imperialism (was) in total collapse and socialism (was) succeeding." And, it would have been worse if, instead of the proxy war in Vietnam, a direct conflict between the Soviet Union and the United States had broken out in 1967 as appeared inevitable to UN Secretary General U Thant. Instead of a direct conflict between these two superpowers the proxy war in Vietnam continued until 1975 when Moscow's proxy state (North Vietnam) eventually prevailed. However, the win by this proxy state was actually a setback for Moscow because it was during this Cold War battle that Beijing joined the United States in an attempt to stop Soviet hegemony.

Not to be deterred by the loss of Beijing as an ally (or maybe because of this loss) the Soviet Union took the Cold War to another level when it invaded Afghanistan in 1979 creating what President Jimmy Carter referred to as "the most serious threat to the peace since the Second World War." Carter then immediately addressed this threat with economic sanctions, trade embargos, and aid to the Afghan opposition.[mlxiii]

When Ronald Reagan became president in January 1981 he went on the offensive in the Cold War and, in so doing, took further aim at Russia's economy noting that:

> In an ironic sense Karl Marx was right. We are witnessing today a great revolutionary crisis, a crisis where the demands of the economic order are conflicting directly with those of the political order. But [it is the Soviet Union that] … is in deep economic difficulty. The rate of growth in [their] national product has been steadily declining since the fifties and is less than half of what it was then…
>
> The decay of the Soviet experiment should come as no surprise to us. Wherever the comparisons have been made between free and closed societies…it is the democratic countries that are prosperous and responsive to the needs of their people. …[mlxiv]

To help accelerate Russia's economic decline Reagan caused Soviet income from natural gas and oil sources to decline by reducing the world-wide demand for these exports.[mlxv] Furthermore, the United States sponsored opposition forces in Afghanistan, Angola, Nicaragua and Cambodia at a cost of a billion dollars a year, while the cost to the Soviet Union was eight billion dollars a year.[mlxvi]

When the Soviet Union's economy started to crumble the iron curtain finally began to crack in 1989 when the Berlin Wall came down; it cracked further when the Warsaw Pact completely dissolved in July 1991, and it came crashing to the ground on December 25, 1991, when Gorbachev resigned. The fall of the Soviet Union and the end of the Cold War, however, did not come easily; after all, it was a country that had lost 27,000,000 men and women in World War II but, in spite of that loss, it had not only prevailed it had become stronger.

What it took to win the Cold War was "a military coalition of every great power in the world...the United States, its major allies, Japan and [more particularly] Communist China...to pressure the Soviet Union into bankruptcy," and "economic collapse."[mlxvii]

Russia's Cold War loss was not a pretty sight, but if the tables had been turned it would have been much worse. The United States may or may not have been hungry, but it most certainly would have lost its freedom and its democracy. Because, as President Eisenhower said in 1957, "the Communist goal of conquering the world ... never changed."

Battles in the Cold War, like battles in conventional wars, often had to be fought on unfriendly terrain and battles in the Cold War, like in conventional wars, were not always won. But the United States stayed in the fight:

> by sending a naval task force to the Turkish Straits in 1946; by financially backing Greece in 1947; by investing $12 billion in rebuilding Western Europe in 1948; by resisting the Soviet blockade of West Berlin in 1948; by adopting a Senate

resolution (the Vandenberg Resolution) in June 1948 to secure as many mutual defense arrangements as possible; by (belatedly) assisting Nationalist China in 1949; by establishing NATO in 1949; by aiding Taiwan (Nationalist China) in 1950; by aiding South Korea in 1950; by financially aiding France in Indochina in 1950; by helping defeat communism in the Philippines in 1953; by helping defeat a pro-Marxist regime in Guatemala in 1954; by signing a Mutual Defense Treaty with Nationalist China in 1954; by forming the Southeast Asia Defense Treaty with Australia, France, New Zealand, Pakistan, Thailand, the Philippines and the United Kingdom in 1954; by inserting training forces into South Vietnam when the French left in 1954; by winning duels with the Soviet Union in the Congo, Ghana, Guinea, and Mali between 1956 and 1964; by committing to defend the Middle East from communist aggression in January 1957 (the Eisenhower Doctrine); by (unsuccessfully) attempting to retain control of Cuba in 1959; by (unsuccessfully) attempting to regain control of Cuba in 1961; by attempting to neutralize Laos in 1961; by opposing a second Soviet attempt to take control of West Berlin in 1961; by confronting the Soviet attempt to put missiles on Cuba in 1962; by enacting the Southeast Asia (Gulf of Tonkin) Resolution in 1964; by committing combat troops to South Vietnam in 1965; by having secured Senate approved mutual defense alliances with 42 countries by 1965; by being the first to put men on the moon—and bring them back, in 1969; by normalizing relations with Communist China in 1972; by reaching an arms reduction agreement with Russia in 1972; by brokering a peace treaty between North and South Vietnam in 1973; by supporting Israel in the 1973 Yom Kipper War and forcing the Soviets to back off when they threatened to intervene; by exchanging embassies with China in 1979; by backing Afghanistan in its ten-year war against Russia; by participating in NATO's 1980 "Euro missile" response to the Russian missiles threatening Europe; by backing anticommunist forces in Nicaragua, Angola and Cambodia in 1981; by overthrowing a communist regime in Grenada in 1983; by initiating an antiballistic missile program in attempt to combat the "evil empire's" significant tactical advantage in nuclear and conventional weapons; by challenging the Soviets "to tear down [the Berlin] wall" in 1987; by helping Afghanistan resist the Soviet invasion and by helping negotiate the Soviet withdrawal after ten years of fighting; by causing the reduction of Soviet oil and natural gas income which, along with costs of the Nicaragua Angola and Cambodia conflicts, helped drive the Soviet economy into shambles; by standing as a symbol of freedom when the "Berlin Wall" came down in 1989; by, along with its allies, causing the Soviet Union to disband on July 1, 1991, which, in turn, caused the Cold War to come to an end on December 25, 1991, and by being there at the end of the Cold War to help rebuild a bankrupt and destitute Russia that still had many nuclear weapons at its disposal.

The Cold War was about trying to establish "lines of containment," and in so doing the United States did not win every battle or do everything right. The United States, for example, did not prevail in 1949 when the communists took control of mainland China; it did not prevail in 1959 when the communists took control of Cuba; it did not prevail in 1961 when it attempted to regain control of Cuba; it did not prevail in 1963 when the communists took control of Laos, and it did not prevail in 1975 when the U.S. Congress abandoned South

Vietnam. But fortunately, the U.S. was able to win enough Cold War battles *and make enough alliances* to finally contain the Soviet Union.

Most Americans opposed communist totalitarianism during the Cold War that followed World War II. But many, then and now, contend that it was not necessary to make the Vietnam boundary, initially established at Potsdam, a line of containment in that war. The same, however, could be said about protecting the "Potsdam boundaries" in West Berlin in 1947 and in 1961 where the U.S. risked World Wars on two occasions to protect boundaries in a city 200 miles inside Soviet territory. The same could also be said about protecting the "Potsdam boundary" in Korea where 36,500 American lives were lost. In truth, the same could be said about almost any of these Cold War battles.

In Korea the spread of communism was completely stopped in 1953; it was also stopped in Vietnam in 1960 where the *New York Times* reported that, "Vietnam [was] free and [was] becoming stronger in defense of its freedom and of ours," and it was stopped in 1973 when the Pairs Peace Treaty created a sovereign South Vietnam. In the end, however, the battle was lost in Vietnam in 1975 when the U.S. withdrew its support. Even so, fighting this battle helped the United States win the Cold War sixteen years later.[mlxviii]

While there was a temporary crack in the line of containment when South Vietnam fell in 1975 the overall line in Asia held firm, and America was able to carry the Cold War into the 1980s where President Reagan stressed the continuing need to oppose the *evil empire* saying:

No President no Congress, no Prime Minister, no Parliament can spend a day entirely free of this threat…"

> We see around us today ... totalitarian forces in the world who seek subversion and conflict around the globe to further their barbarous assault on the human spirit. What, then, is our course? Must civilization perish in a hail of fiery atoms? Must freedom wither in a quiet, deadening accommodation with totalitarian evil?[mlxix]

The answer to those questions, fortunately, was no. Instead, it was the Soviet Union that fell because of the Cold War waged by the United States and its allies. Concededly, there were many casualties in the Cold War (particularly the human loss in Korea, Vietnam and Cambodia) but, as John Gaddis said, it could:

> ...have been worse---much worse. It began with the return of fear [in 1946] and ended in a triumph of hope, an unusual trajectory for great upheavals. It could easily have been otherwise: the world spent the last half of the 20th century having its deepest anxieties not confirmed. The binoculars of a distant future will confirm this for had the Cold War taken a different course there might have been no one left to look back through them. That is something. [Because]...most of us survived.[mlxx]

Even though South Vietnam fell what the United States gained during that war was an unlikely alliance with China and this alliance eventually brought the Cold War to a favorable conclusion. As Herman Melville said "This is a world of chance, free will and necessity ...but chance...has the last featuring blow at events."

In the end, the United States, by free will and by necessity but mostly by chance, was able to prevail in:

the third world war of the twentieth century—a world war fought in the form of arms races, covert action, and proxy wars because the destructiveness of conventional…weapons ruled out direct conflict between the two superpowers, the United States and the Soviet Union.[mlxxi]

CONCLUSION

The United States not only did the right thing in backing South Vietnam when it was attacked by a Sino/Soviet backed North Vietnam, it was obligated to do so under Article IV of the SEATO treaty. The United States also acted correctly when it helped bring this war to a conclusion in 1973 with two sovereign nations.

The United States, however, failed in its responsibility in 1975 when it abandoned South Vietnam. Even so, *while at the expense of its South Vietnamese allies*, the United States achieved a geopolitical victory by backing South Vietnam because it was during this "Cold War battle" that China came to recognize the threat of Russia's expansionist goals, and join forces with the United States to stop Soviet hegemony.

As this book goes to press, the Sino/Soviet bloc has realigned and Russia is attempting to take control of Ukraine as part of its new expansion plans. However, an independent Ukraine, that most certainly remembers the 3.5 million Ukrainians starved to death under Stalin's regime, is fiercely resisting, with help from the United States and many other allies. But, the outcome is far from certain.

It is hoped that this renewed Russian attempt at expansion will be contained. However, if it is not, hopefully, it will not be because the United States tires of the challenge.

EPILOGUE

Congressman Riegle could not bring himself to tell constituents of his who lost their son in Vietnam that their loss was in the "national interest." President Reagan, on the other hand, felt differently. He made this clear, during his first inaugural address, while gazing at the white headstones in Arlington National Cemetery from the West Front of the Nation's Capital. It was then Reagan reminded the nation that the graves on those sloping hills represented:

> … the price that has been paid for our freedom.

> …Their lives [he said] ended in places called Belleau Wood, The Argonne, Omaha Beach, Salerno, and halfway around the world on Guadalcanal, Tarawa, Pork Chop Hill, the Chosin Reservoir, and in a hundred rice paddies and jungles of a place called Vietnam.[mlxxii]

Three years later on Memorial Day 1984, President Reagan recognized Vietnam veterans for their service saying:

> Not long ago, when a memorial was dedicated here in Washington to our Vietnam veterans… the rolls of those who died and are still missing were read for 3 days in a candlelight ceremony at the National Cathedral. And the veterans of Vietnam who were never welcomed home with speeches and bands, but who were never defeated in battle and were heroes as surely as any who have ever fought in a noble cause, staged their own parade on Constitution Avenue. As America watched them—some in wheelchairs, all of them proud—there was a feeling that this nation—that as a nation we were coming

together again and that we had, at long last, welcomed the boys home.[mlxxiii]

Later the same year, while dedicating a statute added to the Vietnam Memorial, Reagan told all Vietnam Veterans that they had:

…performed with a steadfastness and valor that veterans of other wars salute, and you are forever in the ranks of that special number of Americans in every generation that the Nation records as true patriots…

…When you returned home [he said] little solace was given to you. Some of your countrymen were unable to distinguish between our native distaste for war and the stainless patriotism of those who suffered the scars. But there's been a rethinking there too. And now we can say to you, and say as a nation: Thank you for your courage. Thank you for being patient with your countrymen. Thank you. Thank you for continuing to stand with us together.

The men and women of Vietnam fought for freedom in a place where liberty was in danger. They put their lives in danger to help people in a land far away from their own. Many sacrificed their lives in the name of duty, honor, and country. All were patriots who lit the world with their fidelity and courage.

They were both our children and our heroes. We will never forget them. We will never forget their devotion and sacrifice. They stand before us marching into time and into shared memory, forever. May God bless their souls.[mlxxiv]

And, a CBS/*NYT* poll taken a year after this dedication revealed that, by then, the American public had also come to appreciate the sacrifices made by those who served in Vietnam, as 94% of those responding said that they believed Vietnam Veterans deserved the same respect as World War II Veterans.[mlxxv]

DOCUMENTS

1. President Nixon's August 3, 1973 letter to Congress expressing his concerns about the dangerous consequences of cutting off funding for Indochina.

Dear Mr. Speaker:

August 1973

By legislative action the Congress has required an end to American bombing in Cambodia on Aug. 15. The wording of the Cambodia rider is unmistakable; its intent clear. The Congress has expressed its will in the form of law and the Administration will obey that law.

I cannot do so, however, without stating my grave personal reservations concerning the dangerous potential consequences of this measure. I would be remiss in my Constitutional responsibilities if I did not warn of the hazards that lie in the path chosen by Congress.

Since entering office in January of 1969, I have worked ceaselessly to secure an honorable peace in Southeast Asia. Thanks to the support of the American people and the gallantry of our fighting men and allies, a cease-fire agreement in Vietnam and a political settlement in Laos have already been achieved. The attainment of a settlement in Cambodia has been the unremitting effort of this Administration, and we have had every confidence of being able to achieve that goal. With the passage of the Congressional act, the incentive to negotiate a settlement in Cambodia has been undermined, and Aug. 15 will accelerate this process.

This abandonment of a friend will have a profound impact in other countries, such as Thailand, which have relied on the constancy and determination of the United States, and I want the Congress to be fully aware of the consequences of its action. For my part, I assure America's allies that this Administration will do everything permitted by Congressional action to achieve a lasting peace in Indochina. In particular, I want the brave and beleaguered Cambodian people to know that the end to the bombing in Cambodia does not signal an abdication of America's determination to work for a lasting peace in Indochina. We will continue to provide all possible support permitted under the law. We will continue to work for a durable peace with all cthe legal means at our disposal.

I can only hope that the North Vietnamese will not draw the erroneous conclusion from this Congressional action that they are free to launch a military offensive in other areas in Indochina. North Vietnam would be making a very dangerous error if it mistook the cessation of bombing in Cambodia for an invitation to fresh aggression or further violations of the Paris agreements. The American people would respond to such aggression with appropriate action.

I have sent an identical letter to the majority leader of the Senate.

RICHARD NIXON [mlxxvi]

2. Secret August 1973 cable from Embassy in Saigon to Secretary of State protesting the reduction of aid to South Vietnam.

THE RECENT ACTION ON THE HOUSE FLOOR FURTHER REDUCING THE FY 75 MILITARY ASSISTANCE LEVEL FOR VIETNAM TO $700 MILLION IS DEEPLY DISTRESSING. IT COULD HARDLY HAVE COME AT A MORE INOPPORTUNE TIME FROM THE STANDPOINT OF ENCOURAGING THE NORTH VIATNAMESE TO CONTINUE AND PRESS THEIR MILITARY OPERATIONS.

APPART FROM THE PRACTICAL EFFECTS TOUCHED ON ABOVE THE WORST DAMAGE OF A REDUCTION OF MILITARY ASSISTANCE IN THE ORDER OF MAGNITUDE SUGGESTED BY THE HOUSE VOTE WOULD BE POLITICAL AND PSYCHOLOGICAL. WE ARE AT A CRUCIAL POINT IN THE LONG DRAWN OUT PROCESS OF DECISION MAKING IN HANOI. IT IS EVIDENT THAT HANOI HAS BEEN DISAPPOINTED IN ITS EXPECTATION THAT VERY QUICKLY AFTER THE WITHDRAWAL OF AMERICAN FORCES AND MILITARY ADVISORS SOUTH VIETNAM WOULD FALL INTO ITS HANDS. AFTER ALL IN HANOI'S VIEW IT WAS A COLONIALIST WAR. BUT THIS HAS NOT HAPPENED. THERE HAS BEEN NO COLLAPSE AND HANOI HAS BEEN TAKEN ABACK BY THAT FACT AS WELL AS THE PERSISTENT FAILURE FROM THE CONSTANTLY PREDICTED "MASS UPRISINGS" TO OCCUR. NOR HAS THE POLITICAL ALTERNATIVE OFFERED ANY ADVANTAGE FROM HANOI'S VIEWPOINT. ***RECOGNITION OF THEIR POLITICAL WEAKNESS IS FOR EXAMPLE THE REASON FOR THEIR PERSISTENT REFUSAL TO DISCUSS A DEFINITE TIME***

SCHEDULE FOR THE HOLDING OF ELECTIONS CALLED FOR BY THE PARIS AGREEMENT IN THE LAST YEAR. THEREFORE, THE DECISION MAKERS IN HANOI HAVE BEEN IN A DILEMMA, FACED NOT ONLY WITH DISAPPOINTMENT OF THEIR HOPES IN THE SOUTH BUT ALSO WITH SERIOUS ECONOMIC PROBLEMS AT HOME AND LIMITATION ON THEIR ABILITY TO OBTAIN SUPPORT FROM THE PRC AND THE SOVIET UNION THEY HAVE OBVIOUSLY HAD PROBLEMS IN DECIDING WHAT TO DO NEXT.....ACCORDING TO RECENT INTELLIGENCE REPORTING SHOULD THE NORTH VIETNAMESE CONCLUDE THAT THE US IS DISENGAGING POLITICALLY AND ECONOMICALLY FROM THE SOUTH, THEY WOULD SUSPEND SERIOUS ECONOMIC PLANNING AND HOLD THEIR RESOURCES IN RESERVE TO USE MILITARILY AGAINST SOUTH VIETNAM AT SOME OPPORTUNE MOMENT. SOME INTELLIGENCE SOURCES INDICATE, IN FACT, THAT THE COMMUNISTS ARE ANTICIPATING A "DECISIVE" POLITICAL OR MILITARY BREAK-THROUGH AS EARLY AS THE SPRING OF 1975 WHEN THE SOUTH VIETNAMESE GOVERNMENT'S EQUIPMENT AND MATERIAL SHORTAGES COULD BE MOST SEVERE IF THERE IS NO ADDITIONAL ASSISTANCE. HANOI'S LONG AND SHORT-TERM INTENTIONS THUS HINGE CRITICALLY ON ITS CURRENT ESTIMATES OF THE EXTENT AND DURABILITY OF US COMMITMENTS TO THE SOUTH VIETNAMESE.

WE BELIEVE IT LIKELY THAT A REDUCTION IN MILITARY ASSISTANCE TO THE RVN BY OVER 50 PERCENT OF THE ADMINISTRATION'S REQUEST WILL

TIP THE BALANCE IN HANOI IRREVOCABLY IN FAVOR OF THE MILITARY OPTION.[mlxxvii] (Emphasis mine)

SELECTED BIBLIOGRAPHY

Andrew, Rod, Jr., Col. U.S.M.C., *The First Fight, U.S. Marines in Operation Starlight*, August 1965, 2015, Government Printing Office bookstore.

Applebaum, Anne, *Red Famine*, (New York, Anchor Books, A Division of Penguin Random House LLC, 2018).

Benton, Major T., *Pieces of My Puzzle*, (Amazon Books, 2020).

Boot, Max, *The Road Not Taken* (New York, Liverright Publishing Company, 2018).

Brown, David D., Lt. Col., and Holmes, Tiffany Brown, *Battlelines*, (Lincoln, NE, iUniverse Inc, 2005).

Burns, Ken and Ward, Geoffrey C., *The Vietnam War*, (New York, Alfred A. Knopf, a division of Random House, 2017).

Buttinger, Joseph, Vietnam: *A Dragon Embattled Vol. 1*, (New York; Frederick A. Prager, Publishers, 1967).

Clodfelter, Mark, *A Case Study* (Washington D.C., National Defense University Press, 2016).

Dean, John W., *The Nixon Defense, What He Knew And When He Knew It* (New York, Penguin Books, 2014).

Demmer, Amanda C., *After Saigon's Fall*, (United Kingdom, Cambridge University Press, 2021).

Edwards, Lee, *A Brief History of the Cold War* (Washington DC, Regnery History, 2016).

Falk, Richard A. Editor, *The Vietnam War and International Law*, Volume 1 (Princeton, NJ Princeton Paper Backs, 1968).

Falk, Editor, Richard A., Editor, *The Vietnam War and International Law*, Volume 4 (Princeton, NJ, Princeton University Press, 1976).

Fall, Bernard B, *Street Without Joy* (Guilford, CT, Stackpole Books, 1961, 2d ed., 2018).

Ford, Gerald *A time to Heal*, (New York, Berkley Books, 1980).

Gehard, Karyn, Editor, *Smithsonian, The Vietnam War*, (New York, Penguin Random House, 2017).

Gilbert, Marc Jason and Head, William, editors *The Tet Offensive* (Westport, CT, Praeger Publishers, 1996).

Gladdis, John Lewis, *The Cold War, A New History* (London, Penguin Books, 2005).

Goulden, Joseph C., *Korea, The Untold Story of The War* (New York, Mc Graw-Hill Book Company, 1983).

Gravel edition, *The Pentagon Papers*, (Boston, Beacon Press, Vols. I-IV, 1971).

Herring, George C., *America's Longest War, The United States and Vietnam*, Fourth Edition (New York, McGraw Hill, 2002).

Herring, George C., *America's Longest War, The United States and Vietnam 1950-1975,* Fifth Edition (New York, McGraw Hill, 2014).

Isaacson, Walter. *Kissinger* (New York, Simon & Schuster Paperbacks, 1992, 2005).

Jacobs, Seth, *America's Miracle Man in Vietnam* (Durham, Duke University Press, 2004).

Leary, Brad, *Triangle of Death* (Nashville, WND Books, 2003).

Lodge, Henry Cabot, *The Storm Has Many Eyes*, (New York, W.W. Norton & Company, Inc., 1973).

Lodge, Henry Cabot, *As It Was* (New York, W.W. Norton & company, Inc., 1976).

Li, Danhui, *Mao and the Sino-Soviet Split 1959-1973, A New History*, (Lanham, MD, Lexington Books, 2018).

Luthi, Lorenz M., *The Sino-Soviet Split Cold War in the Communist World* (Princeton, NJ, Princeton University Press, 2008).

Mazov, Sergey, *a distant front in the cold war* (Washington DC, Woodrow Wilson Center Press; Chicago, Stanford University Press, 2010).

McCullough, David, *Truman* (New York, Simon & Schuster Paperbacks, 1992).

McNamara, Robert S. *In Retrospect, The Tragedy and lessons of Vietnam* (New York, Vintage Books a division of Random House, 1996).

Mitter, Bana, *China's World War II, 1937-1945, FORGOTTEN ALLY* (New York, Mariner Books, Houghton Miffin Harcourt, 2013).

Moore, John N. editor, *The Real Lessons of the Vietnam War*, Reflections Twenty-Five Years After the Fall of Saigon (Durham, Carolina Academic Press, 2002).

Moyar, Mark, *Triumph Forsaken, The Vietnam War, 1954-1965* (New York, Cambridge University Press, 2006).

Murphy, Edward F., *Dak To, America's Sky Soldiers in South Vietnam's Central Highlands* (New York, Ballantine Books, 1993).

Nashel, Jonathan, *Edward Lansdale's Cold War* (Boston, University of Massachusetts press, 2005).

Nolting, Frederick, *From Trust To Tragedy* (New York, Praeger Publishers, 1988).

Kelsey Orestis, Marianne Kelsey, *My Brother Steve A Marine's Untold Story*, (Bloomington IN, AuthorHouse LLC, 2014).

Pike, Douglas, *Viet Cong* (Cambridge, Massachusetts, The MIT Press, 1966).

Polansky, Daniel, *The Vietnam War* (New York, Scholastic Inc., 2013).

Randall M. Romine, Randall M., *A Vietnam War Chronology* (Book Surge, LLC, 2003).

Sagan, Ginetta and Denney, Stephen, *Violations Of Human Rights in The Socialist Republic Of Vietnam April 30, 1975-April 30, 1983* (California, Aurora Foundation, 1983).

Sorley, Lewis, *A Better War* (Orlando, Harcourt, 1999).

Tuchman, Barbara W., *The March of Folly, From Troy to Vietnam* (New York, Alfred A. Knoff publishers, 1984).

Willbanks, James H., *Vietnam War Almanac*, (New York, Skyhorse Publishing, 2013).

ENDNOTES

PROLOGUE

[i] Amanda C. Demmer, *The Washington Post (online)* With Afghanistan's fall, the U.S. confronts a moral necessity it faced before, August 16, 2021. https://www.proquest.com/docview/2561707368/7501A7760CE4489APQ/5?accountid=189667.

[ii] Amanda C. Demmer, *The Washington Post,* What does the U.S. owe the Afghans who supported it? B.3 August 22, 2021, https://www.proquest.com/docview/2563229509/7501A7760CE4489APQ/1?accountid=189667; *The Washington Post* (online) Maria Sacchetti, Missy Ryan, Alex Horton, August 18, 2021, https://www.proquest.com/docview/2565938162/C8C862DF2E324682PQ/1?accountid=189667.

[iii] Gerald Ford, *A time to Heal*, (New York, Berkley Books, 1980), 248.

[iv] *Ibid.,* 250.

[v] . *Ibid.*

[vi] Amanda C. Demmer, *After Saigon's Fall*, (United Kingdom, Cambridge University Press, 2021), 144.

[vii] *Ibid.,* 160.

[viii] *Ibid.,* 208.

[ix] *Ibid.,* 224.

[x] James H. Willbanks, *Vietnam War Almanac* (New York, Skyhorse Publishing, 2013), 458.

[xi] Thomesa Maresca, USA Today, 40 years later, Vietnam still deeply divided over war, April 30, 2015, https://www.usatoday.com/story/news/world/2015/04/28/fall-of-saigon-vietnam-40-years-later/26447943/, last visited September 18, 2021.

[xii] James Guild, *Why is Vietnam's Vin Fast building an EV Factory in the United States?* The Diplomat, July 26, 2022, https://thediplomat.com/2022/07/why-is-vietnams-vinfast-building-an-ev-factory-in-the-united-states/.

[xiii] Human Rights Watch, Afghanistan: Taliban's Catastrophic Year of Rule, August 11, 2022, https://www.hrw.org/news/2022/08/11/afghanistan-talibans-catastrophic-year-rule.

xiv Isabelle Khurshudyan, Gerry Shih, U.S. allies and foes hold off recognizing new rulers, The Washington Post, A. 18, August 22, 2021, https://www.proquest.com/docview/2563229674/AF988390773B4971PQ/25?accountid=189667.

xv Ibid.

xvi Human Rights Watch, Afghanistan: Taliban's Catastrophic Year of Rule, August 11, 2022, https://www.hrw.org/news/2022/08/11/afghanistan-talibans-catastrophic-year-rule.

PREFACE

xvii Barbara Tuchman, *The March of Folly, From Troy To Vietnam* (New York, Alfred A. Knopf, Inc., 1984), 377.
xviii Dan Bale, *The Washington Post,* Watergate happened 50 years ago, Its legacies echo to this very day, Front Page, June 22, 2022.

CHAPTER ONE

xix Tuchman, *The March of Folly*, 234-235.
xx *Ibid.,* 237.
xxi Mark Moyar, *Triumph Forsaken, The Vietnam War, 1954-1965* (New York, Cambridge University Press, 2006), 15.
xxii David McCullough, *Truman* (New York, Simon & Schuster Paperbacks, 1992), 372.
xxiii The Pentagon Papers, Gravel edition (Boston, Beacon Press, 1971), Vol. 1, 76.
xxiv Joseph Buttinger, Vietnam: *A Dragon Embattled Vol. 1* (New York, Frederick A. Prager, Publishers, 1967), 309.
xxv The Yalta Conference, Milestones: 1937–1945 - Office of the Historian (state.gov last visited August 28, 2021; Lee Edwards and Elizabeth Edwards Spalding, *A Brief History of the Cold War* (Washington D.C., Regnery History, 2016), 22.
xxvi The Pentagon Papers, 1 Gravel, 16.
xxvii *Ibid.*
xxviii William M. Leary, *The Strategic Air War Against Japan*, 135, https://media.defense.gov/2010/Sep/28/2001329789/-1/-1/0/AFD-100928-060.pdf.
xxix McCullough, *Truman,* 449.
xxx *Ibid.,* 428.
xxxi *Ibid.,* 409.
xxxii John Lewis Gladdis, *The Cold War, A New History* (London, Penguin Books, 2005), 8-9.
xxxiii McCullough, *Truman*, 450.
xxxiv Potsdam Agreement, II A. 1, https://www.nato.int/ebookshop/video/declassified/doc_files/Potsdam%20Agreem ent.pdf.
xxxv John F. Kennedy Presidential Library and Museum, https://www.jfklibrary.org/learn/about-jfk/jfk-in-history/the-cold-war-in-berlin, last visited August 28, 2021.
xxxvi McCullough, *Truman,* 424.

xxxvii *Ibid.*, 430.

xxxviii *Ibid.*, 437.

xxxix Joseph C. Goulden, *Korea, The Untold Story of The War* (New York, Mc Graw-Hill Book Company, 1983), 16.

xl McCullough, *Truman,* 443.

xli Potsdam Agreement, Annex II b, https://www.nato.int/ebookshop/video/declassified/doc_files/Potsdam%20Agreement.pdf; McCullough. 447; William M. Leary, *The Strategic Air War Against Japan,* 133, https://media.defense.gov/2010/Sep/28/2001329789/-1/-1/0/AFD-100928-060.pdf.

xlii McCullough, *Truman,* 447.

xliii *Ibid.*

xliv The Pentagon Papers, 1 Gravel 16.

xlv Goulden, *Korea,* 19.

xlvi *Ibid.*

xlvii McCullough, *Truman,* 459.

xlviii *Ibid.* 460.

xlix Goulden, *Korea,* 19.

l *Ibid.*

li *Ibid.*

lii Encyclopedia Britannica Pacific Theater of World War II, Hiroshima and Nagasaki, https://www.britannica.com/topic/Pacific-War/The-war-against-Japan-1945.

liii McCullough, *Truman,* 461.

liv Goulden, *Korea,* 19, 29, 51.

lv *Ibid.*, 4, 21.

lvi *Ibid.*, 12, 22.

lvii United Nations, https://www.un.org/en/sections/history/history-united-nations/, last visited July 17, 2021.

lviii Teaching American History, https://teachingamericanhistory.org/library/document/the-long-telegram/, last visited July 17, 2021.

lix *Ibid.*

lx *Ibid.*

lxi Edwards, *A Brief History of the Cold War*, 6.

lxii McCullough, *Truman,* 489.

lxiii Tuchman, *The March of Folly,* 246.

lxiv McCullough, *Truman,* 488.

lxv Edwards, *A Brief History of the Cold War,* 38.

lxvi The Office of the Historian, https://history.state.gov/milestones/1945-1952/truman-doctrine, last visited August 26, 2021.

lxvii Edwards, *A Brief History of the Cold War*, 41.

lxviii *Ibid.*, 49.

lxix Max Boot, *The Road Not Taken* (New York, Liverright Publishing Company, 2018), 94; Edwards, *A Brief History of the Cold War*, 49.

lxx Bipartisan Foreign Policy: The Marshall Plan, https://www.archives.gov/exhibits/treasures_of_congress/text/page22_text.html, last visited August 26, 2021.

lxxi Edwards, *A Brief History of the Cold War*, 50.

lxxii Goulden, *Korea,* 12, 26.

lxxiii *Ibid.*, 34.

lxxiv The Encyclopedia Britannica, Division of Korea, Establishment of the two republics. http://www.britannica.com/EBchecked/topic/693609/Korea/35019/The-Tonghak-Uprising-and-government-reform, last visited August 28, 2021.

lxxv *Ibid.*

lxxvi The Encyclopedia Britannica, The Berlin Blockade, https://www.britannica.com/event/Berlin-blockade.

lxxvii *Ibid.*

lxxviii *Ibid.*

lxxix *Ibid.*

lxxx *Ibid.*

lxxxi *Ibid.*

lxxxii Boot, *The Road Not Taken*, 94.

lxxxiii NATO | Founders, History, Purpose, Countries, Map, & Facts | Britannica, last visited September 6, 2022.

lxxxiv The Encyclopedia Britannica, The Berlin Blockade, https://www.britannica.com/event/Berlin-bloc.

lxxxv Edwards, *A Brief History of the Cold War*, 54.

lxxxvi *Ibid.*

lxxxvii Bana Mitter, *China's World War II, 1937-1945, FORGOTTEN ALLY* (New York, Mariner Books, Houghton Miffin Harcourt, 2013), 5; Edwards, *A Brief History of the Cold War,* 20.

lxxxviii Edwards, *A Brief History of the Cold War*, 54.

lxxxix *Ibid.*, 55.

xc Encyclopedia Britannica, Indonesia, https://www.britannica.com/place/Indonesia; Boot, *The Road Not Taken*, 42.

xci Boot, *The Road Not Taken*, 94.

xcii U.S. Department of State, Office of the Historian, http://history.state.gov/milestones/1945-1952/chinese-rev; Boot, *The Road Not Taken*, 94; Edwards, *A Brief History of the Cold War*, 22.

xciii George C. Herring, *America's Longest War, The United States and Vietnam,* Fourth Edition, (New York, McGraw Hill, 2002), 16.

xciv The Pentagon Papers, 85; Edwards, *A Brief History of the Cold War*, 55.

xcv Edwards, *A Brief History of the Cold War*, 67.

xcvi Goulden, *Korea*, 100-105.

xcvii Tuchman, *The March of Folly,* 253.

xcviii The Encyclopedia Britannica, The Final Push, http://www.britannica.com/EBchecked/topic/322419/Korean-War/229865/The-final-push.

xcix The Tonghak Uprising and reform, Armistice and aid, http://www.britannica.com/EBchecked/topic/693609/Korea/35019/The-Tonghak-Uprising-and-government-reform, last visited August 26, 2021.

c Goulden, *Korea,* quoting Richard H. Rovere, 647.

CHAPTER TWO

ci Encyclopedia Britannica, Vietnam under Chinese rule, http://www.britannica.com/EBchecked/topic/628349/Vietnam/52727/Vietnam-under-Chinese-rule, last visited August 29, 2021.

cii *Ibid.*

ciii *Ibid.*

civ *Ibid.*

cv Encyclopedia Britannica, Two Divisions of Dai Vet http://www.britannica.com/EBchecked/topic/628349/Vietnam/52727/Vietnam-under-Chinese-rule, last visited August 30, 2021.

cvi *Ibid.*

cvii Moyar, *Triumph Forsaken,* 5, 6; Encyclopedia Britannica, Two Divisions, http://www.britannica.com/EBchecked/topic/628349/Vietnam/52693/Climate, last visited August 30, 2021.

cviii Moyar, *Triumph Forsaken,* 5.

cix Encyclopedia Britannica, Two Divisions, http://www.britannica.com/EBchecked/topic/628349/Vietnam/52693/Climate, last visited August 30, 2021.

cx *Ibid.*

cxi Encyclopedia Britannica, Two Divisions of Vietnam, http://www.britannica.com/EBchecked/topic/628349/Vietnam/52727/Vietnam-under-Chinese-rule.

cxii Moyar, *Triumph Forsaken,* 6.

cxiii Smithsonian, Editors Karyn Gehard, Margaret Parrish, *The Vietnam War* (New York, Penguin Random House, 2017), 14.

cxiv Willbanks, *Vietnam War Almanac*, 4.

cxv Willbanks, *Vietnam War Almanac*, 4; Smithsonian, 16.

cxvi Willbanks, *Vietnam War Almanac*, 4.

cxvii Willbanks, *Vietnam War Almanac*, 5; Smithsonian, 17.

cxviii *Ibid.*

cxix Smithsonian, 14.

cxx *Ibid.*, 17.

cxxi John S. Bowman, General Editor, *The World Almanac of the Vietnam War* (New York, World Almanac, A Bison Book, 1985), 14.

cxxiicxxii The Pentagon Papers, 1 Gravel, 7, 8.

cxxiii George C. Herring, *America's Longest War* (Fourth Edition), *9.*

cxxiv The Pentagon Papers, 1 Gravel, 8.

cxxv *Ibid.*

cxxvi *Ibid.*

cxxvii Encyclopedia Britannica, Japanese Policy 1939-41, https://www.britannica.com/event/World-War-II/Invasion-of-the-Soviet-Union-1941.

cxxviii The Pentagon Papers, 1 Gravel, 9.

cxxix *Ibid.*

cxxx John Norton Moore and Robert F. Turner, Editors, *The Real Lessons of the Vietnam War, Reflections Twenty-Five Years After the Fall of Saigon* (Durham, Carolina Academic Press, 2002), 80; Willbanks, *Vietnam War Almanac*, 480.

cxxxi Encyclopedia Britannica, Vietnamese Communism, http://www.britannica.com/EBchecked/topic/628349/Vietnam/52736/The-conquest-of-Vietnam-by-France.

cxxxii Moyar, *Triumph Forsaken*, 10.

cxxxiii *Ibid.*

cxxxiv Moore, *The Real Lessons of the Vietnam War*, 232.

cxxxv Moyar, *Triumph Forsaken*, 14.

cxxxvi Smithsonian, 19.

cxxxvii Moyar, *Triumph Forsaken*, 15.

cxxxviii Smithsonian, 19.

cxxxix Daniel Polansky, *The Vietnam War* (New York, Scholastic Inc., 2013), 54, 55.

cxl Moyar, *Triumph Forsaken*, 16.

cxli *Ibid.*, 15.

cxlii Boot, *The Road Not Taken*, 173, 174.

cxliii Moyar, *Triumph Forsaken*, 16.

cxliv *Ibid.*, 17-18.

cxlv The Pentagon Papers, 1 Gravel, 16.

cxlvi *Ibid.*

cxlvii Moore, *The Real Lessons Of The Vietnam War*, 80.

cxlviii The Pentagon Papers, 1 Gravel, 16.

cxlix The Pentagon Papers, 1 Gravel, 16.

cl *Ibid.*, 1 Gravel, 46.

cli Buttinger, *Vietnam: A Dragon Embattled Vol. 1*, 325.

clii *Ibid.*

cliii The Pentagon Papers, 1 Gravel, 16.

cliv *Ibid.* 1 Gravel, 46.

clv Buttinger, *Vietnam: A Dragon Embattled Vol. 1*, 363.

clvi The Pentagon Papers, 1 Gravel, 16-17.

clvii *Ibid.* 1 Gravel, 20.

clviii *Ibid.*

clix Herring, *America's Longest War* (Fourth Edition), 12; Tuchman, *The March of Folly,* 242.

clx Herring, *America's Longest War* (Fourth Edition), 12.

clxi *Ibid.,* 13.

clxii *Ibid.*

clxiii *Ibid.*

clxiv Tuchman, *The March of Folly,* 239.

clxv Herring, *America's Longest War* (Fourth Edition), 13; Tuchman, *The March of Folly,* 243.

clxvi Herring, *America's Longest War* (Fourth Edition), 4, 14.

clxvii Buttinger, *Vietnam: A Dragon Embattled Vol. 1*, 339.

clxviii *Ibid.,* 362.

clxix *Ibid.,* 362-363.

clxx The Pentagon Papers, 1 Gravel, 18-19; see also National Achieves records at https://www.docsteach.org/documents?rt=msz6sV9fzRPy&start=10.

clxxi Encyclopedia Britannica, The Republic of the Philippines, https://www.britannica.com/place/Philippines/The-period-of-U-S-influence, last visited August 30, 2021.

clxxii Edwards, *A Brief History of the Cold War*, 203.

clxxiii Richard A. Falk, Editor, *The Vietnam War and International Law*, Volume 1 (Princeton, NJ Princeton Paper Backs, 1968), 202; The Pentagon Papers, 1 Gravel, 31.

clxxiv The Pentagon Papers, 1 Gravel, 31.

clxxv The Pentagon Papers, 1 Gravel, 27; Falk, *The Vietnam War and International Law* (Vol.1), 202, 203, 209.

clxxvi The Pentagon Papers, 1 Gravel, 58.

clxxvii Herring, *America's Longest War* (Fifth Edition), 18.

clxxviii Moore, *The Real Lessons of the Vietnam War*, 81.

clxxix *Ibid.*, 84.

clxxx Falk, Editor, *The Vietnam War and International Law* (Vol.4), (Princeton, NJ, Princeton University Press, 1976), 54.

clxxxi Falk, *The Vietnam War; International Law* (Vol. 1), 203.

clxxxii This Day in History, https://www.history.com/this-day-in-history/ussr-and-prc-sign-mutual-defense-treaty, last visited July 20, 2021.

clxxxiii Falk, *The Vietnam War and International Law* (Vol. 4), 55.

clxxxiv Falk, *The Vietnam War and International Law* (Vol. 4), 55-56.

clxxxv U.S. Department of State, Office of the Historian, https://history.state.gov/milestones/1945-1952/NSC68.

clxxxvi Edwards, *A Brief History of the Cold War*, 61.

clxxxvii The Pentagon Papers, 1 Gravel, 187.

clxxxviii Moyar, *Triumph Forsaken,* 24.

clxxxix The Pentagon Papers, 1 Gravel, 65.

cxc *Ibid.* 1 Gravel, 66.

cxci Moore, *The Real Lessons Of The Vietnam War*, 430.

cxcii *Ibid.*, 431.

cxciii Willbanks, *Vietnam War Almanac*, 12.

cxciv Bowman, *The World Almanac of the Vietnam War*, 34; Willbanks, *Vietnam War Almanac*, 12.

cxcv Willbanks, *Vietnam War Almanac*, 13.

cxcvi Boot, *The Road Not Taken*, 118-119, 126.

cxcvii *Ibid.*, 134.

cxcviii Bowman, *The World Almanac of the Vietnam War*, 34.

cxcix *Ibid.*, 34-35.

cc *Ibid.*

cci Boot, *The Road Not Taken,* 182.

ccii Herring, *America's Longest War* (Fifth Edition), xi; Quoting from W. Scott Thompson and Donald D. Frizzell, *The Lessons of Vietnam* (New York, 1977), 43.

cciii National Archives https://www.archives.gov/historical-docs/todays-doc/?dod-date=727; Bowman, *The World Almanac of the Vietnam War*, 35.

cciv Tuchman, *The March of Folly,* 254, 258.

ccv https://www.history.com/topics/cold-war/nikita-sergeyevich-khrushchev.

ccvi The Pentagon Papers, 1 Gravel, 85-86.

ccvii *Ibid.*, 1 Gravel, 86.

ccviii Tuchman, *The March of Folly,* 259.

ccix Bowman, *The World Almanac of the Vietnam War*, 35.

ccx Boot, *The Road Not Taken*, 163.

ccxi *Ibid.*, *The Road Not Taken*, 162-164.

ccxii Tuchman, *The March of Folly,* 260.

ccxiii BBC, https://www.bbc.com/news/world-asia-pacific-15355605, last viewed February 27, 2021.

ccxiv Falk, *The Vietnam War and International Law* (Vol.1), 557.

ccxv Edwards, *A Brief History of the Cold War*, 74.

ccxvi Falk, *The Vietnam War and International Law* (Vol.1), 204.

ccxvii Bowman, *The World Almanac of the Vietnam War*, 35.

ccxviii Tuchman, *The March of Folly,* 262; Herring, *America's Longest War* (Fourth Edition), 42.

ccxix Herring, *America's Longest War* (Fourth Edition), 41.

ccxx *Ibid.*, 42.

ccxxi Bowman, *The World Almanac of the Vietnam War*, 36; Smithsonian, 15.

ccxxii Herring, *America's Longest War* (Fifth Edition), 44.

ccxxiii *Ibid.*, 44 and 49.

ccxxiv Moyar, *Triumph Forsaken,* 11.

ccxxv Moyar, *Triumph Forsaken,* 11; Willbanks, *Vietnam War Almanac*, 497.

ccxxvi Edward Miller, *Misalliance* (Cambridge, MA, Harvard University Press, 2013), 23.

ccxxvii *Ibid.*, 23.

ccxxviii Moyar, *Triumph Forsaken,* 11-12.

ccxxix Miller, *Misalliance*, 21.

ccxxx Moyar, *Triumph Forsaken,* 12.

ccxxxi Boot, *The Road Not Taken,* 206.

ccxxxii Boot, *The Road Not Taken,* 206; Moyar, *Triumph Forsaken,* 12.

ccxxxiii Moyar, *Triumph Forsaken,* 12.

ccxxxiv Miller, *Misalliance*, 24.

ccxxxv Moyar, *Triumph Forsaken,* 12.

ccxxxvi Polansky, *The Vietnam War*, 10.

ccxxxvii Moyar, *Triumph Forsaken,* 12; The Pentagon Papers, 2 Gravel, 315.

ccxxxviii Boot, *The Road Not Taken*, 206.

ccxxxix Moyar, *Triumph Forsaken*, 11 and 13.

ccxl Moyar, *Triumph Forsaken,* 11.

ccxli *Ibid.*

ccxlii Moyar, *Triumph Forsaken,* 13; Polansky, *The Vietnam War*, 11.

ccxliii Miller, *Misalliance*, 26; Smithsonian, 41.

ccxliv Smithsonian, 40; Moyar, *Triumph Forsaken,* 13.

ccxlv Moyar, *Triumph Forsaken,* 13.

ccxlvi Smithsonian, 40.

ccxlvii Miller, *Misalliance*, 26.

ccxlviii Polansky, *The Vietnam War*, 12.

ccxlix Miller, *Misalliance*, 26.

ccl Miller, *Misalliance*, 28.

ccli Polansky, *The Vietnam War*, 14.

cclii Moyar, *Triumph Forsaken,* 18.

ccliii Seth Jacobs, *America's Miracle Man in Vietnam* (Durham, Duke University Press, 2004), 29.

ccliv Moyar, *Triumph Forsaken,* 18.

cclv *Ibid.*

cclvi Miller, *Misalliance*, 31.

cclvii *Ibid.*, 33.

cclviii Jacobs, *America's Miracle Man in Vietnam*, 29-30, citing Stanley Karnow, *Vietnam: A History* 216-217, New York, Viking Press, 1987.

cclix Moyar, *Triumph Forsaken,* 13.

cclx Moyar, *Triumph Forsaken,* 17-18; Jacobs, *America's Miracle Man in Vietnam*, 29.

cclxi *Vietnam*, Published in 1955 by the Embassy of Vietnam in Washington, D.C., 1, 5.

cclxii Moyar, *Triumph Forsaken,* 18.

cclxiii Miller, *Misalliance*, 34.

cclxiv The Pentagon Papers, 1 Gravel, 296.

cclxv The Pentagon Papers, 1 Gravel, 296; Smithsonian, 40.

cclxvi The Pentagon Papers, 1 Gravel, 59.

cclxvii Miller, *Misalliance*, 36.

cclxviii *Ibid.*

cclxix *Ibid.*, 37.

cclxx Smithsonian, 41.

cclxxi Miller, *Misalliance*, 37.

cclxxii *Ibid.*, 38.

cclxxiii *Ibid.*, 40-43.

cclxxiv *Ibid.*, 48-49.

cclxxv *Ibid.*, 50-51.

cclxxvi *Ibid.*, 51.

cclxxvii Moyar, *Triumph Forsaken,* 33.

cclxxviii *Ibid.*

cclxxix Falk, *The Vietnam War and International Law*, (Vol. 1), 204; Smithsonian, 15.

cclxxx Jonathan Nashel, *Edward Lansdale's Cold War* (Boston, University of Massachusetts press, 2005), 1.

cclxxxi Boot, *The Road Not Taken*, 196, 197-198.

cclxxxii Boot, *The Road Not Taken*, 215; The Pentagon Papers, 2 Gravel, 440.

cclxxxiii Falk, *The Vietnam War and International Law* (Vol.1), 209 n. 27.

cclxxxiv *Ibid.*, 410.

cclxxxv *Ibid.,* 260.

cclxxxvi The Pentagon Papers, 1 Gravel, 162.

cclxxxvii *Ibid.*, 163.

cclxxxviii Miller, *Misalliance*, 53.

cclxxxix The Pentagon Papers, 1Gravel, 296.

ccxc Bernard B. Fall, Street Without Joy (Guilford, CT, Stackpole Books, 1961, 2d ed., 2018), 185-235.

ccxci Falk, *The Vietnam War and International Law* (Vol.1), 204.

ccxcii *Ibid.*, 204 and 556.

ccxciii *Ibid.*, 320.

ccxciv Falk, *The Vietnam War and International Law* (Vol.1), The Geneva Accords, Articles 1 & 14, at 543, 546.

ccxcv Falk, *The Vietnam War and International Law* (Vol.1), 204-206.

ccxcvi *Ibid.*, 162.

ccxcvii Falk, *The Vietnam War and International* Law (Vol.1), 410.

ccxcviii *Ibid.*, 205.

ccxcix The Pentagon Papers, 1 Gravel, 163; Falk, *The Vietnam War and International Law*, (Vol.1), 213.

ccc The Pentagon Papers, 1 Gravel, 162.

ccci Falk, *The Vietnam War and International Law* (Vol.1), 564.

ccccii *Ibid.*, 230 and 561-564.

ccciii The Pentagon Papers, 1 Gravel, 586, 608.

ccciv *Ibid.*, 641

cccv Bowman, *The World Almanac of the Vietnam War*, 41.

cccvi Boot, *The Road Not Taken*, 271.

cccvii The Pentagon Papers, 1 Gravel, 297.

cccviii Falk, The Vietnam War and International Law (Vol.4), 69.

cccix *Ibid.*, 70.

cccx *Ibid.*

cccxi Moyar, *Triumph Forsaken*, 54-55.

cccxii The Pentagon Papers, 1 Gravel 162; 2 Gravel 408, 431.

cccxiii *Ibid.*, 2 Gravel, 415, 416, 433-34.

cccxiv *Ibid.*, 2 Gravel, 432.

cccxv *Ibid.*, 2 Gravel, 431.

cccxvi *Ibid.*, 2 Gravel, 431-432.

cccxvii Falk, *The Vietnam War and International Law* (Vol.1), 209.

cccxviii Douglas Pike, *Viet Cong* (Massachusetts, The MIT Press, 1966), 58.

cccxix *Ibid.*

cccxx Robert S. McNamara, *In Retrospect, The Tragedy and Lessons of Vietnam* (New York, Vintage Books a division of Random House, 1996), 438.

cccxxi Moyar, *Triumph Forsaken*, 34.

cccxxii *Ibid.*, 34-35, 249.

cccxxiii *Ibid.*, 35.

cccxxiv Frederick Nolting, *From Trust To Tragedy* (New York, Praeger Publishers, 1988), 107; Moyar, *Triumph Forsaken*, 35.

cccxxv Moyar, *Triumph Forsaken*, 43, 45.

cccxxvi *Ibid.*, 53.

cccxxvii John Lewis Gaddis, *The Cold War* (New York, Penguin Books, 2007), 130.

cccxxviii Sergey Mazov, *a distant front in the cold war* (Washington D.C. , Woodrow Wilson Center Press; Chicago, Stanford University Press, 2010), 14.

CHAPTER THREE (Pages to)

cccxxix Lorenz M. Luthi, *The Sino-Soviet Split Cold War in the Communist World* (Princeton, NJ, Princeton University Press, 2008), 46.

cccxxx The Pentagon Papers, 1 Gravel, 261-263.

cccxxxi Bowman, *The World Almanac of the Vietnam War*, 44-45.

cccxxxii Nolting, *From Trust To Tragedy*, 61.

cccxxxiii *Ibid.*, 93.

cccxxxiv Moyar, *Triumph Forsaken*, 81.

cccxxxv Boot, *The Road Not Taken*, 296.

cccxxxvi Edwards, *A Brief History of the Cold War*, 210.

cccxxxvii Lindesay Parrot, *New York Times*, SOVIET UNION INSISTS U.N. TAKE SPLIT LANDS; Both Koreas and Vietnams or None is Sobolev Stand on Membership Issue, SOVIET INSISTS U.N. TAKE SPLIT LANDS; Both Koreas and Vietnams or None, Is Sobolev Stand on Membership Issue - The New York Times (nytimes.com), last visited July 26, 2021.

cccxxxviii Moore, *The Real Lessons Of The Vietnam War*, 102.

cccxxxix *Ibid.*

cccxl Moore, *The Real Lessons of the Vietnam War*, 102; Falk, *The Vietnam War and International Law* (Vol. 1), 239-240.

cccxli The Pentagon Papers, 1 Gravel, 262.

cccxlii The Pentagon Papers, 1 Gravel, 613.

cccxliii Smithsonian, 41.

cccxliv The Pentagon Papers, 4 Gravel, 641-642; Falk, *The Vietnam War and International Law* (Vol.1), 593.

cccxlv Edwards, *A Brief History of the Cold War*, 87.

cccxlvi The Pentagon Papers, 1 Gravel, 261-262.

cccxlvii *Ibid.*, 1 Gravel, 263.

cccxlviii Mazov, *a distant front in the cold war*, 66.

cccxlix The Pentagon papers, 1 Gravel, 623.

cccl Pike, *Viet Cong*, 78.

cccli Boot, *The Road Not Taken*, 337.

ccclii Moyar, *Triumph Forsaken,* 81.

cccliii The Pentagon Papers, 1 Gravel, 628-629.

cccliv Boot, *The Road Not Taken,* 336-338.

ccclv Pike, *Viet Cong*, 74.

ccclvi Moyar, *Triumph Forsaken,* 438, n. 47.

ccclvii Moyar, *Triumph Forsaken,* 104

ccclviii *Ibid.,* 104, 438 n. 47.

ccclix Tuchman, *The March of Folly,* 284.

ccclx The Pentagon Papers, 2 Gravel, 636.

ccclxi Tuchman, *The March of Folly,* 284.

ccclxii Edwards, *A Brief History of the Cold War*, 94-95.

ccclxiii Encyclopedia Britannica, Bay of Pigs invasion, http://www.britannica.com/EBchecked/topic/56682/Bay-of-Pigs-invasion.

ccclxiv Moyar, *Triumph Forsaken,* 133; Smithsonian, *The Vietnam War*, 48.

ccclxv *Ibid.,*

ccclxvi Falk, *The Vietnam War and International Law* (Vol. 1), 565-573.

ccclxvii Moyar, *Triumph Forsaken,* 131-132.

ccclxviii President John F. Kennedy July 25, 1961: Report on the Berlin Crisis | Miller Center.

ccclxix Mazov, *a distant front in the cold war*, 15.

ccclxx *Ibid.,* (Bookcover).

ccclxxiThe Pentagon Papers, 2 Gravel, 417, 440.

ccclxxii *Ibid.* 440-441.

ccclxxiii *Ibid.,* 440.

ccclxxiv Boot, *The Road Not Taken,* 353; The Pentagon Papers, 2 Gravel, 442.

ccclxxv The Pentagon Papers, 2 Gravel, 441.

ccclxxvi *Ibid.,* 442.

ccclxxvii *Ibid.,* 4 Gravel, 642.

ccclxxviii Smithsonian, 48.

ccclxxix The Pentagon Papers, 4 Gravel, 642.

ccclxxx Falk, *The Vietnam War and International Law* (Vol. 4), 72, 73.

ccclxxxi Herring, *America's Longest War* (Fifth Edition), 188, 275.

ccclxxxii Smithsonian, 49.

ccclxxxiii https://www.forbes.com/sites/nicolefisher/2018/05/28/the-shocking-health-effects-of-agent-orange-now-a-legacy-of-military-death/#27f2464321c6; Willbanks, *Vietnam War Almanac,* 455-456.

ccclxxxiv Fall, *Street Without Joy,* 374.

ccclxxxv Boot, *The Road Not Taken,* Prologue, xxxviii.

ccclxxxvi *Ibid.,* 401.

ccclxxxvii The Pentagon Papers, 2 Gravel, 165.

ccclxxxviii *Ibid.,* 150.

ccclxxxix Boot, *The Road Not Taken,* 402.

cccxc Willbanks, *Vietnam War Almanac,* 45.

cccxci Boot, *The Road Not Taken,* 401.

cccxcii Edwards, *A Brief History of the Cold War,* 97-99.

cccxciii Moore, *The Real Lessons of the Vietnam War,* 12; Danhui Li, *Mao and the Sino-Soviet Split 1959-1973, A New History* (Lanham, MD, Lexington Books, 2018), 63: Edwards, *A Brief History of the Cold War,* 99.

cccxciv Li, *Mao and the Sino-Soviet Split,* 64, 68.

cccxcv Willbanks, *Vietnam War Almanac,* 45.

cccxcvi Herring, *America's Longest War* (Fifth Edition), 188, 275.

cccxcvii Lorenz M. Luthi, *The Sino-Soviet Split* (Princeton, NJ, Princeton University Press, 2008), 305.

cccxcviii Nolting, *From Trust To Tragedy,* 106; Moyar, *Triumph Forsaken,* 212.

cccxcix The Pentagon Papers, 2 Gravel 226.

cd The Pentagon Papers, 2 Gravel 226; Moyar, *Triumph Forsaken,* 212.

cdi The Pentagon Papers, 2 Gravel 226.

cdii *Ibid,* 208.

cdiii *Ibid.,* 209.

cdiv *Ibid.,* 227.

cdv Bowman, *The World Almanac of the Vietnam War,* 60.

cdvi Moyar, *Triumph Forsaken,* 226-227, 459 n. 84.

cdvii Moyar, *Triumph Forsaken,* 170.

[cdviii] Peter Braestrup, *Big Story* (Novato, CA, Presidio Press, 1994), 446-447.

[cdix] Nolting, *From Trust To Tragedy*, 88.

[cdx] *Ibid.*, 8.

[cdxi] Moyar, *Triumph Forsaken*, 233.

[cdxii] The Pentagon Papers, 2 Gravel, 211.

[cdxiii] McNamara, *In Retrospect*, 52; Moyar, *Triumph Forsaken*, 237.

[cdxiv] The Pentagon Papers, 2 Gravel, 211.

[cdxv] *Ibid.*, 236.

[cdxvi] *Ibid.*, 213-214.

[cdxvii] *Ibid.*, 214.

[cdxviii] Boot, *The Road Not Taken*, 408-409.

[cdxix] *Ibid.*

[cdxx] The Pentagon Papers, 2 Gravel 214, 245; *Moyar, Triumph Forsaken*, 250.

[cdxxi] The Pentagon Papers, 2 Gravel, 214-215.

[cdxxii] *Ibid.*, 215.

[cdxxiii] Moyar, *Triumph Forsaken*, 240.

[cdxxiv] The Pentagon Papers, 2 Gravel 215.

[cdxxv] McNamara, *In Retrospect*, 52, 70.

[cdxxvi] The Pentagon Papers, 2 Gravel, 751-752.

[cdxxvii] *Ibid.*, 763, 766.

[cdxxviii] Boot, *The Road Not Taken*, 568.

[cdxxix] The Pentagon Papers, 2 Gravel, 767-768.

[cdxxx] Moyar, *Triumph Forsaken*, 258-259.

[cdxxxi] The Pentagon Papers, 2 Gravel, 218.

[cdxxxii] Moyar, *Triumph Forsaken*, 261.

[cdxxxiii] *Ibid.*

[cdxxxiv] *Ibid.*

[cdxxxv] *Ibid.*, 262.

[cdxxxvi] The Pentagon Papers, 2 Gravel, 219.

[cdxxxvii] *Ibid.*, 261.

[cdxxxviii] *Ibid.*, 220.

[cdxxxix] Moyar, *Triumph Forsaken*, 265.

[cdxl] *Ibid.*, 266.

[cdxli] The Pentagon Papers, 2 Gravel, 220.

[cdxlii] McNamara, *In Retrospect*, 83.

[cdxliii] *Ibid.*

[cdxliv] *Ibid.*

[cdxlv] Moyar, *Triumph Forsaken*, 273.

[cdxlvi] *Ibid.*

[cdxlvii] *Ibid.*, 272.

[cdxlviii] *Ibid.*, 273.

[cdxlix] *Ibid.*, 272.

[cdl] Herring, *America's Longest War* (Fifth Edition), 275.

cdli Moore, *The Real Lessons of the Vietnam War*, 469.

cdlii The Pentagon Papers, 2 Gravel, 270.

cdliii *Ibid.,* 222.

cdliv Brad O'Leary, *Triangle of Death* (Nashville, WND Books, 2003), 39.

cdlv Bowman, The World Almanac of the Vietnam War, 63; Herring, *America's Longest War* (Fifth Edition), 188.

cdlvi The Pentagon Papers, 2 Gravel 170.

cdlvii *Ibid.,* 315.

cdlviii The Pentagon Papers, 2 Gravel, 193; 3 Gravel, 31.

cdlix Herring, *America's Longest War* (Fifth Edition), 188 and 275.

cdlx Bowman, *The World Almanac of the Vietnam War*, 65.

cdlxi *Ibid.,* 67.

cdlxii The Pentagon Papers, 3 Gravel, 8.

cdlxiii Bowman, *The World Almanac of the Vietnam War*, 76.

cdlxiv Willbanks, *Vietnam War Almanac*, 74.

cdlxv *Ibid.,* 510.

cdlxvi *Ibid.,* 75.

cdlxvii *Ibid.,* 80.

cdlxviii Moyar, *Triumph Forsaken,* 81.

cdlxix The Pentagon Papers, 1 Gravel, 252-253.

cdlxx Falk, *The Vietnam War and International Law* (Vol.1), 583, 591-592.

cdlxxi Boot, *The Road Not Taken*, 280; Gaddis, *The Cold War,* 129.

cdlxxii Edwards, *A Brief History of the Cold War*, 138 making reference to Jeanne J. Kilpatrick, *Dictatorships and Double Standards Rationalism and Reason in Politics* (New York: AEI Simon and Shuster, 1982), 49.

cdlxxiii Boot, *The Road Not Taken*, xxxviii.

cdlxxiv Moore, *The Real Lessons of the Vietnam War*, 468.

cdlxxv Moyar, *Triumph Forsaken,* 273.

cdlxxvi Tuchman, *The March of Folly,* 309.

cdlxxvii The Pentagon Papers, 2 Gravel, 270.

CHAPTER FOUR

cdlxxviii The Pentagon Papers, 3 Gravel, 12; Moore, *The Real Lessons of The Vietnam War*, 121; Moyar, *Triumph Forsaken,* 310 and Willbanks, *Vietnam War Almanac*, 79.

cdlxxix Willbanks, *Vietnam War Almanac*, 80-81.

cdlxxx *Ibid.*

cdlxxxi *Ibid.,* 83.

cdlxxxii Bowman, *The World Almanac of the Vietnam War*, 86.

cdlxxxiii Willbanks, *Vietnam War Almanac*, 85.

cdlxxxiv Bowman, *The World Almanac of the Vietnam War*, 88.

cdlxxxv *Ibid.,* 89.

cdlxxxvi *Ibid.,* 93.

cdlxxxvii *Ibid.,* 94.

cdlxxxviii Bowman, *The World Almanac of The Vietnam War,* 94; LI, *Mao and the Sino-Soviet Split,* 110-111.

cdlxxxix Edwards, *A Brief History of the Cold War,* 107.

cdxc Bowman, *The World Almanac of the Vietnam War,* 95.

cdxci *Ibid.,* 99.

cdxcii The Pentagon Papers, 3 Gravel, 240.

cdxciii *Ibid.*

cdxciv *Ibid.*

cdxcv Herring, *America's Longest War* (Fifth Edition), 188, 275.

cdxcvi Moyar, *Triumph Forsaken,* 352.

cdxcvii Willbanks, *Vietnam War Almanac,* 103.

cdxcviii Bowman, *The World Almanac of the Vietnam War,* 104.

cdxcix Willbanks, *Vietnam War Almanac,* 104.

d Bowman, *The World Almanac of the Vietnam War,* 104.

di Herring, America's Longest War (Fifth Edition), 159.

dii *Ibid.*

diii Bowman, *The World Almanac of the Vietnam War,* 104.

div Willbanks, *Vietnam War Almanac,* 106.

dv The Pentagon Papers, 3 Gravel, 404, 417-418.

dvi *Ibid.,* 419.

dvii Bowman, *The World Almanac of the Vietnam War,* 107.

dviii The Pentagon Papers, 3 Gravel, 423.

dix *Ibid.,* 278, 280, 352.

dx *Ibid.,* 447.

dxi *Ibid.,* 281-282.

dxii Falk, *The Vietnam War and International Law* (Vol.4), 485.

dxiii Moore, *The Real Lessons of the Vietnam War,* 102; Falk, *The Vietnam War and International Law* (Vol. 1), 239-240.

dxiv Falk, *The Vietnam War and International Law* (Vol.1), 175.

dxv *Ibid.,* 562, 564.

dxvi The Pentagon Papers, 4 Gravel, 641-642; Falk, *The Vietnam War and International Law* (Vol.1), 593.

dxvii Falk, *The Vietnam War and International Law* (Vol.1), 583.

dxviii *Ibid.,* 593.

dxix *Ibid.,* 583.

dxx *Ibid.,* 591-592.

dxxi *Ibid.,* 583.

dxxii Pike, *Viet Cong,* 76, 78, 79, 82, 102.

dxxiii Falk, *The Vietnam War and International Law* (Vol.1), 579.

dxxiv President John F. Kennedy July 25, 1961: Report on the Berlin Crisis | Miller Center.

dxxv Falk, *The Vietnam War and International Law* (Vol.1), Introduction at 11,460; *The Real Lessons Of The Vietnam War*, 30.

dxxvi The Pentagon Papers, 1 Gravel, 265.

dxxvii Pike, *Viet Cong*, 74.

dxxviii Moyar, *Triumph Forsaken,* 438.

dxxix *Ibid.*

dxxx Smithsonian, 332.

dxxxi Tuchman, *The March of Folly,* 366.

CHAPTER FIVE

dxxxii Bowman, *The World Almanac of the Vietnam War*, 113; Rod Andrew, Jr., Col. U.S.M.C., *The First Fight, U.S. Marines in Operation Starlight*, August 1965, 2015, 4, 17, https://www.usmcu.edu/Portals/218/The_First_Fight_Starlite.pdf; Government Printing Office bookstore.GPO.gov., 1-866-512-1800, 202-512-1800.

dxxxiii Willbanks, *Vietnam War Almanac*, 127, 500.

dxxxiv *Ibid.,* 127.

dxxxv Moyar, *Triumph Forsaken,* 402.

dxxxvi Bowman, *The World Almanac of the Vietnam War*, 119.

dxxxvii Tuchman, *March of Folly*, 325.

dxxxviii Bowman, *The World Almanac of the Vietnam War*, 120.

dxxxix Andrew, *The First Fight*, 5.

dxl Andrew, *The First Fight*, 17.

dxli Braestrup, *Big Story*, 250-251.

dxlii Andrew, *The First Fight*, 5, 6, 14, 15, 17, 18, 20.

dxliii Andrew, *The First Fight*, 35.

dxliv Major T. Benton, Pieces of My Puzzle, 19.

dxlv Andrew, *The First Fight*, 520.

dxlvi *Ibid.,* 22.

dxlvii *Ibid.,* 30-31.

dxlviii *Ibid.*

dxlix *Ibid.,* 34.

dl *Ibid.*

dli *Ibid.*

dlii *Ibid.,* 35.

dliii *Ibid.,* 36-37.

dliv *Ibid.,* 37, 42.

dlv *Ibid.,* 42-44.

dlvi Benton, *Pieces of My Puzzle*, 15, 27, 30.

dlvii Andrew, *The First Fight*, 33, 36, 44.

dlviii Benton, *Pieces of My Puzzle*, 27.

dlix *Ibid.,* 33.

dlx Andrew, *The First Fight*, 47.

dlxi Benton, *Pieces of My Puzzle*, 32.

dlxii *Ibid.,* 16-17.

dlxiii *Ibid.,* ix-xi.

dlxiv *Ibid.,* 2.

dlxv *Ibid.*

dlxvi Andrew, *The First Fight*, 27.

dlxvii The Pentagon Papers, 2 Gravel, 297.

dlxviii *Ibid.,* 4 Gravel, 635-638.

dlxix *Ibid.,* 4 Gravel, 6-7 and 128-129.

dlxx Herring, *America's Longest War* (Fifth Edition), 188, 275.

dlxxi Willbanks, *Vietnam War Almanac*, 150-151.

dlxxii O'Leary, Triangle of Death, 39; Herring, *Americas Longest War,* (Fourth Edition), 192; Moyar, *Triumph Forsaken,* 403.

dlxxiii Willbanks, *Vietnam War Almanac*, 161.

dlxxiv Bowman, *The World Almanac of the Vietnam War*, 140.

dlxxv Bowman, *The World Almanac of the Vietnam War*, 141; Wilbanks, *Vietnam War Almanac*, 500.

dlxxvi Herring, *America's Longest War* (Fifth Edition), 201.

dlxxvii Henry Cabot Lodge, *The Storm Has Many Eyes,* (New York, W.W. Norton & Company, Inc., 1973), 214.

dlxxviii Lodge, *The Storm Has Many Eyes*, 216-217.

dlxxix The Pentagon Papers, 2 Gravel, 384.

dlxxx *Ibid.*

dlxxxi *Ibid.*

dlxxxii Moyar, *Triumph Forsaken,* 216.

dlxxxiii Moore, *The Real Lessons of the Vietnam War*, 468.

dlxxxiv McNamara, *In Retrospect*, 83.

dlxxxv Boot, *The Road Not Taken*, xxxviii.

CHAPTER SIX

dlxxxvi The Pentagon Papers, 4 Gravel, 6, 7, 127-128.

dlxxxvii *Ibid.,* 127-128.

dlxxxviii Bowman, *The World Almanac of the Vietnam War*, 152-153.

dlxxxix The Pentagon Papers, 4 Gravel, 138.

dxc Bowman, *The World Almanac of the Vietnam War*, 155-157.

dxci Herring, *America's Longest War* (Fifth Edition), 188, 275.

dxcii Bowman, *The World Almanac of the Vietnam War*, 164.

dxciii *Ibid.,* 166.

dxciv Moore, *The Real Lessons Of The Vietnam War*, 477-479.

dxcv Bowman, *The World Almanac of the Vietnam War*, 167.

dxcvi The Pentagon Papers, 4 Gravel, 10.

dxcvii McNamara, *In Retrospect*, 264-270.

dxcviii The Pentagon Papers, 4 Gravel, 11.

dxcix *Ibid.*

dc *Ibid.,* 12, 184.

dci *Ibid.,* 12.

dcii Marianne Kelsey Orestis, *My Brother Stevie A Marine's Untold Story* (Bloomington IN, AuthorHouse LLC, 2014), 72.

dciii Kelsey Orestis, *My Brother Stevie,* 30.

dciv Kelsey Orestis, *My Brother Stevie,* 58.

dcv Kelsey Orestis, *My Brother Steve,* 50, 59, 73.

dcvi *Ibid.,* 65-66.

dcvii Lt. Col. David D. Brown, Tiffany Brown Holmes, *Battlelines* (Lincoln, NE, iUniverse Inc, 2005), 86.

dcviii *Ibid.,* 86-87.

dcix *Ibid.,* 88.

dcx *Ibid.,* 88, 91-94.

dcxi *Ibid.,* 100.

dcxii Kelsey Orestis, *My Brother Stevie,* 76.

dcxiii *Ibid.,* 86.

dcxiv Brown, *Battlelines,* 88.

dcxv *Ibid.,*117.

dcxvi Kelsey Orestis, *My Brother Stevie,* vii

dcxvii Bowman, *The World Almanac of the Vietnam War,* 173; Herring, *America's Longest War* (Fourth Edition), 196.

dcxviii McNamara, *In Retrospect,* 284.

dcxix The Pentagon Papers, 4 Gravel, 198.

dcxx *Ibid.,* 199.

dcxxi *Ibid.*

dcxxii *Ibid.,* 203.

dcxxiii *Ibid.,* 203-204.

dcxxiv Bowman, *The World Almanac of the Vietnam War,* 180; Herring, *America's Longest War* (Fourth Edition), 196.

dcxxv Bowman, *The World Almanac of the Vietnam War,* 181.

dcxxvi The Pentagon Papers, 4 Gravel, 206.

dcxxvii *Ibid.*

dcxxviii Marc J. Gilbert and William Head, Editors, *The Tet Offensive* (Westport, CT, Praeger Publishers, 1996), 193.

dcxxix Bowman, *The World Almanac of the Vietnam War,* 183.

dcxxx The Pentagon Papers, 4 Gravel, 206-207.

dcxxxi Herring, *America's Longest War* (Fourth Edition), 209; McNamara, *In Retrospect,* 302.

dcxxxii McNamara, *In Retrospect,* 307-308.

dcxxxiii *Ibid.,* 308.

dcxxxiv Bowman, *The World Almanac of the Vietnam War,* 186.

dcxxxv Bowman, *The World Almanac of the Vietnam War*, 187; Edward F. Murphy, *Dak To, America's Sky Soldiers in South Vietnam's Central Highlands* (New York, Ballantine Books, 1993), 326.

dcxxxvi Braestrup, *Big Story*, 49.

dcxxxvii Bowman, *The World Almanac of the Vietnam War*, 188.

dcxxxviii Braestrup, *Big Story*, 63.

dcxxxix *Ibid.*

dcxl McNamara, *In Retrospect,* 311.

dcxli McNamara, *In Retrospect,* 311; Bowman, *The World Almanac of the Vietnam War*, 188.

dcxlii Herring, *America's Longest War* (Fourth Edition), 217.

dcxliii *Ibid.,*163.

dcxliv Peter Braestrup, *Big Story*, xvii.

dcxlv Herring, *America's Longest War* (Fifth Edition), 188, 275.

dcxlvi Gilbert, *The Tet Offensive,* 197.

dcxlvii *Ibid.,* 197-198.

dcxlviii *Ibid.,* 18, 98.

dcxlix Braestrup, *Big Story*, xvii, 67.

dcl The Pentagon Papers, 4 Gravel, 15.

dcli Gilbert, *The Tet Offensive*, 20.

dclii Bowman, *The World Almanac of the Vietnam War*, 194.

dcliii The Pentagon Papers, 4 Gravel, 15, 234.

dcliv Gilbert, *The Tet Offensive*, 24-25.

dclv Braestrup, *Big Story*, 116, 599-600.

dclvi Gillbert, *Tet offensive*, 127.

dclvii *Ibid.,* 128.

dclviii *Ibid.*

dclix The Pentagon Papers, 4 Gravel, 15, 234-235.

dclx The Pentagon Papers, 4 Gravel, 539.

dclxi WALTER CRONKITE'S "WE ARE MIRED IN STALEMATE" BROADCAST, FEBRUARY 27, 1968 https://facultystaff.richmond.edu/~ebolt/history398/cronkite_1968.html; last visited September 3, 2021; Brestrup, *Big Story*, 601.

dclxii WALTER CRONKITE'S "WE ARE MIRED IN STALEMATE" BROADCAST, FEBRUARY 27, 1968, https://facultystaff.richmond.edu/~ebolt/history398/cronkite_1968.html; Peter Brestrup, *Big Story*, 601.

dclxiii Edwards, *A Brief History of the Cold War*, 105.

dclxiv *Ibid.*

dclxv The Pentagon Papers, 4 Gravel, 235.

dclxvi Braestrup, *Big Story*, 473.

dclxvii Bowman, *The World Almanac of the Vietnam War*, 198.

dclxviii The Pentagon Papers, 4 Gravel, 575-576.

[dclxix] Braestrup, *Big Story*, 453, 601.

[dclxx] Bowman, *The World Almanac of the Vietnam War*, 198.

[dclxxi] Braestrup, *Big Story*, xviii.

[dclxxii] *Ibid.*, 272-273, 571 quoting UPI, 017A—Cushman NX, by Robert C. Miller, March 11, 1968.

[dclxxiii] *Ibid.,* 250-251.

[dclxxiv] *Ibid,*

[dclxxv] *Ibid.,* xviii.

[dclxxvi] Bowman, *The World Almanac of the Vietnam War*, 200.

[dclxxvii] The Pentagon Papers, 4 Gravel, 596-602.

[dclxxviii] Braestrup, *Big Story*, 334.

[dclxxix] Gilbert, *The Tet Offensive*, 206, 209.

[dclxxx] *Ibid.,* 208.

[dclxxxi] *Ibid.,* 206, 209.

[dclxxxii] Herring, *America's Longest War* (Fifth Edition) 240; Gilbert, *The Tet Offensive*. 84.

[dclxxxiii] Herring, *Americas Longest War* (Fourth Edition), 249.

[dclxxxiv] *Ibid.*

[dclxxxv] Lewis Sorley, *A Better War* (Orlando, FL, Harvest Book, Harcourt, Inc., 1999), 16.

[dclxxxvi] Bowman, *The World Almanac of the Vietnam War*, 202.

[dclxxxvii] *Ibid.,* 203.

[dclxxxviii] Sorley, *A Better War*, 14.

[dclxxxix] Willbanks, *Vietnam War Almanac*, 260.

[dcxc] Willbanks, *Vietnam War Almanac*, 261; Sorley, *A Better War*, 93, quoting from Stephen Young, *How North Won The War*, interview with Bui Tin, *Wall Street Journal* (3 August 1995).

[dcxci] Sorley, *A Better War*, 93.

[dcxcii] Moore, *The Real Lessons Of The Vietnam War*, 230.

[dcxciii] Sorley, *A Better War*, 93 quoting from Stephen Young, *How North Won The War*, interview with Bui Tin, *Wall Street Journal* (3 August 1995).

[dcxciv] Bowman, *The World Almanac of the Vietnam War*, 204.

[dcxcv] *Ibid.,* 206.

[dcxcvi] Sorley, *A Better War*, 107, quoting from President Nixon's memoir, *No More Vietnams*, 20.

[dcxcvii] Sorley, *A Better War*, 107, quoting from President Nixon's memoir, *No More Vietnams*, 22.

[dcxcviii] Willbanks, *Vietnam War Almanac*, 264.

[dcxcix] Willbanks, *Vietnam War Almanac*, 265; Sorley, *A Better War*, 127.

[dcc] Bowman, *The World Almanac of the Vietnam War*, 210.

[dcci] *Ibid.*

[dccii] *Ibid.,* 211.

[dcciii] *Ibid.*

dcciv *Ibid.,* 212.

dccv *Ibid.,* 213.

dccvi *Ibid.*

dccvii *Ibid.*

dccviii *Ibid.,* 215.

dccix Mark Clodfelter, Case Study, National War College, National Defense University Press, 2016, 4, http://inss.ndu.edu/Portals/68/Documents/casestudies/nwc_casestudy-1.pdf.

dccx *Ibid.*

dccxi Bowman, *The World Almanac of the Vietnam War,* 215.

dccxii *Ibid.*

dccxiii *Ibid.,* 216.

dccxiv *Ibid.*

dccxv Herring, *America's Longest War* (Fifth Edition), 188, 275.

dccxvi Bowman, *The World Almanac of the Vietnam War,* 217.

dccxvii Moore, *The Real Lessons Of The Vietnam War,* 479.

dccxviii Bowman, *The World Almanac of the Vietnam War,* 217; Sorley, *A Better War,* 97.

dccxix Gilbert, *Tet offensive,* 129.

dccxx *Ibid.,* 133.

dccxxi Braestrup, *Big Story,* 137; Herring, *America's Longest War* (Fifth Edition), 248.

dccxxii Herring, *America's Longest War* (Fifth Edition), 248.

dccxxiii Braestrup, *Big Story,* 508.

CHAPTER SEVEN

dccxxiv *Ibid.,* 206.

dccxxv Bowman, *The World Almanac of the Vietnam War,* 219.

dccxxvi Walter Isaacson, *Kissinger* (New York, Simon & Schuster Paperbacks, 2005), 335-336.

dccxxvii *Ibid.,* 336.

dccxxviii Bowman, *The World Almanac of the Vietnam War,* 220.

dccxxix *Ibid.*

dccxxx *Ibid.*

dccxxxi Sorley, *A Better War,* 114.

dccxxxii *Ibid.,* 104-106.

dccxxxiii *Ibid.,* quoting from President Nixon's memoir, *No More Vietnams,* 107.

dccxxxiv Sorley, *A Better War,* 107, 420 n. 19.

dccxxxv *Ibid.,* 117-118.

dccxxxvi *Ibid.,* 382.

dccxxxvii Bowman, *The World Almanac of the Vietnam War,* 224.

dccxxxviii *Ibid.,* 225.

dccxxxix Sorley, *A Better War*, 119.

dccxl Bowman, *The World Almanac of the Vietnam War*, 225.

dccxli Herring, The Longest War (Fifth Edition), 188.

dccxlii Bowman, *The World Almanac of the Vietnam War*, 226.

dccxliii *Ibid.*

dccxliv *Ibid.*, 227.

dccxlv *Ibid.*

dccxlvi *Ibid.*

dccxlvii *Ibid.*, 228; Sorley, *A Better War*, 141.

dccxlviii Sorley, *A Better War*, 142.

dccxlix Bowman, *The World Almanac of the Vietnam War*, 228.

dccl *Ibid.*

dccli *Ibid.*, 230.

dcclii Sorley, *A Better War*, 128; Bowman, *The World Almanac of the Vietnam War*, 229; Randall M. Romine, *A Vietnam War Chronology* (Book Surge, LLC, 2003), 391.

dccliii Bowman, *The World Almanac of the Vietnam War*, 229.

dccliv *Ibid.*

dcclv *Ibid.*

dcclvi Falk, *The Vietnam War and International Law* (Vol, 1), 175.

dcclvii Bowman, *The World Almanac of the Vietnam War*, 230.

dcclviii *Ibid.*, 231.

dcclix *Ibid.*, 232.

dcclx *NASA*, https://www.nasa.gov/mission_pages/apollo/apollo11.html.

dcclxi Bowman, *The World Almanac of the Vietnam War*, 233.

dcclxii *Ibid.*

dcclxiii Isaacson, *Kissinger*, 338.

dcclxiv Bowman, 233-234.

dcclxv *Ibid.*, 232.

dcclxvi Murphy, *America's Sky Soldier, 36.*

dcclxvii *Ibid.*

dcclxviii Bowman, *The World Almanac of the Vietnam War*, 237.

dcclxix *Ibid.*

dcclxx *Ibid.*, 238.

dcclxxi *Ibid.*

dcclxxii *Ibid.*

dcclxxiii *Ibid.*

dcclxxiv *Ibid.*, 239.

dcclxxv *Ibid.*

dcclxxvi *Ibid.*, 240.

dcclxxvii President Nixon Address to the Nation on the War in Vietnam, http://www.presidency.ucsb.edu/ws/?pid=2303, last visited September 3, 2021.

dcclxxviii Bowman, *The World Almanac of the Vietnam War*, 242.

dcclxxix *Ibid.*

dcclxxx *Ibid.*, 244.

dcclxxxi *Ibid.*

dcclxxxii *Ibid.*, 246.

dcclxxxiii Isaacson, *Kissinger*, 336-337.

dcclxxxiv Bowman, *The World Almanac of the Vietnam War*, 246; Herring, Americas Longest War (Fifth Edition), 188.

dcclxxxv Herring, *America's Longest War* (Fifth Edition), 275.

dcclxxxvi Bowman, *The World Almanac of the Vietnam War*, 249.

dcclxxxvii *Ibid.*, 250.

dcclxxxviii *Ibid.*, 250, 328.

dcclxxxix *Ibid.*, 251.

dccxc *Ibid.*

dccxci *Ibid.*, 252

dccxcii *Ibid.*

dccxciii Vietnam War Travel, https://namwartravel.com/dak-po-km-15/.

dccxciv Vietnam War Travel, https://namwartravel.com/dak-po-km-15/; Bernard B. Fall, *Street Without Joy* (Guilford, Connecticut, Stackpole Books, 1961, 2d ed., 2018), 185-250.

dccxcv Fall, *Street Without Joy,* viii.

dccxcvi *Ibid.*, vii.

dccxcvii *Ibid.*, 185-186, 206.

dccxcviii *Ibid.*, 205-207.

dccxcix *Ibid.*, 210-211.

dccc *Ibid.*, 211-212.

dccci *Ibid.*, 210, 211, 212, 214, 215, 216, 217, 220.

dcccii *Ibid.*, 234-235.

dccciii Bowman, *The World Almanac of the Vietnam War*, 254.

dccciv *Ibid.*, 255.

dcccv *Ibid.*

dcccvi *Ibid.*

dcccvii *Ibid.*, 257.

dcccviii *Ibid.*, 255 and 257.

dcccix Romine, *A Vietnam War Chronology*, 466.

dcccx *Ibid.*

dcccxi Bowman, *The World Almanac of the Vietnam War*, 255.

dcccxii *Ibid.*, 257.

dcccxiii Bowman, *The World Almanac of the Vietnam War*, 257.

dcccxiv *Ibid.*, 257- 258.

dcccxv *Ibid.*, 258.

dcccxvi Isaacson, *Kissinger*, 337.

dcccxvii *Ibid.*, 259.

dcccxviii *Ibid.*

dcccxix *Ibid.*

dcccxx *Ibid.*, 261.

dcccxxi *Ibid.*

dcccxxii Base attack An Khe/Camp Radcliff, August 1979, *https://www.freewebs.com/jim4jet/baseattackaug70.htm*, last visited September 3, 2021.

dcccxxiii Bowman, *The World Almanac of the Vietnam War*, 263.

dcccxxiv *Ibid.*, 265.

dcccxxv *Ibid.*, 263-264.

dcccxxvi *Ibid.*, 265.

dcccxxvii Isaacson, *Kissinger*, 338.

dcccxxviii Bowman, *The World Almanac of the Vietnam War*, 268.

dcccxxix *Ibid.*, 269-270.

dcccxxx Isaacson, *Kissinger*, 338.

dcccxxxi *Ibid.*

dcccxxxii Bowman, *The World Almanac of the Vietnam War*, 272.

dcccxxxiii Herring, *America's Longest War* (Fifth Edition), 188, 275.

dcccxxxiv Bowman, *The World Almanac of the Vietnam War*, 273.

dcccxxxv Gulf of Tonkin Resolution, https://constitutioncenter.org/blog/the-gulf-of-tonkin-and-the-limits-of-presidential-power/, last visited September 3, 2021.

dcccxxxvi This Day in History, https://www.history.com/this-day-in-history/senate-repeals-tonkin-gulf-resolution.

dcccxxxvii Bowman, *The World Almanac of the Vietnam War*, 276.

dcccxxxviii *Ibid.*

dcccxxxix *Ibid.*, 277.

dcccxl *Ibid.*

dcccxli *Ibid.*, 274.

dcccxlii Bowman, *The World Almanac of the Vietnam War*, 274.

dcccxliii Washington Post, *Army Reduces Calley's Term to 20 years*, https://www.washingtonpost.com/wp-srv/inatl/longterm/flash/articles/aug96/mylai71.htm History, https://www.history.com/this-day-in-history/calley-charged-for-my-lai-massacre.

dcccxliv *History*, https://www.history.com/this-day-in-history/calley-found-guilty-of-my-lai-murders, last visited August 15, 2021.

dcccxlv Isaacson, *Kissinger*, 339.

dcccxlvi *Ibid.*

dcccxlvii Isaacson, *Kissinger*, 339.

dcccxlviii *Ibid.*, 340.

dcccxlix *Ibid.*

dcccl *Ibid.*

dcccli Bowman, *The World Almanac of the Vietnam War*, 284.

dccclii Mark Opsasnick, *The Lizard King was Here* (Trenton, New Jersey, Book Locker, 2022) 127-129.

dcccliii Isaacson, *Kissinger*, 344.

dcccliv Bowman, *The World Almanac of the Vietnam War*, 287.

dccclv Isaacson, *Kissinger*, 346.

dccclvi Bowman, *The World Almanac of the Vietnam War*, 288.

dccclvii Bowman, *The World Almanac of the Vietnam War*, 290.

dccclviii Willbanks, *Vietnam War Almanac*, 381.

dccclix *Ibid.*, 291.

dccclx Isaacson, *Kissinger*, 351.

dccclxi Isaacson, *Kissinger*, 353.

dccclxii Bowman, *The World Almanac of the Vietnam War*, 293.

dccclxiii Herring, *America's Longest War* (Fifth Edition), 188, 275.

dccclxiv Bowman, *The World Almanac of the Vietnam War*, 296.

dccclxv *Ibid.*, 297-298.

dccclxvi *Ibid.*, 298.

dccclxvii *Ibid.*

dccclxviii Isaacson, *Kissinger*, 399, 402-403.

dccclxix Bowman, *The World Almanac of the Vietnam War*, 300.

dccclxx Isaacson, *Kissinger*, 353.

dccclxxi Bowman, *The World Almanac of the Vietnam War*, 301.

dccclxxii *Ibid.*, 302.

dccclxxiii *Ibid.*, 302-303.

dccclxxiv *Ibid.*, 304.

dccclxxv *Ibid.*

dccclxxvi Smithsonian, 290.

dccclxxvii Bowman, *The World Almanac of the Vietnam War*, 304.

dccclxxviii *Ibid.*, 307.

dccclxxix *Ibid.*, 308.

dccclxxx *Ibid.*, 309-310.

dccclxxxi Smithsonian, 291.

dccclxxxii *Ibid.*

dccclxxxiii Bowman, *The World Almanac of the Vietnam War*, 310.

dccclxxxiv *Ibid.*

dccclxxxv Isaacson, *Kissinger*, 424.

dccclxxxvi *Ibid.*

dccclxxxvii *Ibid.*, 425.

dccclxxxviii History, Détente - Definition, Policy & Cold War - HISTORY

dccclxxxix Boot, *The Road Not Taken*, 553.

dcccxc Herring, *Americas Longest War* (Fifth Edition), 318.

dcccxci Bowman, *The World Almanac of the Vietnam War*, 314.

dcccxcii *Ibid.*, 333.

dcccxciii *Ibid.*, 335.

dcccxciv Tuchman, *The March of Folly,* 372.

dcccxcv Bowman, *The World Almanac of the Vietnam War*, 337.

dcccxcvi Willbanks, *Vietnam War Almanac*, 434.

dcccxcvii Bowman, *The World Almanac of the Vietnam War*, 338.

dcccxcviii *Ibid.*

dcccxcix *Ibid.*, 297.

cm Isaacson, *Kissinger*, 486.

cmi *Ibid.*

cmii Herring, *America's Longest War* (Fifth Edition), 330.

cmiii Isaacson, *Kissinger*, 486.

cmiv Gaddis, *The Cold War*, 176.

cmv *Ibid.*

CHAPTER EIGHT

cmvi *The New York Times*, He calls '73 pledge to Hanoi invalid, *https://www.nytimes.com/1977/05/20/archives/he-calls-73-pledge-of-aid-to-hanoi-invalid-nixon-calls-pledge-of.html*, last visited September 7, 2021, Amanda C. Demmer, *After Saigon's Fall* (United Kingdom, Cambridge University Press, 2021), 63, 252.

cmvii Li, *Mao and the Sino-Soviet Split,* 260

cmviii *Ibid.*

cmix Bowman, *The World Almanac of the Vietnam War*, 337-338.

cmx *Ibid.*, 338.

cmxi Li, *Mao and the Sino-Soviet Split,* 260.

cmxii Bowman, *The World Almanac of the Vietnam War*, 340.

cmxiii Bowman, *The World Almanac of the Vietnam War*, 315; Tuchman, *The March of Folly,* 370.

cmxiv *History*, https://www.history.com/news/watergate-nixon-john-dean-tapes; Los Angeles Times, https://www.latimes.com/politics/la-na-pol-john-dean-watergate-russia-investigation-20190610-story.html.

cmxv Bowman, *The World Almanac of the Vietnam War*, 340.

cmxvi *Ibid.*

cmxvii Edwards, *A Brief History of the Cold War*, 123.

cmxviii Bowman, *The World Almanac of the Vietnam War*, 340-341.

cmxix *Ibid.*, 341.

cmxx *Ibid.*, 340.

cmxxi Willbanks, *Vietnam War Almanac*, 441.

cmxxii Herring, *Americas Longest War* (Fifth Edition), 275.

cmxxiii Willbanks, *Vietnam War Almanac*, 441.

cmxxiv Bowman, *The World Almanac of the Vietnam War*, 341.

cmxxv *Ibid.*

cmxxvi *Ibid.*

cmxxvii Bowman, *The World Almanac of the Vietnam War,* 341; Boot, *The Road Not Taken*, 564-565.

[cmxxviii] Willbanks, *Vietnam War Almanac*, 443.

[cmxxix] *Ibid.*

[cmxxx] *Ibid.*, 444.

[cmxxxi] *Ibid.*

[cmxxxii] Herring, America's Longest War (Fifth Edition), 275; Bowman, *The World Almanac of the Vietnam War*, 343.

[cmxxxiii] Willbanks, *Vietnam War Almanac,* 444.

[cmxxxiv] *Ibid.*, 445.

[cmxxxv] *Ibid.*, 446.

[cmxxxvi] *Ibid.*

[cmxxxvii] *Ibid.,* 448.

[cmxxxviii] Smithsonian, 326.

[cmxxxix] Smithsonian, 320.

[cmxl] Willbanks, *Vietnam War Almanac*, 448; See the entire speech at https://www.fordlibrarymuseum.gov/library/speeches/750179.asp; taken from the Gerald R. Ford; Presidential Library; Geoffrey C. Ward and Ken Burns, *The Vietnam War* (New York, Alfred A. Knopf, a division of Random House, 2017), 543; *The New York Times*, https://www.nytimes.com/1975/04/11/archives/reaction-is-cool-but-many-in-congress-support-request-for.html.

[cmxli] Willbanks, *Vietnam War Almanac*, 449.

[cmxlii] *Ibid.*

[cmxliii] Bowman, *The World Almanac of the Vietnam War*, 341.

[cmxliv] *Ibid.*

[cmxlv] Moore, *The Real Lessons of the Vietnam War*, 483-484.

[cmxlvi] Bowman, *The World Almanac of the Vietnam War*, 341.

[cmxlvii] Boot, *The Road Not Taken*, 566.

[cmxlviii] *Ibid.*

[cmxlix] *Ibid.*

CHAPTER NINE

[cml] Amanda C. Demmer, *After Saigon's Fall* (United Kingdom, Cambridge University Press, 2021), 134.

[cmli] *Ibid.,* 111.

[cmlii] Smithsonian, 340; Herring, *America's Longest War* (Fifth Edition), 356.

[cmliii] Willbanks, *Vietnam War Almanac*, 453.

[cmliv] Bowman, *The World Almanac of the Vietnam War*, 347.

[cmlv] Edwards, *A Brief History of the Cold War*, 218.

[cmlvi] Willbanks, *Vietnam War Almanac*, 453.

[cmlvii] *Ibid.*, 454.

[cmlviii] Office of the Historian, https://history.state.gov/milestones/1969-1976/rapprochement-china; Willbanks, *Vietnam War Almanac*, 454.

[cmlix] Willbanks, *Vietnam War Almanac*, 454-455.

cmlx *Ibid.*

cmlxi *Ibid.*, 455.

cmlxii Edwards, *A Brief History of the Cold War*, 218.

cmlxiii Edwards, *A Brief History of the Cold War*, 141-142, 219.

cmlxiv *Ibid.*, 139.

cmlxv The University of Virginia Miller Center Presidential Speeches, Jimmy Carter, https//millercenter.org/the-presidency/presedential-speeches/January-23-1980-state-union-address.

cmlxvi Willbanks, *Vietnam War Almanac*, 456.

cmlxvii *Ibid.*

cmlxviii *Ibid.*

cmlxix *Ibid.*

cmlxx Boot, *The Road Not Taken*, 589.

cmlxxi The University of Virginia Miller Center of Presidential speeches, Ronald Reagan, https://millercenter.org/the-presidency/presidential-speeches/january-29-1981-first-press-conference.

cmlxxii The University of Virginia Miller Center of presidential speeches, Ronald Reagan https://millercenter.org/the-presidency/presidential-speeches/june-8-1982-address-british-parliament last visited September 4, 2021.

cmlxxiii Edwards, *A Brief History of the Cold War*, 220.

cmlxxiv The University of Virginia Miller Center of Presidential Speeches, Ronald Reagan, https://millercenter.org/the-presidency/presidential-speeches/march-8-1983-evil-empire-speech, last visited September 4, 2021.

cmlxxv The University of Virginia Miller Center of Presidential Speeches, Ronald Reagan, https://millercenter.org/the-presidency/presidential-speeches/march-23-1983-address-nation-national-security.

cmlxxvi Edwards, *A Brief History of the Cold War*, 220.

cmlxxvii *Ibid.*, 221.

cmlxxviii Willbanks, *Vietnam War Almanac*, 459.

cmlxxix Edwards, *A Brief History of the Cold War*, 221.

cmlxxx Demmer, *After Saigon's Fall*, 144.

cmlxxxiDemmer, *After Saigon's Fall*, 145; Willbanks, *Vietnam War Almanac*, 461.

cmlxxxii Willbanks, *Vietnam War Almanac*, 461.

cmlxxxiii University of Virginia, Miller Center Presidential Speeches, Ronald Reagan, https://millercenter.org/the-presidency/presidential-speeches/june-12-1987-address-brandenburg-gate-berlin-wall.

cmlxxxiv Demmer, *After Saigon's Fall*, 148.

cmlxxxv Edwards, *A Brief History of the Cold War*, 223

cmlxxxvi Willbanks, *Vietnam War Almanac*, 463.

cmlxxxvii Demmer, *After Saigon's Fall*, 168.

cmlxxxviii *Ibid.*, 186-187.

cmlxxxix *Ibid.*, 187.

cmxc Edwards, *A Brief History of the Cold War*, 224.

cmxci Demmer, *After Saigon's Fall*, 201.

cmxcii Edwards, *A Brief History of the Cold War*, 224

cmxciii *Ibid.*

cmxciv Willbanks, *Vietnam War Almanac*, 463.

cmxcv Demmer, *After Saigon's Fall*, 201, 288.

cmxcvi *Ibid.*, 201.

cmxcvii *Ibid.*

cmxcviii *Ibid.*

cmxcix Willbanks, *Vietnam War Almanac*, 463.

m *Ibid.*

mi *Ibid.*, 464.

mii *Ibid.*

miii Smithsonian, 325.

miv Smithsonian, 341.

mv Amanda C. Demmer, *The Washington Post,* What does the U.S. owe the Afghans who supported it? August 22, 2021. https://www.proquest.com/docview/2563229509/7501A7760CE4489APQ/1?accountid=189667

mvi Demmer, *After Saigon's Fall*, 220.

mvii Willbanks, *Vietnam War Almanac*, 464.

mviii *Ibid.*

mix Amanda C. Demmer, *After Saigon's Fall*, 198.

mx Smithsonian, 340.

mxi Willbanks, *Vietnam War Almanac*, 455

mxii Willbanks, *Vietnam War Almanac*, 456

mxiii Moore, *The Real Lessons of the Vietnam War*, 454.

mxiv *Ibid.*, 238.

mxv Willbanks, *Vietnam War Almanac* 463.

mxvi *Ibid.*

mxvii Thomesa Maresca, USA Today, 40 years later, Vietnam still deeply divided over war, April 30, 2015, https://www.usatoday.com/story/news/world/2015/04/28/fall-of-saigon-vietnam-40-years-later/26447943/, last visited September 18, 2021.

mxviii Demmer, *After Saigon's Fall*, 195-196.

mxix *Ibid.*

mxx Burns, *The Vietnam War*, 384.

CHAPTER TEN

mxxi Pike, *Viet Cong*, xi-xii.

mxxii University of Virginia, Miller Center Presidential Speeches Gerald Ford: https://millercenter.org/the-presidency/presidential-speeches/april-10-1975-address-us-foreign-policy

mxxiii Gerald R. Ford, *A Time To Heal* (New York, Berkley Books, 1980), 247.

mxxiv Willbanks, *Vietnam War Almanac*, 449.

mxxv Ford, *A Time To Heal*, 250.

mxxvi *Ibid.*

mxxvii *Ibid.*

mxxviii Moore, *The Real Lessons of the Vietnam War*, 104 quoting from Jacqueline Desbarats, "Repression in the Socialist Republic of Vietnam: Executions and Population Relocation."

mxxix Smithsonian, 337; Wilbanks, *Vietnam War Almanac*, 449; Boot, *The Road Not Taken*, 571.

mxxx Smithsonian, 309, 333.

mxxxi *Ibid.,* 332.

mxxxii *Ibid.,*

mxxxiii Encyclopedia of Buddhism, Buddhism in Vietnam, https://encyclopediaofbuddhism.org/wiki/Buddhism_in_Vietnam, last visited on 8/21/21.

mxxxiv Smithsonian, 333.

mxxxv Boot, *The Road Not Taken*, 571.

mxxxvi Ginetta Sagan and Stephen Denney, *Violations Of Human Rights in The Socialist Republic Of Vietnam April 30, 1975-April 30, 1983* (California, Aurora Foundation, 1983), Introduction, 3.

mxxxvii Boot, *The Road Not Taken*, 572.

mxxxviii *Ibid.*

mxxxix Sagan and Denney, *Violations of Human Rights,* 12-13.

mxlmxl *Ibid.,* 13.

mxli *Ibid.,* 7.

mxlii Vietnamkrigen, As printed in the *New York Times*, https://vietnamkrigen.wordpress.com/dokumentsamling/open-letter-to-the-socialist-republic-of-vietnam/, last visited 8/23/21.

mxliii *Ibid.,* 15.

mxliv Willbanks, *Vietnam War Almanac*, 458.

mxlv *Ibid.*

mxlvi Burns, The Vietnam War, "The Huge Mistake" (unnumbered page after Epilogue).

mxlvii Gaddis, *The Cold War*, 177 quoting Henry Kissinger, *Years of Upheaval*, (Boston, Little Brown, 1982), 307-8.

mxlviii Isaacson, *Kissinger,* 487.

mxlix *Ibid.*

CHAPTER ELEVEN

ml The Pentagon Papers, 1 Gravel, xvi as quoted in the Letter of Transmittal by Leslie H. Gelb, Director of Pentagon Papers Task Force.

mli CBS News Poll, https://www.cbsnews.com/news/cbs-news-poll-u-s-involvement-in-vietnam/, September 4, 2021.

mlii *Ibid.*

mliii Inspiring quotes, https://www.inspiringquotes.us/quotes/qDuO_gulFIPaD, last visited 2/9/21

mliv The Pentagon Papers, 1 Gravel, 8.

mlv Edwards, *A Brief History of the Cold War,* back book cover.

mlvi Moore, *The Real Lessons Of The Vietnam War,* 11.

mlvii Edwards, *A Brief History of the Cold War*, 100.

mlviii *Ibid.*

mlix History, https://www.history.com/this-day-in-history/the-hitler-stalin-pact; Edwards, *A Brief History of the Cold War*, 202.

mlx The University of Virginia Miller Center, Presidential Speeches, last visited February 25, 2021; https://millercenter.org/the-presidency/presidential-speeches/march-12-1947-truman-doctrine, last visited August 23, 2021.

mlxi Moore, *The Real Lessons Of The Vietnam War*, 11.

mlxii *Ibid.,* 439.

mlxiii Office of the Historian, https://history.state.gov/milestones/1977-1980/soviet-invasion-afghanistan.

mlxiv The University of Virginia Miller Center of presidential speeches, Ronald Reagan. https://millercenter.org/the-presidency/presidential-speeches/june-8-1982-address-british-parliament.

mlxv History, Soviet Union: Stalin, Cold War & Collapse | HISTORY - HISTORY, last visited 8/23/2021; Edwards, https://www.heritage.org/conservatism/commentary/how-ronald-reagan-won-the-cold-war, last visited March 8, 2021.

mlxvi Edwards, https://www.heritage.org/conservatism/commentary/how-ronald-reagan-won-the-cold-war, last visited 6/20/2021.

mlxvii Encyclopedia Britannica, https://www.britannica.com/place/Russia/Ethnic-relations-and-Russias-near-abroad.

mlxviii Moore, *The Real Lessons Of The Vietnam War*, 14.

mlxix The University of Virginia Miller Center of presidential speeches, Ronald Reagan https://millercenter.org/the-presidency/presidential-speeches/june-8-1982-address-british-parliament, last visited September 4, 2021.

mlxx Gaddis, *The Cold War, A New History*, 266.

mlxxi Moore, *The Real Lessons Of The Vietnam War,* 425.

Epilogue

[mlxxii] The University of Virginia Miller Center Presidential Speeches, Ronald Reagan https://millercenter.org/the-presidency/presidential-speeches/january-20-1981-first-inaugural-address, last visited August 22, 2021.

[mlxxiii] The University of Virginia Miller Center Presidential Speeches, Ronald Reagan, May 28, 1984, Remarks Honoring the Vietnam War's Unknown Soldier: Miller Center, https://millercenter.org/the-presidency/presidential-speeches/may-28-1984-remarks-honoring-vietnam-wars-unknown-soldier, last visited August 22, 2021.

[mlxxiv] President Reagan's November 11, 1984, Remarks at the Dedication Ceremonies for the Vietnam Veteran's Memorial statute, UC Santa Barbara, https://www.presidency.ucsb.edu/documents/remarks-dedication-ceremonies-for-the-vietnam-veterans-memorial-statue, last visited August 22, 2021.

[mlxxv] Roper Center for Public Opinion Research at Cornell University, https://ropercenter.cornell.edu/heros-welcome-american-public-and-attitudes-toward-veterans

DOCUMENTS

[mlxxvi] *New York Times*, August 4, 1973, Text of Nixon's Letter on Bombing Halt, https//www.nytimes.com1973/08/04/archives/text-of-nixons-letter-on-bombing-halt.html, last visited September 4, 2021.

[mlxxvii] Moore, *The Real Lessons of the Vietnam War*, 483-484.

ABOUT THE AUTHOR

Mr. Maney was in the Judge Advocate General's Corps in Vietnam where he served as a trial lawyer and as Chief of Military Justice in the 4th Infantry Division. After the Army, he joined the Department of Justice where he began as a line prosecutor and finished as Chief of the Tax Division's Southern Criminal Enforcement Section.

Upon retiring from DOJ, Mr. Maney joined a program at the Treasury Department which, upon request from foreign officials, sent him and other team members to the requesting nations to help them determine whether economic crime statutes such as money laundering, criminal tax, terrorist financing, organized crime, and political corruption might be useful fits in their legal framework and, if so, how to best implement them.

CPSIA information can be obtained
at www.ICGtesting.com
Printed in the USA
JSHW010328050523
41190JS00001B/1